This 63rd Edition is dedicated to all those professional and aspiring amateur mixologists throughout the world who seek the most authoritative, accurate, and complete source for perfect drinks.

MR. BOSTON

OFFICIAL

BARTENDER'S

GUIDE

63rd Edition

REVISED AND UPDATED

WARNER BOOKS

A Warner Communications Company

Acknowledgments

Appreciation is acknowledged to Leo Cotton, who served as originator and editor of the first *Mr. Boston Bartender's Guide,* which was published in 1935. He continued as editor through the guide's 49th printing—a period of over thirty-five years, until his retirement in 1970.

Further appreciation and acknowledgment is extended to: Jamie Rothstein, Editor; James Overall, Creative Director; Albert Justiniano, Art Director; Marina P. Freyer, Photo Stylist; Andrius Balukas, Book Design; Robert Marinelli, Illustration; Roland Grybauskas, Donna-Ann P. Hayden, Patricia McCafferty, Marketing and Development; The Pottery Barn, Glassware.

Mr. Boston Official Bartender's Guide
Copyright © 1988 by Glenmore Distilleries Company

Material from Mr. Boston Bartender's Guide, copyright © 1935, 1936, 1940, 1941, 1946, 1948, 1949, 1951, 1953, 1955, 1957, 1959, 1960, 1961, 1962, 1963, 1964, 1965, 1966, 1967, 1968, 1969, 1970, 1974, 1976, 1977, 1978, 1981, 1984 by Mr. Boston Distiller Corporation.

Warner Books, Inc., 666 Fifth Avenue, New York, NY 10103
Ⓦ A Warner Communications Company

Printed in the United States of America
First Printing: November 1988
10   9   8   7   6   5   4   3

63rd Edition revised and updated by Elin McCoy
and John Frederick Walker

Photos by William Hubell, Photography, Greenwich, Connecticut

Library of Congress Cataloging-in-Publication Data
Main entry under title:
Mr. Boston official bartender's guide.

Includes index.
1. Liquors.   2. Cocktails.   3. Alcoholic beverages.
I. Mister Boston official bartender's guide.
TX951.M7   1988   641.8'74   88-17392
ISBN 0-446-38763-0

CONTENTS

List of Illustrations 7

Introduction 8

The Basic Bar: Supplies and Methods 11

Measurements 24

Calorie Counts 27

America's Favorite Drinks 28

New Drinks 32

Drink Recipes (listed alphabetically) 37

Special Sections 204
    Eggnog 205
    No-Alcohol Drinks 208

The Liquor Dictionary 212
    Brandy 213
    Liqueurs 214
    Gin 216
    Rum 217
    Whiskey 218
    Vodka 221

Beer 223

Wine 226
    How Wine Is Made 227
    Wine Appreciation 227
    Wine Tasting 228
    Wine Storage 228
    Wine Service 229
    Wine and Food 230
    A Glossary of Basic Wine Terms 232
    Wines of the United States 234

Wines of France 237
Wines of Germany 242
Wines of Italy 244
Wines of Spain 246
Wines of Portugal 248
Wines of Other Countries 250

Shopping Suggestions 251

Index 254

LIST OF
ILLUSTRATIONS

Home Bar set-up / *10*
Gin and Tonic, Black Russian, Margarita,
  Screwdriver / *28*
Tom Collins, Manhattan, Brandy Alexander,
  Whiskey Sour / *29*
Martini, Tequila Sunrise, Dacquiri, Bloody Mary / *31*
Fuzzy Navel, Passion Mimosa, Indian Summer,
  Kamikaze / *33*
Melon Ball, Cape Codder, Blue Margarita / *34*
Grape Berry, Lemon Squash / *36*
Strawberry Sunrise, Apple Colada, Rum Swizzle / *43*
Brandy / *47*
White Russian, Grasshopper, Toasted Almond / *53*
Sparkling Wine / *67*
Creme de menthe, Creme de cacao, Amaretto / *77*
Strawberry Margarita / *92*
Gin Highball / *96*
Mulled Claret, Tropical Heat / *102*
Bellini, Pineapple Cooler, Adonis / *114*
Kir / *119*
Mexican Coffee / *126*
Martini / *127*
Bourbon Straight-Up, Mint Julep, Bourbon on Rocks / *135*
Pousse Café / *144*
Rum Fix, Planter's Punch, Rum Daisy / *154*
Royal Purple Punch, Brandy Punch, Banana Punch / *157*
Scotch Mist, Scotch Bishop / *166*
Chilled Vodka / *179*
Vermouth Cassis, Vermouth Cocktail / *188*
Wine / *196*
Eggnog / *206*
Beer / *222*

INTRODUCTION

Welcome. You are holding in your hands the 63rd Edition of the definitive guide to mixing perfect drinks. The *Mr. Boston Bartender's Guide* has been the official manual of bartenders and spirits professionals since it was first published in 1935. It has been endorsed, consulted, and considered a basic tool for bartenders for decades. In fact, over ten million copies have been sold since it first appeared shortly after the repeal of Prohibition as an urgently needed source of answers to questions such as: How much is a dash? How do you make a dry Martini? How do you frost glasses?

Even experienced bartenders had trouble making the same drink taste the same way each time they mixed it. So Mr. Boston collected the best-known and best-loved drink recipes, tested and standardized the measurements, and presented, in alphabetical order, recipes with such clear, easy-to-follow directions that, at last, anyone could be an expert at cocktail time.

Of course the book was copied. But originators stay original. With this, our 63rd Edition, we not only have updated our comprehensive sections on spirits, wines, beers, and liqueurs of the world, but included a selection of popular no-alcohol drinks. In addition, light drinks—those that contain $1/3$ to $1/2$ less alcohol than a standard drink (5 oz. of wine, 12 oz. of beer, or a drink containing $1^1/_2$ oz. of spirits)—are marked with the symbol **◐**, signifying lower alcohol content.

With this book as your guide, you can look at almost any wine and spirits label from any country and know what you are buying, what it will taste like, where it is from, and what foods it complements. You will know how to store and serve wine and beer and a bit about the process and unique conditions that produced them.

None of this is stuffy or complicated. Drinks are meant to go with good times and good friends. So is the *Mr. Boston Bartender's Guide.* Informative but fun to read, complete but concise, it is the only book you need to make memorable drinks for your parties and perfect wine choices for intimate or elegant occasions.

So congratulations! You have made an excellent selection to enhance your expertise as a professional bartender or a well-informed host. Simply turn the page and you are on your way to making your friends'—and your own—favorite drinks superbly.

Home Bar set-up

THE BASIC BAR: SUPPLIES AND METHODS

Since the repeal of Prohibition, *Mr. Boston Bartender's Guides* have passed down the secrets of mixing the perfect drink. This newly revised edition now contains over a thousand recipes, including many new cocktail recipes, made easily accessible by fingertip indexing.

The winning methods are gathered here for you to use with complete confidence. You need only follow this advice to achieve the extra artistry that will mark you as a professional.

There are a few practical rules to follow for stocking your bar and mixing drinks. You'll want to be able to satisfy the tastes of your guests quickly, so that you can enjoy the conviviality of good spirits. Here you'll find the supplies you'll need to keep on hand to take care of anyone's request. And with the mastery of a few simple techniques carefully explained here, you'll find it easy to quickly concoct any drink calling for mixing, mashing, muddling, or simple stirring.

Equipment

The right tools make the job easier. For home or professional bar you'll need to have handy:

1. Can and bottle openers
2. Easy-to-use corkscrew
3. Waiter's corkscrew
4. Glass stirring rod or long spoon
5. Coil-rimmed bar strainer
6. A tall, heavy-duty mixing glass or shaker
7. Small, sharp stainless-steel paring knife for cutting fruit or for shearing off rind
8. Wooden muddler or the back of a large wooden spoon for mashing herbs, fruit, etc.
9. Large pitcher
10. Fruit juice extractor
11. Set of measuring spoons
12. A jigger measure with easy-to-read half- and quarter-ounce measures
13. Ice bucket and ice tongs

    Electric blender (optional)
    Glassware

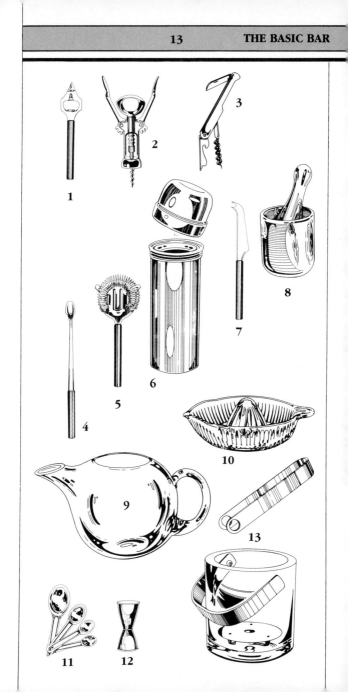

1

2

3

4

5   6

7

8

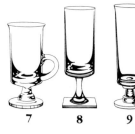
9

10   11

12   13

14   15

16   17

Glassware

The best glasses should be thin-lipped, transparent, and sound off in high registers when "pinged." Clean, sparkling glasses show off good drinks to great advantage. The proper glass enhances a drink. Here are illustrations showing a comprehensive selection. In practice, however, only a few basic types are necessary. Nos. 1, 4, 7, 11, 14, and 17, for example, will answer virtually all your needs. Beside each recipe in the recipe section are line drawings of the classic shape used for each drink.

You might also need a coffee cup, coffee mug, or punch cup for some of the recipes.

Glass Name

1. **Collins**
2. **Shot**
3. **Highball**
4. **Old-Fashioned**

5. **Beer Mug**
6. **Beer Pilsner**
7. **Irish Coffee Cup**
8. **Pousse Café**
9. **Parfait**

10. **Red Wine**
11. **White Wine**
12. **Sherry**
13. **Champagne Flute**

14. **Brandy Snifter**
15. **Cocktail**
16. **Cordial or Pony**
17. **Whiskey Sour**

Stocking a Bar

If you keep a 750-milliliter bottle of each of the spirits mentioned here, you'll be able to create just about any combination of drinks and *that* should satisfy just about everybody.

- Gin
- Vodka
- Rum (Light and Dark)
- Bourbon
- Scotch
- Tequila
- Vermouth (Sweet and Dry)
- Red and White Wine (Dry)
- Brandy, Port, Sherry
- Any assortment of liqueurs popular in your crowd

When you want to get fancier you can diversify the standards with sophisticated variations: Irish whiskey as well as Scotch; Puerto Rican as well as Jamaican rum, etc. Time, experience, and your most frequent guests' tastes will shape your bar offerings.

Choose a selection of mixers from the following:

Mineral water
Colas
Ginger Ale
Club Soda or Seltzer
Tonic or Quinine Water
Lemon/Lime Sodas
Fresh fruit juices, especially:
    Orange, grapefruit, lemon, lime
Other juices: Tomato, pineapple, cranberry
Sugar syrup (See p. 17 for recipe)
Water (in a small pitcher)

To garnish you'll need:

- Jar of cocktail onions
- Jar of stuffed olives
- Lemons
- Limes
- Oranges
- Strawberries
- Celery stalks
- Bitters
- Cassis (black currant syrup)
- Cinnamon sticks (for hot, mulled wines)
- Mint leaves (for juleps)
- Tabasco sauce
- Worcestershire sauce
- Horseradish
- Maraschino cherries
- Cucumber
- Pineapple
- Coarse salt

Certain fancy tropical-type drinks require these exotic additions to your potable collections:

> Bananas (for banana daiquiries)
> Coconut milk
> Grenadine syrup (made from pomegranates)
> Orange flower water (or substitute Triple Sec)
> Orgeat syrup (almond-flavor syrup)
> Papaya juice
> Passion fruit juice
> Raspberry syrup
> Light cream
> Heavy cream
> Whipping cream

You'll also need: table salt, pepper, granulated sugar, and powdered sugar.

To Make Simple Syrup or Sugar Syrup

In saucepan, gradually stir one pound granulated sugar into 13 oz. hot water to make 16 oz. simple syrup.

About Bitters

A little goes a long way. Made from numerous and intricate combinations of growing things (roots, barks, berries, and herbs) which are each uniquely flavored, they add zest to mixed drinks.

Angostura Bitters—Made from a Trinidadian secret recipe.

Abbott's Aged Bitters—Made in Baltimore since 1865.

Peychaud's Bitters—These come from New Orleans.

Orange Bitters—Made from the dried peel of mouth-puckering Seville oranges and sold by several English firms.

Vermouth

Vermouth is a white appetizer wine flavored with as many as thirty to forty different herbs, roots, berries, flowers, and seeds. There are nearly as many vermouth formulas as there are brand labels.

The dry variety (French) is light gold in color and has a delightful nutty flavor. Sweet (Italian) vermouth is red, richer in flavor, and more syrupy. Both are perishable and will lose their freshness if left too long in an opened bottle. Refrigerate after opening. Use with care and discretion in mixed drinks—be sure to follow the recipe since most people now prefer "drier" cocktails.

Ice

Bar ice must be clean and fresh and free of any flavor save water. If necessary, use bottled spring water.

Rule of thumb: For parties, you will always need more ice than you have. Buy or make extra.

Ice goes in the cocktail glass first. That way the spirits get cooled on the way in without any unnecessary splashing. Ice can be crushed, shaved, cracked, or cubed, depending on the drink. If you can store only one kind of ice, buy cubes. Most highballs, old-fashioneds, and on-the-rocks drinks call for ice cubes. Use cracked or cubed ice for stirring and shaking; crushed or shaved ice for special tall drinks, frappes, and other drinks to be sipped through straws.

Techniques

How to Chill a Glass

Always chill before you fill. There are three ways to make a cocktail glass cold:

1. Put the glasses in the refrigerator or freezer a couple of hours before using them.
2. Fill the glasses with crushed ice just before using.
3. Fill the glasses with cracked ice and stir it around before pouring in the drink.

If refrigerator space is not available for pre-chilling, fill each glass with ice before mixing. When the drink is ready, empty the glass, shake out all of the melted ice, and then pour in the drink.

How to Frost a Glass

There are two types of "frosted" glass. For "frosted" drinks, glasses should be stored in a refrigerator or buried in shaved ice long enough to give each glass a white, frosted, ice-cold look and feel.

For a "sugar-frosted" glass, moisten the rim of a pre-chilled glass with a slice of lime or lemon and then dip the rim into powdered sugar.

For margaritas, rub the rim of the glass with a lime, invert glass, and dip into coarse salt.

How to Muddle

Muddling is a simple mashing technique for grinding herbs such as mint smooth in the bottom of a glass. You can buy a wooden muddler in a bar supply store. It crushes the herbs, much as the back of a soup spoon might, without scarring your glassware.

To Stir or Not to Stir

Pitchers of cocktails need at least ten seconds of stirring to mix properly. Carbonated mixers in drinks do much of their own stirring just by naturally bubbling. Two stirs from you will complete the job.

When to Shake

Shake any drink made with juices, sugar, eggs, or cream, or use an electric blender. Strain cocktails from shaker or blender to a glass through a coil-rimmed strainer.

Pouring

Pour drinks as soon as you make them or they will wilt. Leftovers should be discarded or they will be too diluted by the time you get to "seconds."

When making a batch of drinks at once, set up the glasses in a row. Pour until each glass is half full, then backtrack until the shaker is empty. That way everyone gets the same amount, thoroughly mixed.

Floating Liqueurs

Creating a rainbow effect in a glass with different colored cordials requires a special pouring technique. Simply pour each liqueur slowly over an inverted teaspoon (rounded side up) into a glass: Start with the heaviest liqueur first. (Recipes will give proper order.) Pour *slowly.* The rounded

surface of the spoon will spread each liqueur over the one beneath without mixing them. You can accomplish the same trick using a glass rod. Pour slowly down the rod.

The Secret of Flaming

The secret to setting brandy (or other high-alcohol spirits) aflame is first to warm it and its glass until almost hot. You can warm a glass by holding it by its stem above the flame or electric coil on your stove until the glass feels warm. (Avoid touching the glass to the flame or coil; that could char or crack the glass.)

Next, heat some brandy in a saucepan above the flame (or in a cooking pan). When the brandy is hot, ignite it with a match. If it's hot enough, it will flame instantly. Pour the flaming liquid carefully into the other brandy you want flamed. If all the liquid is warm enough, it will ignite.

Warning: Flames can shoot high suddenly. Look up and be sure there's nothing "en route" that can ignite. That includes your hair. Have an open box of baking soda handy in case of accidents. Pour it over flames to extinguish them. Use pot holders to protect your hands from the hot glass, spoon, or pan.

When Using Eggs

Eggs go into the shaker before the liquor (so that you can make sure the egg is fresh). To separate yolk from white, crack the egg in half on the edge of a glass. Pour the egg yolk from one half-shell to the other, back and forth, until the white runs down into the glass below and only the yolk is left in the shell.

Use cracked ice to blend egg with other ingredients you need chilled.

Using Fruit and Fruit Juices

Whenever possible, use only *fresh* fruit. Wash the outside peel before using. Fruit can be cut in wedges or in slices. If slices are used, they should be cut about one-quarter-inch thick and slit toward the center to fix slice on rim of glass. Make sure garnishes are fresh and cold.

When mixing drinks containing fruit juices, *always* pour the liquor last. Squeeze and strain fruit juices just before

using to ensure freshness and good taste. Avoid artificial, concentrated substitutes.

When recipes call for a twist of lemon peel, rub a narrow strip of peel around the rim of the glass to deposit the oil on it. Then twist the peel so that the oil (usually one small drop) will drop into the drink. Then drop in the peel. The lemon oil gives added character to the cocktail, which many prefer.

To Open Champagne or Sparkling Wine

When the bottle is well chilled, wrap it in a clean towel and undo the wire around the cork. Pointing the bottle away from people and priceless objects, hold the cork with one hand, grasp the bottle by the indentation on the bottom, and slowly turn the bottle (not the cork!) until the cork comes free with a pop! Pour slowly into the center of the glass.

To Open Wine

Cut the seal neatly around the neck with a sharp knife just below the top. Peel off, exposing the cork. Wipe off cork and bottle lip. Insert the corkscrew and turn until the corkscrew is completely inside the cork. With a steady pull, remove cork. If the cork crumbles or breaks, pour the wine through a tea strainer into another container for serving. The host or hostess should taste the wine to check its quality before offering it to guests.

MEASUREMENTS

A Buying Guide

Use the following as a reference for determining approximately how many bottles of liquor and wine you may need for various occasions.

For Cocktails	You'll Need at Least	For Buffet or Dinner	You'll Need at Least	For an After-Dinner Party	You'll Need at Least
10 to 16 drinks	1-750 ml	8 cocktails	1-750 ml	12 to 16 drinks	1-750 ml for 4 people
		8 glasses wine	2 bottles		
		4 liqueurs	1-500 ml		
		8 highballs	1-750 ml		
15 to 22 drinks	2-750 mls	12 cocktails	1-750 ml	18 to 26 drinks	2-750 mls for 6 people
		12 glasses wine	2 bottles		
		8 liqueurs	1-750 ml		
		18 highballs	2-750 mls		
18 to 24 drinks	2-750 mls	16 cocktails	1-750 ml	20 to 34 drinks	2-750 mls for 8 people
		16 glasses wine	3 bottles		
		10 liqueurs	1-750 ml		
		18 highballs	2-750 mls		
20 to 40 drinks	3-750 mls	24 cocktails	2-750 mls	25 to 45 drinks	3-750 mls for 12 people
		24 glasses wine	4 bottles		
		16 liqueurs	1-750 ml		
		30 highballs	3-750 mls		
40 to 65 drinks	4-750 mls	40 cocktails	3-750 mls	45 to 75 drinks	5-750 mls for 20 people
		40 glasses wine	7 bottles		
		25 liqueurs	2-750 mls		
		50 highballs	4-750 mls		

Measuring

Even the most professional bartender measures the ingredients of every drink, even though experience may permit some to do this by eye and by skillful freehand pouring. However, to make a perfect drink every time, measure all ingredients. Remember, too, that many drinks can be spoiled by being too strong as well as too weak.

Some standard bar measures:

1 Dash (or splash)	1/6 teaspoon (1/32 ounce)
1 Teaspoon (bar spoon)	1/8 ounce
1 Tablespoon	3/8 ounce
1 Pony	1 ounce
1 Jigger (barglass)	$1^{1}/_{2}$ ounces
1 Wineglass	4 ounces
1 Split	6 ounces
1 Cup	8 ounces

Metric Standards of Fill for Distilled Spirits

Metric Size	Fluid Ounces	Nearest U.S. Equivalent	Fluid Ounces	Number of Bottles per Case
50 ml.	1.7	miniature	1.6	120
100 ml.	3.4	1/4 pint	4	48
200 ml.	6.8	1/2 pint	8	48
375 ml.	12.7	3/4 pint	12	24
500 ml.	16.9	1 pint	16	24
750 ml.	25.4	4/5 quart	25.6	12
1 liter	33.8	1 quart	32	12
1.75 liters	59.2	1/2 gallon	64	6

Metric Sizes for Wine

Name of Package	New Metric Size	Equivalent Fluid Oz.	Bottles Per Case
Split	187 ml.	6.34	48
Tenth	375 ml.	12.68	24
Fifth	750 ml.	25.36	12
Quart	1 liter	33.81	12
Magnum	1.5 liters	50.72	6
Jeroboam	3 liters	101.44	4

ml. = milliliters   1 liter = 1,000 milliliters

Liquid Measures

Metric Units

10 milliliters	=	1 centiliter
10 centiliters	=	1 deciliter
10 deciliters	=	1 liter
10 liters	=	1 decaliter
10 decaliters	=	1 hectoliter
10 hectoliters	=	1 kiloliter

Metric and United States Equivalents

U.S. Unit	Metric Unit
1 fluid ounce	= 29.573 milliliters
1 quart	= 9.4635 deciliters 0.94635 liter
1 gallon	= 3.7854 liters
3.3814 fluid ounces	= 1 milliliter
0.033814 fluid ounce	= 1 decaliter
33.814 fluid ounces 1.0567 quarts 0.26417 gallon	= 1 liter

CALORIE COUNTS

To determine the caloric intake of your favorite cocktail, use the following chart as a guide.

Beverage	Calories per 1 oz. Serving
White wine (24 proof)	23
Red wine (24 proof)	23
Beer (typical American)	12
Champagne (25 proof)	26
Liqueurs (34–48 proof)	86–105
All Straight Spirits:	
80 proof	65
86 proof	70
90 proof	74

AMERICA'S FAVORITE DRINKS

a) Gin and Tonic b) Black Russian
c) Margarita d) Screwdriver

a) Tom Collins b) Manhattan c) Brandy Alexander d) Whiskey Sour

BLACK RUSSIAN
1½ oz.   Vodka
¾ oz.   Coffee Liqueur
Pour over ice cubes in old-fashioned cocktail glass.

BLOODY MARY
1½ oz. Vodka
3 oz.   Tomato Juice
1 dash Lemon Juice
½ tsp. Worcestershire
      Sauce
2 or 3 drops Tabasco
      Sauce
Pepper and Salt
Shake with ice and strain
into old-fashioned glass
over ice cubes. A wedge of
lime may be added.

BRANDY ALEXANDER
½ oz. Crème de Cacao
    (Brown)
½ oz. Brandy
½ oz. Heavy Cream
Shake well with cracked ice
and strain into a cocktail
glass.

DAIQUIRI
Juice of 1 Lime
1 tsp. Powdered Sugar
1½ oz. Light Rum
Shake with ice and strain
into cocktail glass.

GIMLET
1 oz. Lime Juice
1 tsp. Powdered Sugar
1½ oz. Gin
Shake with ice and strain into cocktail glass.

GIN AND TONIC
2 oz. Gin
Tonic
Pour gin into highball glass over ice cubes and fill with tonic water. Stir.

MANHATTAN
¾ oz. Sweet Vermouth
1½ oz. Blended Whiskey
Stir with ice and strain into cocktail glass. Serve with a cherry.

MARGARITA
1½ oz. Tequila
½ oz. Triple Sec
1 oz. Lemon or Lime Juice
Rub rim of cocktail glass with rind of lemon or lime, dip rim in salt. Shake ingredients with ice and strain into the salt-rimmed glass.

MARTINI (Extra Dry) (8-to-1)
2 oz. Gin
¼ oz. Dry Vermouth
Stir vermouth and gin over ice cubes in a mixing glass. Strain into cocktail glass. Serve with a twist of lemon peel or olive, if desired.

PIÑA COLADA
3 oz. Rum
3 tbsp. Coconut Milk
3 tbsp. Crushed Pineapple
Place in an electric blender with two cups of crushed ice and blend at high speed for a short time. Strain into collins glass and serve with straw.

SCREWDRIVER
Put two or three cubes of ice into highball glass. Add 2 oz. Vodka. Fill balance of glass with orange juice and stir.

TEQUILA SUNRISE
2 oz. Tequila
4 oz. Orange Juice
¾ oz. Grenadine
Stir tequila and orange juice with ice and strain into highball glass. Add ice cubes. Pour in grenadine slowly and allow to settle. Before drinking, stir to complete your sunrise.

TOM COLLINS
Juice of ¹/₂ Lemon
1 tsp. Powdered Sugar
2 oz. Gin

Shake with ice and strain into collins glass. Add several ice cubes, fill with carbonated water, and stir. Decorate with slices of lemon, orange, and a cherry. Serve with straw.

WHISKEY SOUR
Juice of ¹/₂ Lemon
¹/₂ tsp. Powdered Sugar
2 oz. Blended Whiskey

Shake with ice and strain into sour glass. Decorate with a half-slice of lemon and a cherry.

a) Martini b) Tequila Sunrise
c) Dacquiri d) Bloody Mary

NEW DRINKS

ALABAMA SLAMMER
1 oz. Amaretto
1 oz. Southern Comfort
$^1/_2$ oz. Sloe Gin
Stir in a highball glass over ice and add a splash of lemon juice.

BLUE MARGARITA
$1^1/_2$ oz. Tequila
$^1/_2$ oz. Blue Curaçao
1 oz. Lime Juice
Rub rim of cocktail glass with lime juice. Dip rim in coarse salt. Shake ingredients with ice and strain into glass.

CAPE CODDER
$1^1/_2$ oz. Vodka
5 oz. Cranberry Juice
Pour into highball glass over ice. Stir well. Garnish with a wedge of lime.

FUZZY NAVEL
3 oz. 48-Proof Peach Schnapps
3 oz. Orange Juice
Combine orange juice and schnapps and pour over ice in highball glass. Garnish with orange slice.

BAHAMA MAMA
$^1/_2$ oz. Dark Rum
$^1/_2$ oz. Coconut Liqueur
$^1/_4$ oz. 151-Proof Rum
$^1/_4$ oz. Coffee Liqueur
Juice of $^1/_2$ Lemon
4 oz. Pineapple Juice
Combine ingredients and pour over cracked ice in highball glass. Garnish with strawberry or cherry.

BELLINI ⓛ
3 oz. Italian White Peach Juice (or Peach Nectar)
1 dash Lemon Juice
3 oz. Chilled Sparkling Wine (Dry)
1 dash Black Currant Juice or Grenadine
Pour chilled white peach juice into champagne flute. Add dash of lemon juice (more if peach nectar is substituted) and dash of black currant juice or grenadine for color. Fill with chilled sparkling wine.

ⓛ indicates lower alcohol content

a) Fuzzy Navel b) Passion Mimosa c) Indian Summer d) Kamikaze

a) Melon Ball b) Cape Codder
c) Blue Margarita

INDIAN SUMMER 🍸

Wet sour glass edge and rim and then dip in cinnamon. Add **2 ounces Apple Schnapps**. Top off with hot apple cider. Add cinnamon stick if desired.

KAMIKAZE

1 oz.   Lime Juice
1 oz.   Triple Sec
1 oz.   Vodka

Shake and serve over ice in old-fashioned glass.

LONG ISLAND TEA

$^1/_2$ oz. Vodka
$^1/_2$ oz. Gin
$^1/_2$ oz. Light Rum
$^1/_2$ oz. Tequila
Juice of $^1/_2$ Lemon

Combine ingredients and pour over ice in highball glass. Add a dash of cola for color. Garnish with slice of lemon.

MELON BALL

1 oz.   Melon Liqueur
1 oz.   Vodka
2 oz.   Pineapple Juice

Pour over ice in a highball glass and garnish with an orange, pineapple, or watermelon slice.

PASSION MIMOSA 🅛

2 oz.   Chilled Passion
        Fruit Juice
Chilled Champagne

Pour chilled juice into flute, fill with chilled champagne. Garnish with strawberry.

TOASTED ALMOND

$1^1/_2$ oz.   Coffee Liqueur
1 oz.   Amaretto
$1^1/_2$ oz.   Cream or Milk

Add all ingredients over ice in an old-fashioned glass.

WOO WOO

$1^1/_2$ oz. Hot Shot
        Tropical Fruit Liqueur
        or Peach Schnapps
$1^1/_2$ oz. Vodka
$3^1/_2$ oz. Cranberry Juice

Pour ingredients over ice in a highball glass and stir.

🅛 indicates lower alcohol content

a) Grape Berry b) Lemon Squash

A

ABBEY COCKTAIL
$1^1/_2$ oz. Gin
Juice of $^1/_4$ Orange
1 dash Orange Bitters
Shake with ice and strain into cocktail glass. Add a maraschino cherry.

ABSINTHE DRIP COCKTAIL
$1^1/_2$ oz. Anis
1 Sugar Cube
Pour Anis into special drip glass or old-fashioned cocktail glass. Place sugar cube over hole of drip spoon (or in silver tea strainer). Pack spoon or strainer with cracked ice, pour cold water to fill. When water has dripped through, drink is ready.

ABSINTHE SPECIAL COCKTAIL
$1^1/_2$ oz. Anis
1 oz. Water
$^1/_4$ tsp. Powdered Sugar
1 dash Orange Bitters
Shake with ice and strain into cocktail glass.

ACAPULCO
$1^1/_2$ oz. Light Rum
1 tbsp. Lime Juice
$1^1/_2$ tsp. Triple Sec
1 tsp. Sugar
1 Egg White
Combine and shake all ingredients with ice and strain into old-fashioned glass over ice cubes. Add a sprig of mint.

ADAM AND EVE
1 oz. Forbidden Fruit
1 oz. Gin
1 oz. Brandy
1 dash Lemon Juice
Shake well with cracked ice and strain into cocktail glass.

ADONIS COCKTAIL
1 dash Orange Bitters
$^3/_4$ oz. Sweet Vermouth
$1^1/_2$ oz. Dry Sherry
Stir with ice and strain into cocktail glass.

AFFAIR
2 oz. Strawberry Schnapps
2 oz. Cranberry Juice
2 oz. Orange Juice
Pour over ice in a highball glass and top wth club soda if desired.

AFFINITY COCKTAIL
1 oz. Dry Vermouth
1 oz. Sweet Vermouth
1 oz. Scotch
3 dashes Orange Bitters
Stir with ice and strain into cocktail glass.

AFTER DINNER COCKTAIL
1 oz. Apricot-Flavored Brandy
1 oz. Triple Sec
Juice of 1 Lime
Shake with ice and strain into cocktail glass. Leave lime in glass.

AFTER SUPPER COCKTAIL
1 oz. Apricot-Flavored Brandy
1 oz. Triple Sec
$^1/_2$ tsp. Lemon Juice
Shake with ice and strain into cocktail glass.

A.J.
$1^1/_2$ oz. Applejack
1 oz. Grapefruit Juice
Shake with ice and strain into cocktail glass.

ALABAMA FIZZ
Juice of $^1/_2$ Lemon
1 tsp. Powdered Sugar
2 oz. Gin
Shake well with cracked ice and strain into highball glass over two ice cubes. Fill with carbonated water. Add two sprigs of fresh mint.

ALABAMA SLAMMER
1 oz. Amaretto
1 oz. Southern Comfort
$^1/_2$ oz. Sloe Gin
Stir in a highball glass over ice and add a splash of lemon juice.

ALASKA COCKTAIL
2 dashes Orange Bitters
$1^1/_2$ oz. Gin
$^3/_4$ oz. Chartreuse (Yellow)
Stir with ice and strain into cocktail glass.

ALBEMARLE FIZZ
Juice of $^1/_2$ Lemon
1 tsp. Powdered Sugar
2 oz. Gin
1 tsp. Raspberry Syrup
Shake with ice and strain into highball glass over two ice cubes. Fill with carbonated water.

ALEXANDER COCKTAIL NO. 1
1 oz. Gin
1 oz. Crème de Cacao (White)
1 oz. Light Cream
Shake with ice and strain into cocktail glass. Sprinkle nutmeg on top.

ALEXANDER COCKTAIL NO. 2
1 oz. Crème de Cacao (White)
1 oz. Brandy
1 oz. Light Cream
Shake with ice and strain into cocktail glass. Sprinkle nutmeg on top.

ALEXANDER'S SISTER COCKTAIL
1 oz. Dry Gin
1 oz. Crème de Menthe (Green)
1 oz. Light Cream
Shake with ice and strain into cocktail glass. Sprinkle nutmeg on top.

ALFIE COCKTAIL
1½ oz. Lemon Vodka
1 tbsp. Pineapple Juice
1 dash Triple Sec
Shake with ice and strain into cocktail glass.

ALGONQUIN
1½ oz. Blended Whiskey
1 oz. Dry Vermouth
1 oz. Pineapple Juice
Shake with ice and strain into cocktail glass.

ALLEGHENY
1 oz. Bourbon
1 oz. Dry Vermouth
1½ tsp. Blackberry-Flavored Brandy
1½ tsp. Lemon Juice
Shake with ice and strain into cocktail glass. Add a twist of lemon peel on top.

ALLEN COCKTAIL
1½ tsp. Lemon Juice
¾ oz. Maraschino
1½ oz. Gin
Shake with ice and strain into cocktail glass.

ALLIES COCKTAIL
1 oz. Dry Vermouth
1 oz. Gin
½ tsp. Kümmel
Stir with ice and strain into cocktail glass.

ALMERIA
1½ oz. Rum
1 oz. Coffee-Flavored Liqueur
1 Egg White
Shake all ingredients with cracked ice and strain into cocktail glass.

AMARETTO AND CREAM
1½ oz. Amaretto
1½ oz. Light Cream
Shake well with cracked ice. Strain and serve in cocktail glass.

AMARETTO MIST
1½ oz. Amaretto
Serve in an old-fashioned glass over crushed ice with a twist of lemon or a wedge of lime, if desired.

AMARETTO ROSE
1½ oz. Amaretto
½ oz. Rose's Lime Juice
Club Soda
Pour Amaretto and lime juice over ice in a collins glass and fill with club soda.

AMARETTO SOUR

$1^1/_2$ oz.   Amaretto
$^3/_4$ oz. Lemon Juice (No
   Sugar)

Shake well with cracked ice
and strain into sour glass.
Garnish with a slice of
orange.

AMARETTO STINGER

$1^1/_2$ oz.   Amaretto
$^3/_4$ oz. Crème de Menthe
   (White)

Shake well with ice. Strain
and serve in cocktail glass.

AMARETTO TEA

6 oz.   Hot Tea
$1^1/_2$ to 2 oz. Amaretto
   Whipped Cream

Pour hot tea into a
stemmed glass, using a
spoon in glass to prevent
cracking. Add Amaretto but
do not stir. Top with
chilled whipped cream.

AMBASSADOR'S MORNING LIFT

32 oz. Prepared Dairy
   Eggnog
6 oz.   Cognac
3 oz.   Jamaica Rum
3 oz.   Crème de Cacao
   (Brown)

Combine in large punch
bowl and serve. Brandy or
bourbon may be
substituted for cognac.

AMBROSIA

1 oz.   Applejack
1 oz.   Brandy
1 dash Triple Sec
Juice of 1 Lemon
Chilled champagne

Shake all ingredients
except champagne. Pour
contents into highball glass
with cubed ice. Fill with
chilled champagne.

AMERICAN BEAUTY COCKTAIL

1 tbsp. Orange Juice
1 tbsp. Grenadine
$^1/_2$ oz. Dry Vermouth
$^1/_2$ oz. Brandy
$^1/_4$ tsp. Crème de Menthe
   (White)
1 dash Port

Shake with ice and strain
into cocktail glass and top
with a dash of port.

AMERICAN GROG

1 lump Sugar
Juice of $^1/_4$ Lemon
$1^1/_2$ oz.   Light Rum

Pour ingredients into hot
mug and fill with hot water.
Stir.

AMERICANO

2 oz.   Sweet Vermouth
2 oz.   Campari

Pour sweet vermouth and
Campari into highball glass
over ice cubes. Fill with
carbonated water and stir.
Add a twist of lemon peel.

AMER PICON COCKTAIL

Juice of 1 Lime   **L**
1 tsp.   Grenadine
$1^1/_2$ oz.   Amer Picon
Shake with ice and strain
into cocktail glass.

ANDALUSIA

$1^1/_2$ oz.   Dry Sherry
$^1/_2$ oz.   Brandy
$^1/_2$ oz.   Light Rum
Stir well with cracked ice
and strain into cocktail
glass.

ANGEL FACE **L**

1 oz.   Gin
$^1/_2$ oz.   Apricot-Flavored
     Brandy
$^1/_2$ oz.   Apple Brandy
Shake well with cracked ice
and strain into cocktail
glass.

ANGEL'S DELIGHT

$1^1/_2$ tsp.   Grenadine
$1^1/_2$ tsp.   Triple Sec
$1^1/_2$ tsp.   Sloe Gin
$1^1/_2$ tsp.   Light Cream
Pour carefully, in order
given, into pousse-café
glass so that each
ingredient floats on
preceding one without
mixing.

ANGEL'S KISS

$^1/_4$ oz.   Crème de Cacao
     (White)
$^1/_4$ oz.   Sloe Gin
$^1/_4$ oz.   Brandy
$^1/_4$ oz.   Light Cream
Pour ingredients carefully,
in order given, so that they
do not mix. Use pousse-
café glass.

ANGEL'S TIP

$^3/_4$ oz.   Crème de Cacao
     (White)
$^1/_4$ oz.   Light Cream
Float cream and insert
toothpick in cherry and put
on top. Use pousse-café
glass.

ANGEL'S WING

$^1/_2$ oz.   Crème de Cacao
     (White)
$^1/_2$ oz.   Brandy
1 tbsp.   Light Cream
Pour ingredients carefully,
in order given, so that they
do not mix. Use pousse-
café glass.

ANGLER'S COCKTAIL

2 dashes Bitters
3 dashes Orange Bitters
$1^1/_2$ oz.   Gin
1 dash   Grenadine
Shake with cracked ice and
pour into old-fashioned
glass over ice cubes.

ANTE

Y 1 oz. Apple Brandy
1/2 oz. Triple Sec
1 oz. Dubonnet®

Stir well with cracked ice and strain into cocktail glass.

ANTOINE SPECIAL

1 1/2 oz. Dubonnet®
1 1/2 oz. Dry Vermouth

Float vermouth on top of chilled Dubonnet® in a wine glass.

APPLE BLOW FIZZ

1 Egg White
Juice of 1/2 Lemon
1 tsp. Powdered Sugar
2 oz. Apple Brandy

Shake with ice and strain into highball glass with two ice cubes. Fill with carbonated water.

APPLE BRANDY COCKTAIL

Y 1 1/2 oz. Apple Brandy
1 tsp. Grenadine
1 tsp. Lemon Juice

Shake with ice and strain into cocktail glass.

APPLE BRANDY HIGHBALL

2 oz. Apple Brandy

Pour over ice cubes in a highball glass. Fill with ginger ale or carbonated water. Add a twist of lemon peel, if desired, and stir.

APPLE BRANDY RICKEY

Juice of 1/2 Lime
1 1/2 oz. Apple Brandy

Fill highball glass with carbonated water and ice cubes. Leave lime in glass. Stir.

APPLE BRANDY SOUR

Juice of 1/2 Lemon
1/2 tsp. Powdered Sugar
2 oz. Apple Brandy

Shake with ice and strain into sour glass. Decorate with a half-slice of lemon and a cherry.

APPLECAR

Y 1 oz. Applejack
1 oz. Triple Sec
1 oz. Lemon Juice

Shake with ice and strain into cocktail glass.

APPLE COLADA

2 oz. Apple Schnapps
1 oz. Cream of Coconut
1 oz. Half-and-Half

Blend all ingredients with two cups of crushed ice in an electric blender at a high speed. Pour into a tall glass and serve with a straw. Garnish with an apple slice and cherry.

a) Strawberry Sunrise b) Apple Colada
c) Rum Swizzle

APPLEJACK PUNCH
1.75 liter Applejack
4 oz. Grenadine
16 oz. Orange Juice
64 oz. Ginger Ale

Combine first three ingredients in punch bowl with large block of ice. Add ginger ale and slices of apple.

APPLE PIE NO. 1
3/4 oz. Light Rum
3/4 oz. Sweet Vermouth
1 tsp. Apple Brandy
1/2 tsp. Grenadine
1 tsp. Lemon Juice

Shake with ice and strain into cocktail glass.

APPLE PIE NO. 2
3 oz. Apple Schnapps
1 splash Cinnamon Schnapps

Pour into old-fashioned glass over ice and garnish with an apple slice and sprinkle with cinnamon.

APPLE RUM RICKEY
3/4 oz. Applejack
3/4 oz. Light Rum
1/4 Lime

Pour applejack and rum into highball glass over ice cubes. Fill with carbonated water. Squeeze lime and drop into glass. Stir.

APRICOT ANISE COLLINS
1 1/2 oz. Gin
1/2 oz. Apricot-Flavored Brandy
1 1/2 tsp. Anisette
1 tbsp. Lemon Juice

Shake with ice and strain into collins glass over ice. Fill with carbonated water and stir lightly. Garnish with a slice of lemon.

APRICOT BRANDY RICKEY
Juice of 1/2 Lime
2 oz. Apricot-Flavored Brandy

Pour into highball glass over ice cubes and fill with carbonated water. Drop a rind of lime into glass. Stir.

APRICOT COCKTAIL
Juice of $^1/_4$ Lemon
Juice of $^1/_4$ Orange
1$^1/_2$ oz. Apricot-Flavored Brandy
1 tsp. Gin

Shake with ice and strain into cocktail glass.

APRICOT COOLER
$^1/_2$ tsp. Powdered Sugar
2 oz. Carbonated Water
2 oz. Apricot-Flavored Brandy

In a collins glass, dissolve powdered sugar and carbonated water. Stir and fill glass with cracked ice and add brandy.
Fill with carbonated water or ginger ale and stir again. Insert a spiral of orange or lemon peel (or both) and dangle end over rim of glass.

APRICOT FIZZ
Juice of $^1/_2$ Lemon
Juice of $^1/_2$ Lime
1 tsp. Powdered Sugar
2 oz. Apricot-Flavored Brandy

Shake with cracked ice and strain into highball glass with two ice cubes. Fill with carbonated water.

APRICOT LADY
1$^1/_4$ oz. Light Rum
1 oz. Apricot-Flavored Brandy
$^1/_4$ tsp. Triple Sec
1 tbsp. Lime Juice
1 Egg White

Shake all ingredients with ice and strain into old-fashioned glass over ice cubes. Add an orange slice.

APRIHOT
3 oz. Apricot-Flavored Brandy
3 oz. Boiling Water

Combine in coffee mug with a dash of cinnamon, and garnish with an orange or lemon slice.

AQUARIUS
1$^1/_2$ oz. Blended Whiskey
$^1/_2$ oz. Cherry-Flavored Brandy
1 oz. Cranberry Juice

Shake with ice and strain into old-fashioned glass over ice.

AQUEDUCT
1$^1/_2$ oz. Vodka
1$^1/_2$ tsp. Curaçao (White)
1$^1/_2$ tsp. Apricot-Flavored Brandy
1 tbsp. Lime Juice

Combine and shake all ingredients and strain into cocktail glass. Add a twist of orange peel.

ARISE MY LOVE
1 tsp. Crème de Menthe (Green)
Chilled champagne
Put crème de menthe into champagne flute. Fill with chilled champagne.

ARTILLERY
1½ oz. Gin
1½ tsp. Sweet Vermouth
2 dashes Bitters
Stir with ice and strain into cocktail glass.

AUNT JEMIMA
½ oz. Brandy
½ oz. Crème de Cacao (White)
½ oz. Benedictine
Pour carefully, in order given, into a pousse-café glass so that ingredients do not mix.

Brandy

B

B & B
½ oz. Benedictine
½ oz. Brandy
Use cordial glass and carefully float the brandy on top of the Benedictine.

BABBIE'S SPECIAL COCKTAIL
1 tbsp. Light Cream
1½ oz. Apricot-Flavored Brandy
¼ tsp. Gin
Shake with ice and strain into cocktail glass.

BACARDI COCKTAIL
1½ oz. Bacardi Rum
Juice of ½ Lime
½ tsp. Grenadine
Shake with ice and strain into cocktail glass.

BACHELOR'S BAIT COCKTAIL
1½ oz. Gin
1 Egg White
1 dash Orange Bitters
½ tsp. Grenadine
Shake with ice and strain into cocktail glass.

BAHAMA MAMA
½ oz. Dark Rum
½ oz. Coconut Liqueur
¼ oz. 151-Proof Rum
¼ oz. Coffee Liqueur
Juice of ½ Lemon
4 oz. Pineapple Juice
Combine ingredients and pour over cracked ice in tall glass. Garnish with strawberry or cherry.

BALTIMORE BRACER
1 oz. Anisette
1 oz. Brandy
1 Egg White
Shake with ice and strain into cocktail glass.

BALTIMORE EGGNOG
1 Whole Egg
1 tsp. Powdered Sugar
1 oz. Brandy
1 oz. Jamaica Rum
1 oz. Madeira
¾ cup Milk
Shake well with ice and strain into collins glass. Sprinkle nutmeg on top.

BAMBOO COCKTAIL
1½ oz. Dry Sherry
¾ oz. Dry Vermouth
1 dash Orange Bitters
Stir with ice and strain into cocktail glass.

 indicates lower alcohol content

BANANA COW

▽ 1 oz.   Light Rum
1 oz.   Creme de Banana
1¹/₂ oz.   cream
Dash Grenadine

Shake ingredients with crushed ice and strain into cocktail glass. Garnish with banana slice and top with nutmeg.

BANANA DAIQUIRI

Same as Frozen Daiquiri on page 94 but add a sliced medium-size ripe banana before blending.

BANANA PUNCH

2 oz.   Vodka
1¹/₂ tsp. Apricot-Flavored Brandy
Juice of ¹/₂ Lime

Pour into collins glass filled with crushed ice. Add carbonated water and top with slices of banana and sprigs of mint.

BANSHEE

▽ 1 oz.   Crème de Banana
¹/₂ oz.   Crème de Cacao (White)
¹/₂ oz.   Light Cream

Shake with cracked ice and strain into cocktail glass.

BARBARY COAST

▽ ¹/₂ oz.   Gin
¹/₂ oz.   Rum
¹/₂ oz.   White Crème de Cacao
¹/₂ oz.   Scotch
¹/₂ oz.   Light Cream

Shake with ice and strain into cocktail glass.

BARNABY'S BUFFALO BLIZZARD*

1 oz.   Crème de Cacao (White)
³/₄ oz.   Vodka
1 oz.   Galliano
Vanilla Ice Cream
1 dash Grenadine
Whipped Cream
³/₄ cup   Milk

Shake or blend. Serve in a collins glass.

BARON COCKTAIL

▽ ¹/₂ oz.   Dry Vermouth
1¹/₂ oz.   Gin
1¹/₂ tsp. Triple Sec
¹/₂ tsp.   Sweet Vermouth

Stir with ice and strain into cocktail glass. Add a twist of lemon peel.

BARTON SPECIAL

¹/₂ oz.   Applejack
¹/₄ oz.   Scotch
¹/₄ oz.   Gin

Shake with ice and strain into old-fashioned glass over ice cubes.

BEACHCOMBER*

▽ 1¹/₂ oz.   Light Rum
¹/₂ oz.   Lime Juice
¹/₂ oz.   Triple Sec
1 dash Maraschino

Shake with cracked ice and strain into cocktail glass rimmed with lime juice and sugar.

*Barnaby's Restaurant, Buffalo, N.Y.

BEADLESTONE COCKTAIL

$1^{1}/_{2}$ oz.   Dry Vermouth
$1^{1}/_{2}$ oz.   Scotch
Stir with ice and strain into cocktail glass.

BEALS COCKTAIL

$1^{1}/_{2}$ oz.   Scotch
$^{1}/_{2}$ oz.   Dry Vermouth
$^{1}/_{2}$ oz.   Sweet Vermouth
Stir with ice and strain into cocktail glass.

BEAUTY SPOT COCKTAIL

1 tsp.   Orange Juice
$^{1}/_{2}$ oz.   Sweet Vermouth
$^{1}/_{2}$ oz.   Dry Vermouth
1 oz.   Gin
1 dash Grenadine
Shake first four ingredients with ice and strain into cocktail glass, with a dash of grenadine in bottom of glass.

BEER BUSTER

$1^{1}/_{2}$ oz.   100-proof Vodka
Ice-Cold Beer
2 dashes Tabasco Sauce
Put vodka in a highball glass and fill with beer or ale. Add Tabasco and stir lightly.

BEE STINGER

Substitute blackberry brandy for brandy in a Stinger, page 175.

BELLINI ⓛ

3 oz.   Italian White Peach Juice (or Peach Nectar)
1 dash Lemon Juice
3 oz.   Chilled sparkling Wine (Dry)
1 dash Black Currant Juice or Grenadine
Pour chilled white peach juice into champagne flute. Add dash of lemon juice (more if peach nectar is substituted) and dash of black currant juice or grenadine for color. Fill with chilled sparkling wine.

BELMONT COCKTAIL

2 oz.   Gin
1 tsp.   Raspberry Syrup
$^{3}/_{4}$ oz.   Light Cream
Shake with ice and strain into cocktail glass.

BENNETT COCKTAIL

Juice of $^{1}/_{2}$ Lime
$1^{1}/_{2}$ oz.   Gin
$^{1}/_{2}$ tsp.   Powdered Sugar
2 dashes Orange Bitters
Shake with ice and strain into cocktail glass.

BENTLEY

$1^{1}/_{2}$ oz.   Apple Brandy
1 oz.   Dubonnet®
Stir with cracked ice and strain into cocktail glass. Add a twist of lemon peel.

ⓛ indicates lower alcohol content

BERMUDA BOUQUET
Juice of ¹/₄ Orange
Juice of ¹/₂ Lemon
1 tsp. Powdered Sugar
1¹/₂ oz. Gin
1 oz. Apricot-Flavored Brandy
1 tsp. Grenadine
¹/₂ tsp. Triple Sec
Shake with ice and strain into highball glass with ice cubes.

BERMUDA HIGHBALL
³/₄ oz. Gin
³/₄ oz. Brandy
³/₄ oz. Dry Vermouth
Pour into highball glass over ice cubes. Fill with ginger ale or carbonated water. Add a twist of lemon peel and stir.

BERMUDA ROSE
1¹/₄ oz. Gin
1¹/₂ tsp. Apricot-Flavored Brandy
1¹/₂ tsp. Grenadine
Shake with ice and strain into cocktail glass.

BETSY ROSS
1¹/₂ oz. Brandy
1¹/₂ oz. Port
1 dash Triple Sec
Stir with cracked ice and strain into cocktail glass.

BETWEEN-THE-SHEETS
Juice of ¹/₄ Lemon
¹/₂ oz. Brandy
¹/₂ oz. Triple Sec
¹/₂ oz. Light Rum
Shake with ice and strain into cocktail glass.

BIFFY COCKTAIL
Juice of ¹/₂ Lemon
1 tbsp. Swedish Punch
1¹/₂ oz. Gin
Shake with ice and strain into cocktail glass.

BIJOU COCKTAIL
³/₄ oz. Gin
³/₄ oz. Chartreuse (Green)
³/₄ oz. Sweet Vermouth
1 dash Orange Bitters
Stir with ice and strain into cocktail glass. Add a cherry on top.

BIKINI
2 oz. Vodka
1 oz. Light Rum
¹/₂ oz. Milk
1 tsp. Sugar
Juice of ¹/₂ Lemon
Shake with ice and strain into cocktail glass. Garnish with a lemon twist.

BILLY TAYLOR
Juice of ¹/₂ Lime
2 oz. Gin
Fill collins glass with carbonated water and ice cubes. Stir.

BIRD-OF-PARADISE FIZZ
Juice of ¹/₂ Lemon
1 tsp. Powdered Sugar
1 Egg White
1 tsp. Grenadine
2 oz. Gin
Shake with ice and strain into highball glass over two ice cubes. Fill with carbonated water.

BISHOP
Juice of $1/4$ Lemon
Juice of $1/4$ Orange
1 tsp. Powdered Sugar
Burgundy Wine
Shake with ice and strain
into highball glass. Add
two ice cubes, fill with
burgundy, and stir well.
Decorate with fruits.

BITTERS
HIGHBALL 🅛
$3/4$ oz. Bitters
Ginger Ale or
    Carbonated Water
Fill highball glass with
bitters, ice cubes, and
ginger ale or carbonated
water. Add a twist of lemon
peel, if desired, and stir.

BITTERSWEET 🅛
1 oz. Sweet Vermouth
1 oz. Dry Vermouth
1 dash Bitters
1 dash Orange Bitters
Stir with cracked ice and
strain into cocktail glass.
Add a twist of orange peel.

BLACK DEVIL
2 oz. Light Rum
$1/2$ oz. Dry Vermouth
Stir with cracked ice and
strain into cocktail glass.
Add a black olive.

BLACK HAWK
$1^1/4$ oz. Blended
    Whiskey
$1^1/4$ oz. Sloe Gin
Stir with ice and strain into
cocktail glass. Serve with a
cherry.

BLACKJACK
1 oz. Kirschwasser
$1/2$ oz. Brandy
1 oz. Coffee
Shake with cracked ice and
strain into old-fashioned
glass over ice cubes.

BLACK MAGIC
$1^1/2$ oz. Vodka
$3/4$ oz. Coffee Liqueur
1 dash Lemon Juice
Stir and serve in old-
fashioned glass over ice
cubes and add a twist of
lemon peel.

BLACK MARIA
2 oz. Coffee-Flavored
    Brandy
2 oz. Light Rum
4 oz. Strong Black
    Coffee
2 tsp. Powdered Sugar
Stir in brandy snifter and
add cracked ice.

BLACK RUSSIAN
$1^1/2$ oz. Vodka
$3/4$ oz. Coffee Liqueur
Pour over ice cubes in old-
fashioned cocktail glass.

BLACK SOMBRERO
See Sombrero recipe on
page 172.

BLACKTHORN
$1^1/2$ oz. Sloe Gin
1 oz. Sweet Vermouth
Stir with ice and strain into
cocktail glass. Add a twist of
lemon peel.

🅛 indicates lower alcohol content

a) White Russian b) Grasshopper c) Toasted Almond

BLACK VELVET

5 oz. Chilled Stout
5 oz. Chilled Champagne

Pour very carefully, in order given, into champagne flute so that the stout and champagne don't mix.

BLANCHE

1 oz. Anisette
1 oz. Triple Sec
$^1/_2$ oz. Curaçao (White)

Shake with cracked ice and strain into cocktail glass.

BLARNEY STONE COCKTAIL

2 oz. Irish Whiskey
$^1/_2$ tsp. Anis
$^1/_2$ tsp. Triple Sec
$^1/_4$ tsp. Maraschino
1 dash Bitters

Shake with ice and strain into cocktail glass. Add a twist of orange peel and an olive.

BLOOD-AND-SAND COCKTAIL

1 tbsp. Orange Juice
$^1/_2$ oz. Scotch
$^1/_2$ oz. Cherry-Flavored Brandy
$^1/_2$ oz. Sweet Vermouth

Shake with ice and strain into cocktail glass.

BLOODHOUND COCKTAIL

$^1/_2$ oz. Dry Vermouth
$^1/_2$ oz. Sweet Vermouth
1 oz. Gin

Shake with ice and strain into cocktail glass. Decorate with two or three crushed strawberries.

BLOODY BULL

1 oz. Vodka
$^1/_2$ glass Tomato Juice
$^1/_2$ glass Beef Bouillon

Add all ingredients in a highball glass over ice. Stir and add a squeeze of lemon and a slice of lime.

BLOODY MARIA

1 oz. Tequila
2 oz. Tomato Juice
1 dash Lemon Juice
1 dash Tabasco Sauce
1 dash Celery Salt

Shake all ingredients with cracked ice. Strain into old-fashioned glass over ice cubes. Add a slice of lemon.

BLOODY MARY

$1^1/_2$ oz. Vodka
3 oz. Tomato Juice
1 dash Lemon Juice
$^1/_2$ tsp. Worcestershire Sauce
2 or 3 drops Tabasco Sauce
Pepper and Salt

Shake with ice and strain into old-fashioned glass over ice cubes. A wedge of lime may be added.

BLUE BIRD

1½ oz.   Gin
½ oz.   Triple Sec
1 dash Bitters

Stir with ice cubes and strain into cocktail glass. Add a twist of lemon peel and a cherry.

BLUE BLAZER ☕

Use two large silver-plated mugs, with handles.

2½ oz. Blended Whiskey
2½ oz. Boiling Water
1 tsp. Powdered Sugar

Put the whiskey into one mug and the boiling water into the other. Ignite the whiskey and, while blazing, mix both ingredients by pouring them four or five times from one mug to the other. If done well, this will have the appearance of a continuous stream of liquid fire. Sweeten with powdered sugar and serve with a twist of lemon peel. Serve in a 4-oz. punch cup.

BLUE DEVIL COCKTAIL

1 oz.   Gin
Juice of ½ Lemon or 1 Lime
1 tbsp. Maraschino
½ tsp. Blue Curaçao

Shake with ice and strain into cocktail glass.

BLUE HAWAIIAN

1 oz.   Light Rum
1 oz.   Blue Curaçao
2 oz.   Pineapple Juice
1 oz.   Cream of Coconut

Blend ingredients with one cup ice in blender at high speed. Pour in a highball glass. Garnish with a slice of pineapple and a cherry.

BLUE LAGOON

1 oz.   Vodka
1 oz.   Blue Curaçao
Lemonade

Pour first two ingredients over ice in a highball glass. Fill with lemonade. Garnish with a cherry.

BLUE MARGARITA

1½ oz. Tequila
½ oz. Blue Curaçao
1 oz.   Lime Juice

Rub rim of cocktail glass with lime juice. Dip rim in coarse salt. Shake ingredients with ice and strain into glass.

BLUE MONDAY COCKTAIL

1½ oz. Vodka
¾ oz. Triple Sec
1 dash Blue Food Coloring

Stir with ice and strain into cocktail glass.

BLUE MOON COCKTAIL

1½ oz. Gin
¾ oz. Blue Curaçao

Stir with ice and strain into cocktail glass. Add a twist of lemon peel.

BOBBY BURNS COCKTAIL

$1^1/_2$ oz. Sweet Vermouth
$1^1/_2$ oz. Scotch
$1^1/_4$ tsp. Benedictine

Stir with ice and strain into cocktail glass. Add a twist of lemon peel.

BOCCIE BALL

$1^1/_2$ oz. Amaretto
$1^1/_2$ oz. Orange Juice
2 oz. Club Soda

Serve in a highball glass over ice.

BOLERO

$1^1/_2$ oz. Light Rum
$3/_4$ oz. Apple Brandy
$1/_4$ tsp. Sweet Vermouth

Stir well with cracked ice and strain into cocktail glass.

BOMBAY COCKTAIL

$1/_2$ oz. Dry Vermouth
$1/_2$ oz. Sweet Vermouth
1 oz. Brandy
$1/_4$ tsp. Anis
$1/_2$ tsp. Triple Sec

Stir with ice and strain into cocktail glass.

BOMBAY PUNCH

Juice of 12 Lemons

Add enough powdered sugar to sweeten. Pour over a large block of ice in punch bowl and stir. Then add:

32 oz. Brandy
32 oz. Dry Sherry
$1/_2$ cup Maraschino
$1/_2$ cup Triple Sec
4 750-ml bottles Chilled Champagne
64 oz. Chilled Carbonated Water

Stir well and decorate with fruits in season. Serve in punch glasses.

BOOM BOOM PUNCH

64 oz. Light Rum
32 oz. Orange Juice
1 750-ml bottle Sweet Vermouth
1 750-ml bottle Chilled Champagne

Pour into punch bowl over large block of ice all ingredients except chilled champagne. Stir. Add chilled champagne on top. Decorate with sliced bananas.

BOOMERANG

1 oz. Dry Vermouth
$1^1/_2$ oz. Gin
1 dash Bitters
1 dash Maraschino

Stir with ice cubes and strain into cocktail glass. Add twist of lemon peel.

BORINQUEN
1½ oz. Light Rum
1 tbsp. Passion Fruit Syrup
1 oz. Lime Juice
1 oz. Orange Juice
1 tsp. 151-Proof Rum

Put half a cup of crushed ice into blender. Add all ingredients and blend at low speed. Pour into old-fashioned glass.

BOSOM CARESSER
1 oz. Brandy
1 oz. Madeira
½ oz. Triple Sec

Stir with cracked ice and strain into cocktail glass.

BOSTON BULLET
A Martini substituting an olive stuffed with an almond for the regular olive. See Martini on page 130.

BOSTON COCKTAIL
¾ oz. Gin
¾ oz. Apricot-Flavored Brandy
Juice of ¼ Lemon
1½ tsp. Grenadine

Shake with ice and strain into cocktail glass.

BOSTON COOLER
Into collins glass, put the juice of ½ lemon, 1 tsp. powdered sugar, and 2 oz. carbonated water. Stir. Then fill glass with cracked ice and add **2 oz. Light Rum.** Fill with carbonated water or ginger ale and stir again. Add spiral of orange or lemon peel (or both) and dangle end over rim of glass.

BOSTON GOLD
1 oz. Vodka
½ oz. Crème de Banana Orange Juice

Pour vodka and banana liqueur over ice cubes in highball glass. Fill with orange juice and stir.

BOSTON SIDECAR
¾ oz. Brandy
¾ oz. Light Rum
¾ oz. Triple Sec
Juice of ½ Lime

Shake with ice and strain into cocktail glass.

BOSTON SOUR
Juice of ½ Lemon
1 tsp. Powdered Sugar
2 oz. Blended Whiskey
1 Egg White

Shake with cracked ice and strain into sour glass. Add a slice of lemon and a cherry.

BOURBON HIGHBALL

Fill highball glass with 2 oz. Bourbon, ginger ale or carbonated water, and ice cubes. Add a twist of lemon peel, if desired, and stir.

BRANDIED MADEIRA

1 oz. Brandy
1 oz. Madeira
$^1/_2$ oz. Dry Vermouth
Stir with cracked ice and strain into old-fashioned glass over ice cubes. Add a twist of lemon peel.

BRANDIED PORT

1 oz. Brandy
1 oz. Tawny Port
1 tbsp. Lemon Juice
1 tsp. Maraschino
Shake all ingredients and strain into old-fashioned glass with ice cubes. Add a slice of orange.

BRANDY ALEXANDER

$^1/_2$ oz. Crème de Cacao (Brown)
$^1/_2$ oz. Brandy
$^1/_2$ oz. Heavy Cream
Shake well with cracked ice and strain into a cocktail glass.

BRANDY AND SODA

Pour 2 oz. Brandy into collins glass with ice cubes. Add carbonated water.

BRANDY BLAZER

1 lump Sugar
1 piece Orange Peel
2 oz. Brandy
Combine ingredients in old-fashioned glass. Light the liquid with match, stir with long spoon for a few seconds, and strain into hot punch cup.

BRANDY CASSIS

$1^1/_2$ oz. Brandy
1 oz. Lemon Juice
1 dash Crème de Cassis
Shake with cracked ice and strain into cocktail glass. Add a twist of lemon peel.

BRANDY COBBLER

1 tsp. Powdered Sugar
2 oz. Carbonated Water
2 oz. Brandy
Dissolve powdered sugar in carbonated water. Fill 10-oz. goblet with shaved ice. Add brandy. Stir well and decorate with fruits in season. Serve with straws.

BRANDY COCKTAIL

2 oz. Brandy
$^1/_4$ tsp. Sugar Syrup
2 dashes Bitters
Stir with ice and strain into cocktail glass. Add a twist of lemon peel.

BRANDY COLLINS
Juice of ¹/₂ Lemon
1 tsp. Powdered Sugar
2 oz. Brandy

Shake with cracked ice and strain into collins glass. Add cubes of ice, fill with carbonated water, and stir. Decorate with a slice of orange or lemon and a cherry. Serve with straws.

BRANDY CRUSTA COCKTAIL
Moisten the edge of a cocktail glass with lemon and dip into sugar. Cut the rind of half a lemon in a spiral and place in glass.

1 tsp. Maraschino
1 dash Bitters
1 tsp. Lemon Juice
¹/₂ oz. Triple Sec
2 oz. Brandy

Stir above ingredients with ice and strain into sugar-rimmed glass. Add a slice of orange.

BRANDY DAISY
Juice of ¹/₂ Lemon
¹/₂ tsp. Powdered Sugar
1 tsp. Raspberry Syrup or Grenadine
2 oz. Brandy

Shake with ice and strain into stein or 8-oz. metal cup. Add cubes of ice and decorate with fruit.

BRANDY EGGNOG
1 Whole Egg
1 tsp. Powdered Sugar
2 oz. Brandy

Shake with ice and strain into collins glass. Fill glass with milk. Sprinkle nutmeg on top.

BRANDY FIX
Juice of ¹/₂ Lemon
1 tsp. Powdered Sugar
1 tsp. Water
2¹/₂ oz. Brandy

Mix lemon juice, powdered sugar, and water in a highball glass. Stir. Then fill glass with shaved ice and brandy. Stir, add a slice of lemon. Serve with straws.

BRANDY FIZZ
Juice of ¹/₂ Lemon
1 tsp. Powdered Sugar
2 oz. Brandy

Shake with cracked ice and strain into highball glass over two ice cubes. Fill with carbonated water.

BRANDY FLIP
1 Whole Egg
1 tsp. Powdered Sugar
1¹/₂ oz. Brandy
2 tsps. Light Cream (if desired)

Shake with ice and strain into sour glass. Sprinkle a little nutmeg on top.

BRANDY GUMP COCKTAIL

1½ oz. Brandy
Juice of ½ Lemon
½ tsp. Grenadine

Shake with ice and strain into cocktail glass.

BRANDY HIGHBALL

In a highball glass pour 2 oz. Brandy over ice cubes and fill with ginger ale or carbonated water. Add a twist of lemon peel, if desired, and stir gently.

BRANDY JULEP

Into collins glass put 1 tsp. powdered sugar, five or six leaves fresh mint, and 2½ oz. Brandy. Then fill glass with finely shaved ice, and stir until mint rises to top, being careful not to bruise leaves. (Do not hold glass with hand while stirring.) Decorate with a slice of pineapple, orange, or lemon and a cherry. Serve with straws.

BRANDY MILK PUNCH

1 tsp. Powdered Sugar
2 oz. Brandy
1 cup Milk

Shake with ice, strain into collins glass, and sprinkle nutmeg on top.

BRANDY PUNCH

Juice of 1 dozen Lemons
Juice of 4 Oranges

Add enough sugar to sweeten and mix with:

1 cup Grenadine
32 oz. Carbonated Water

Pour over large block of ice in punch bowl and stir well. Then add:

1 cup Triple Sec
1.75 liter Brandy
2 cups Tea (optional)

Stir well and decorate with fruits in season. Serve in punch glasses.

BRANDY SANGAREE

Dissolve ½ tsp. powdered sugar in 1 tsp. of water, and add 2 oz. Brandy. Pour into highball glass over ice cubes. Fill with carbonated water. Stir. Float a tbsp. of port on top and sprinkle lightly with nutmeg.

BRANDY SLING

Dissolve 1 tsp. powdered sugar in tsp. of water and juice of $1/2$ lemon. Add **2 oz. Brandy**. Serve in old-fashioned cocktail glass with cubed ice and twist of lemon peel.

BRANDY SMASH

Muddle 1 lump sugar with 1 oz. carbonated water and 4 sprigs of fresh mint. Add **2 oz. Brandy** and ice cubes. Stir and decorate with a slice of orange and a cherry. Add a twist of lemon peel on top. Use old-fashioned cocktail glass.

BRANDY SOUR

Juice of $1/2$ Lemon
$1/2$ tsp. Powdered Sugar
2 oz. Brandy
Shake with ice and strain into sour glass. Decorate with a half slice of lemon and a cherry.

BRANDY SQUIRT

$1^1/2$ oz. Brandy
1 tbsp. Powdered Sugar
1 tsp. Grenadine
Shake with ice and strain into highball glass and fill with carbonated water. Decorate with stick of pineapple and strawberries.

BRANDY SWIZZLE

Make same as Gin Swizzle (see page 99), using **2 oz. Brandy**.

BRANDY TODDY

In an old-fashioned glass dissolve:
$1/2$ tsp. Powdered Sugar
1 tsp. Water
Add:
2 oz. Brandy
1 Ice Cube
Stir and add a twist of lemon peel on top.

BRANDY TODDY (HOT)

Put lump of sugar into punch cup and fill two-thirds with boiling water. Add **2 oz. Brandy**. Stir and decorate with a slice of lemon. Sprinkle nutmeg on top.

BRANDY VERMOUTH COCKTAIL

$1/2$ oz. Sweet Vermouth
2 oz. Brandy
1 dash Bitters
Stir with ice and strain into cocktail glass.

BRANTINI

$1^1/2$ oz. Brandy
1 oz. Gin
1 dash Dry Vermouth
Stir with cracked ice and strain into old-fashioned glass with cubed ice. Add a twist of lemon peel.

BRAVE BULL
1½ oz. Tequila
1 oz. Coffee Liqueur
Pour over ice cubes in old-fashioned glass and stir. Add a twist of lemon.

BRAZIL COCKTAIL
1½ oz. Dry Vermouth
1½ oz. Dry Sherry
1 dash Bitters
¼ tsp. Anis
Stir with ice and strain into cocktail glass.

BREAKFAST EGGNOG
1 Whole Egg
½ oz. Triple Sec
2 oz. Apricot-Flavored Brandy
6 oz. Milk
Shake well with cracked ice and strain into collins glass. Sprinkle nutmeg on top.

BRIGHTON PUNCH
¾ oz. Bourbon
¾ oz. Brandy
¾ oz. Benedictine
Juice of ½ Orange
Juice of ½ Lemon
Shake with ice and pour into collins glass nearly filled with shaved ice. Then fill with carbonated water and stir gently. Decorate with orange and lemon slices and serve with straw.

BROKEN SPUR COCKTAIL
¾ oz. Sweet Vermouth
1½ oz. Port
¼ tsp. Triple Sec
Stir with ice and strain into cocktail glass.

BRONX COCKTAIL
1 oz. Gin
½ oz. Dry Vermouth
½ oz. Sweet Vermouth
Juice of ¼ Orange
Shake with ice and strain into cocktail glass. Serve with slice of orange.

BRONX COCKTAIL (DRY)
1 oz. Gin
1 oz. Dry Vermouth
Juice of ¼ Orange
Shake with ice and strain into cocktail glass. Serve with slice of orange.

BRONX GOLDEN COCKTAIL
Same as Bronx Cocktail with the addition of one egg yolk. Use sour glass.

BRONX SILVER COCKTAIL

Juice of $1/2$ Orange
1 Egg White
$1/2$ oz. Dry Vermouth
1 oz. Gin

Shake with ice and strain into sour glass.

BRONX TERRACE COCKTAIL

$1^1/2$ oz. Gin
$1^1/2$ oz. Dry Vermouth
Juice of $1/2$ Lime

Shake with ice and strain into cocktail glass. Add a cherry.

BROWN COCKTAIL

$3/4$ oz. Gin
$3/4$ oz. Light Rum
$3/4$ oz. Dry Vermouth

Stir with ice and strain into cocktail glass.

BUCK JONES

$1^1/2$ oz. Light Rum
1 oz. Sweet Sherry
Juice of $1/2$ Lime

Pour ingredients into highball glass over ice cubes and stir. Fill with ginger ale.

BUCKS FIZZ (MIMOSA) ⑧

Pour 2 oz. orange juice in a collins glass over two cubes of ice, fill with Chilled **Champagne**, and stir very gently.

BUDDY'S FAVORITE

$1^1/2$ oz. Bourbon
6 oz. Cold Water

Pour ingredients in a highball glass. Stir and serve without ice.

BULLDOG COCKTAIL

$1^1/2$ oz. Cherry-Flavored Brandy
$3/4$ oz. Gin
Juice of $1/2$ Lime

Shake with ice and strain into cocktail glass.

BULLDOG HIGHBALL

Juice of $1/2$ Orange
2 oz. Gin

Pour into highball glass over ice cubes and fill with ginger ale. Stir.

BULL FROG

$1^1/2$ oz. Vodka
5 oz. Lemonade

Pour over ice in a tall glass and garnish with a slice of lime.

BULL'S EYE

1 oz. Brandy
2 oz. Hard Cider

Pour into highball glass over ice cubes and fill with ginger ale. Stir.

---

⑧ indicates lower alcohol content

BULL SHOT

1 1/2 oz. Vodka
3 oz.   Chilled Beef
         Bouillon
1 dash Worcestershire
         Sauce
1 dash Salt and Pepper

Shake with cracked ice and strain into old-fashioned glass.

BULL'S MILK

1 tsp.   Powdered Sugar
1 oz.   Light Rum
1 1/2 oz.   Brandy
1 cup Milk

Shake with ice and strain into collins glass. Sprinkle nutmeg and pinch of cinnamon on top.

BURGUNDY BISHOP

Juice of 1/4 Lemon
1 tsp. Powdered Sugar
1 oz.   Light Rum

Shake with ice and strain into highball glass over ice cubes. Fill with red wine and stir. Decorate with fruits.

BUSHRANGER

1 1/2 oz. Light Rum
1 oz.   Dubonnet®
1 dash Bitters

Stir with cracked ice and strain into cocktail glass.

BUTTON HOOK COCKTAIL

1/2 oz. Crème de Menthe
         (White)
1/2 oz. Apricot-Flavored
         Brandy
1/2 oz. Anis
1/2 oz. Brandy

Shake with ice and strain into cocktail glass.

C

CABARET

1½ oz. Gin
2 dashes Bitters
½ tsp. Dry Vermouth
¼ tsp. Benedictine

Stir with ice and strain into cocktail glass. Serve with a cherry.

CABLEGRAM

Juice of ½ Lemon
1 tsp. Powdered Sugar
2 oz. Blended Whiskey

Stir with ice cubes in highball glass and fill with ginger ale.

CADIZ

¾ oz. Dry Sherry
¾ oz. Blackberry-Flavored Brandy
½ oz. Triple Sec
1 tbsp. Light Cream

Shake with ice and strain into old-fashioned glass over ice cubes.

CAFÉ DE PARIS COCKTAIL

1 Egg White
1 tsp. Anis
1 tsp. Light Cream
1½ oz. Gin

Shake with ice and strain into cocktail glass.

CAFÉ DI AMARETTO ☕

Add 1 oz. Amaretto to a cup of black coffee. Top with whipped cream.

CAFÉ ROYALE ☕ 🅛

1 Sugar Cube
Brandy
1 cup Hot Black Coffee

Put cube of sugar, well soaked with brandy, in teaspoon and hold so that it will rest on top of the cup of coffee and ignite. Hold until flame burns out. Drop contents in coffee.

🅛 indicates lower alcohol content

CALEDONIA
1 oz. Crème de Cacao
   (Brown)
1 oz. Brandy
1 oz. Milk
1 Egg Yolk
Shake well with ice and
strain into old-fashioned
glass over ice cubes.
Sprinkle cinnamon on top.

CALIFORNIA LEMONADE
Juice of 1 Lemon
Juice of 1 Lime
1 tbsp. Powdered
   Sugar
2 oz. Blended
   Whiskey
1/4 tsp. Grenadine
Shake with ice and strain
into collins glass over
shaved ice. Fill with
carbonated water and
decorate with slices of
orange and lemon, and a
cherry. Serve with straws.

CALM VOYAGE
1/2 oz. Strega
1/2 oz. Light Rum
1 tbsp. Passion Fruit
   Syrup
2 tsps. Lemon Juice
1/2 Egg White
Put all ingredients in
blender with half a cup of
crushed ice. Blend at low
speed and pour into
champagne flute.

CAMERON'S KICK COCKTAIL
3/4 oz. Scotch
3/4 oz. Irish Whiskey
Juice of 1/4 Lemon
2 dashes Orange Bitters
Shake with ice and strain
into cocktail glass.

CANADIAN CHERRY
1 1/2 oz. Canadian
   Whisky
1/2 oz. Cherry-Flavored
   Brandy
1 1/2 tsps. Lemon Juice
1 1/2 tsps. Orange Juice
Shake all ingredients and
strain into old-fashioned
glass over ice cubes.
Moisten glass rim with
cherry brandy.

CANADIAN COCKTAIL
1 1/2 oz. Canadian
   Whisky
1 dash Bitters
1 1/2 tsps. Triple Sec
1 tsp. Powdered
   Sugar
Shake with ice and strain
into cocktail glass.

CANADIAN PINEAPPLE
1 1/2 oz. Canadian
   Whisky
1 tsp. Pineapple Juice
1 tbsp. Lemon Juice
1/2 tsp. Maraschino
Shake with ice and strain
into old-fashioned glass
over ice cubes. Add a stick
of pineapple.

Sparkling Wine

CANADO SALUDO
- 1½ oz. Light Rum
- 1 oz. Orange Juice
- 1 oz. Pineapple Juice
- 5 dashes Lemon Juice
- 5 dashes Grenadine
- 5 dashes Bitters

Serve in a 6-oz. glass with pineapple slices, orange slice, and a cherry over ice cubes.

CANAL STREET DAISY
- Juice of ¼ Lemon
- Juice of ¼ Orange
- 1 oz. Blended Whiskey

Pour all ingredients into a collins glass over ice cubes. Add carbonated water and an orange slice.

CAPE CODDER
- 1½ oz. Vodka
- 3 oz. Cranberry Juice

Pour into highball glass over ice. Stir well. Garnish with a wedge of lime.

CAPPUCINO COCKTAIL
- ¾ oz. Coffee-Flavored Brandy
- ¾ oz. Vodka
- ¾ oz. Light Cream

Shake well with ice. Strain into cocktail glass.

CAPRI
- ¾ oz. Crème de Cacao (White)
- ¾ oz. Crème de Banana
- ¾ oz. Light Cream

Shake with ice and strain into old-fashioned glass over ice cubes.

CARA SPOSA
- 1 oz. Coffee-Flavored Brandy
- 1 oz. Triple Sec
- ½ oz. Light Cream

Shake with ice and strain into cocktail glass.

CARDINAL PUNCH
- Juice of 1 dozen Lemons

Add enough powdered sugar to sweeten. Pour over large block of ice in punch bowl and stir well. Then add:
- 16 oz. Brandy
- 16 oz. Light Rum
- 1 split Chilled champagne
- 64 oz. Claret or Red Wine
- 32 oz. Carbonated Water
- 8 oz. Sweet Vermouth
- 16 oz. Strong Tea (optional)

Stir well and decorate with fruits in season. Serve in punch glasses.

CARIBBEAN CHAMPAGNE
- ½ tsp. Light Rum
- ½ tsp. Crème de Banana
- Chilled champagne

Pour rum and banana liqueur into champagne flute. Fill with chilled champagne and stir lightly. Add a slice of banana.

CARROL COCKTAIL
1½ oz. Brandy
¾ oz. Sweet Vermouth
Stir with ice and strain into cocktail glass. Serve with a cherry.

CARUSO
1½ oz. Gin
1 oz. Dry Vermouth
½ oz. Crème de Menthe (Green)
Stir with ice and strain into cocktail glass.

CASA BLANCA
2 oz. Light Rum
1½ tsps. Lime Juice
1½ tsps. Triple Sec
1½ tsps. Maraschino
Shake with ice and strain into cocktail glass.

CASINO COCKTAIL
2 dashes Orange Bitters
¼ tsp. Maraschino
¼ tsp. Lemon Juice
2 oz. Gin
Shake with ice and strain into cocktail glass. Serve with a cherry.

CHAMPAGNE COCKTAIL
1 lump Sugar
2 dashes Bitters
Chilled champagne
Place in chilled champagne flute and fill with champagne. Add a twist of lemon peel.

CHAMPAGNE CUP
4 tsps. Powdered Sugar
6 oz. Carbonated Water
1 oz. Triple Sec
2 oz. Brandy
16 oz. Chilled champagne
Fill large glass pitcher with cubes of ice and ingredients above. Add chilled champagne. Stir well and decorate with seasonal fruits and also rind of cucumber inserted on each side of pitcher. Top with a small bunch of mint. Serve in wine glasses.

CHAMPAGNE PUNCH
Juice of 1 dozen Lemons
Add enough powdered sugar to sweeten. Pour over large block of ice in punch bowl and stir well. Then add:
1 cup Maraschino
1 cup Triple Sec
16 oz. Brandy
2 750-ml bottles Chilled champagne
16 oz. Carbonated Water
16 oz. Strong Tea (optional)
Stir well and decorate with fruits in season. Serve in punch glasses.

CHAMPAGNE SHERBET PUNCH
- 2 750-ml bottles Chilled champagne
- 1 750-ml bottle Sauterne
- 32 oz. Lemon or Pineapple Sherbet

Put sherbet in punch bowl. Add sauterne and chilled champagne. Decorate with lemon slices or pineapple chunks.

CHAMPAGNE VELVET
See Black Velvet recipe on page 54.

CHAMPS ÉLYSÉES COCKTAIL
- 1 oz. Brandy
- ½ oz. Chartreuse (Yellow)
- Juice of ¼ Lemon
- ½ tsp. Powdered Sugar
- 1 dash Bitters

Shake with ice and strain into cocktail glass.

CHAPALA
- 1½ oz. Tequila
- 1 tbsp. Orange Juice
- 1 tbsp. Lemon Juice
- 1 dash Triple Sec
- 2 tsps. Grenadine

Shake with ice and strain into old-fashioned glass over ice cubes. Add a slice of orange.

CHAPEL HILL
- 1½ oz. Bourbon
- ½ oz. Triple Sec
- 1 tbsp. Lemon Juice

Shake with ice and strain into cocktail glass. Add twist of orange peel.

CHARLES COCKTAIL
- 1½ oz. Sweet Vermouth
- 1½ oz. Brandy
- 1 dash Bitters

Stir with ice and strain into cocktail glass.

CHARLIE CHAPLIN
- 1 oz. Sloe Gin
- 1 oz. Apricot-Flavored Brandy
- 1 oz. Lemon Juice

Shake with ice and strain into old-fashioned glass over ice cubes.

CHATEAU BRIAND'S RUM COW*
- 1¼ oz. Dark Rum
- 1 tsp. Sugar
- 2 dashes Bitters
- ¾ cup Milk

Blend and strain into a collins glass.

CHELSEA SIDECAR
- Juice of ¼ Lemon
- ¾ oz. Triple Sec
- ¾ oz. Gin

Shake with ice and strain into cocktail glass.

*Chateau Briand,
Dallas, Texas

CHERIE
Juice of 1 Lime
1/2 oz. Triple Sec
1 oz. Light Rum
1/2 oz. Cherry-Flavored
Brandy
Shake with ice and strain
into cocktail glass. Add a
cherry.

CHERRY BLOSSOM
1 1/2 oz. Brandy
1/2 oz. Cherry-Flavored
Brandy
1 1/2 tsps. Triple Sec
1 1/2 tsps. Grenadine
2 tsps. Lemon Juice
Shake with ice and strain
into cocktail glass which
has had its rim moistened
with cherry brandy and
dipped into powdered
sugar. Add a maraschino
cherry.

CHERRY COOLER
2 oz. Cherry Vodka
Cola
Pour cherry vodka into
collins glass over ice cubes.
Fill with cola, add a slice of
lemon, and stir.

CHERRY FIZZ
Juice of 1/2 Lemon
2 oz. Cherry-Flavored
Brandy
Shake with ice and strain
into highball glass with two
ice cubes. Fill with
carbonated water and
decorate with a cherry.

CHERRY FLIP
1 Whole Egg
1 tsp. Powdered Sugar
1 1/2 oz. Cherry-Flavored
Brandy
2 tsps. Light Cream (if
desired)
Shake with ice and strain
into sour glass. Sprinkle a
little nutmeg on top.

CHERRY RUM
1 1/4 oz. Light Rum
1 1/2 tsps. Cherry-
Flavored Brandy
1 tbsp. Light Cream
Shake with ice and strain
into cocktail glass.

CHERRY SLING
2 oz. Cherry-Flavored
Brandy
Juice of 1/2 Lemon
Serve in old-fashioned glass
with ice cubes and stir. Add
a twist of lemon peel.

CHERRY WINE
COCKTAIL
3/4 oz. Danish Cherry
Wine
3/4 oz. Vodka
Juice of 1/2 Lime
Shake with ice and strain
into cocktail glass.

CHI-CHI
1½ oz. Vodka
1 oz. Cream of Coconut
4 oz. Pineapple Juice

Blend ingredients with one cup ice in blender at high speed. Pour in red wine glass. Garnish with a slice of pineapple and a cherry.

CHICAGO COCKTAIL
2 oz. Brandy
1 dash Bitters
¼ tsp. Triple Sec

Prepare old-fashioned glass by rubbing slice of lemon around rim and then dip in powdered sugar. Stir ingredients above with ice and strain into prepared glass.

CHICAGO FIZZ
Juice of ½ Lemon
1 tsp. Powdered Sugar
1 Egg White
1 oz. Port
1 oz. Light Rum

Shake with ice and strain into highball glass over two ice cubes. Fill with carbonated water and stir.

CHINESE COCKTAIL
1 tbsp. Grenadine
1½ oz. Jamaica Rum
1 dash Bitters
1 tsp. Maraschino
1 tsp. Triple Sec

Shake with ice and strain into cocktail glass.

CHOCOLATE COCKTAIL
1½ oz. Port
1½ tsps. Chartreuse (Yellow)
1 Egg Yolk
1 tsp. Powdered Sugar

Shake with ice and strain into sour glass.

CHOCOLATE DAISY
Juice of ½ Lemon
½ tsp. Powdered Sugar
1 tsp. Grenadine
1½ oz. Brandy
1½ oz. Port

Shake with ice and strain into stein or metal cup. Add ice cubes and decorate with fruit.

CHOCOLATE FLIP
1 Whole Egg
1 tsp. Powdered Sugar
¾ oz. Sloe Gin
¾ oz. Brandy
2 tsps. Light Cream (if desired)

Shake with ice and strain into sour glass. Sprinkle a little nutmeg on top.

CHOCOLATE RUM
1 oz. Light Rum
½ oz. Crème de Cacao (Brown)
½ oz. Crème de Menthe (White)
1 tbsp. Light Cream
1 tsp. 151-Proof Rum

Shake with ice and strain into old-fashioned glass over ice cubes.

CHOCOLATE SOLDIER
Juice of $^1/_2$ Lime
$^3/_4$ oz. Dubonnet®
$1^1/_2$ oz. Gin
Shake with ice and strain into cocktail glass.

CHRISTMAS YULE ☙ EGGNOG
Beat first the yolks and then, in a separate bowl, the whites of 1 dozen eggs. Pour them together and add:

  1 pinch Baking Soda
  6 oz. Light Rum
  2 lbs. Granulated Sugar

Beat into stiff batter. Then add:

  32 oz. Milk
  32 oz. Light Cream
  1.75 liter Blended
    Whiskey

Stir. Set in refrigerator overnight. Before serving, stir again, and serve in punch glasses. Sprinkle nutmeg on top.

CIDER CUP
4 tsps. Powdered Sugar
6 oz. Carbonated Water
1 oz. Triple Sec
2 oz. Brandy
16 oz. Apple Cider
Fill large glass pitcher with ice. Stir in the ingredients and decorate with as many fruits as available and a rind of cucumber inserted on each side of pitcher. Top with a small bunch of mint. Serve in red-wine glasses.

CIDER EGGNOG
1 Whole Egg
1 tsp. Powdered Sugar
$^1/_2$ cup Milk
Shake with ice and strain into collins glass. Then fill the glass with cider and stir. Sprinkle nutmeg on top.

CLAMATO COCKTAIL
$1^1/_2$ oz. Vodka
1 oz. Clam Juice
3 oz. Tomato Juice
Shake with ice, strain, and serve over ice cubes in old-fashioned glass.

CLARET COBBLER
1 tsp. Powdered Sugar
2 oz. Carbonated Water
3 oz. Claret
Dissolve powdered sugar in carbonated water and then add claret. Fill goblet with ice and stir. Decorate with fruits in season. Serve with straws.

CLARET CUP
4 tsps. Powdered Sugar
6 oz. Carbonated Water
1 oz. Triple Sec
2 oz. Brandy
16 oz. Claret
Fill large glass pitcher with ice. Stir in the ingredients and decorate with as many fruits as available and a rind of cucumber inserted on each side of pitcher. Top with a small bunch of mint. Serve in red-wine glass.

CLARET PUNCH
Juice of 1 dozen Lemons
Add enough powdered
sugar to sweeten. Pour over
large block of ice in punch
bowl and stir well. Then
add:
    1 cup Triple Sec
    16 oz. Brandy
    3 750-ml bottles Claret
    32 oz. Carbonated Water
    32 oz. Strong Tea
    (optional)
Stir and decorate with fruits
in season. Serve in punch
glasses.

CLARIDGE COCKTAIL
3/4 oz. Gin
3/4 oz. Dry Vermouth
1 tbsp. Apricot-
        Flavored Brandy
1 tbsp. Triple Sec
Stir with ice and strain into
cocktail glass.

CLASSIC COCKTAIL
Juice of 1/4 Lemon
1 1/2 tsps. Curaçao
1 1/2 tsps. Maraschino
1 oz. Brandy
Prepare rim of old-
fashioned glass by rubbing
with lemon and dipping
into powdered sugar. Shake
ingredients with ice and
strain into prepared glass.

CLOVE COCKTAIL
1 oz. Sweet Vermouth
1/2 oz. Sloe Gin
1/2 oz. Muscatel
Stir with ice and strain into
cocktail glass.

CLOVER CLUB COCKTAIL
Juice of 1/2 Lemon
2 tsps. Grenadine
1 Egg White
1 1/2 oz. Gin
Shake with ice and strain
into cocktail glass.

CLOVER LEAF COCKTAIL
Juice of 1 Lime
2 tsps. Grenadine
1 Egg White
1 1/2 oz. Gin
Shake with ice and strain
into cocktail glass. Serve
with mint leaf on top.

CLUB COCKTAIL
1 1/2 oz. Gin
3/4 oz. Sweet Vermouth
Stir with ice and strain into
cocktail glass. Add a cherry
or olive.

COBBLERS
See Index on page 257 for complete list of Cobbler recipes.

COCOMACOQUE
Juice of 1/2 Lemon
2 oz.   Pineapple Juice
2 oz.   Orange Juice
1 1/2 oz. Light Rum
2 oz.   Red Wine
Shake all ingredients except wine. Pour into collins glass over ice cubes and top with wine. Add pineapple stick.

COFFEE COCKTAIL
1 Whole Egg
1 tsp. Powdered Sugar
1 oz.   Port
1 oz.   Brandy
Shake with ice and strain into sour glass. Sprinkle nutmeg on top.

COFFEE FLIP
1 Whole Egg
1 tsp. Powdered Sugar
1 oz.   Brandy
1 oz.   Port
2 tsps. Light Cream (if desired)
Shake with ice and strain into sour glass. Sprinkle a little nutmeg on top.

COFFEE GRASSHOPPER
3/4 oz. Coffee-Flavored Brandy
3/4 oz. Crème de Menthe (White)
3/4 oz. Light Cream
Shake with ice and strain into old-fashioned glass over ice cubes.

COFFEE SOUR
1 1/2 oz. Coffee-Flavored Brandy
1 oz.   Lemon Juice
1 tsp.   Powdered Sugar
1/2 Egg White
Shake with ice and strain into sour glass.

COGNAC COUPLING
2 oz.   Cognac
1 oz.   Tawny Port
1/2 oz. Anis
1 tsp. Lemon Juice
Shake with ice and strain into old-fashioned glass over ice cubes.

COGNAC HIGHBALL
2 oz.   Cognac
Ginger Ale or Carbonated Water
Pour cognac into highball glass over ice cubes and fill with ginger ale or carbonated water. Add a twist of lemon peel, if desired, and stir.

COLD DECK COCKTAIL
$^1/_2$ tsp. Crème de Menthe (White)
$^1/_2$ oz. Sweet Vermouth
1 oz. Brandy
Stir with ice and strain into cocktail glass.

COLE'S RASPBERRY CREAM*
$1^1/_2$ tbsps. Raspberry Yogurt
$1^1/_2$ tbsps Raspberry Ice Cream
$1^1/_2$ oz. Crème de Cacao (White)
$1^1/_2$ oz. Vodka
2 oz. Heavy Cream
Shake or blend.

COLLINS
See Index on page 258 for complete list of Collins recipes.

COLONIAL COCKTAIL
$^1/_2$ oz. Grapefruit Juice
1 tsp. Maraschino
$1^1/_2$ oz. Gin
Shake with ice and strain into cocktail glass. Serve with an olive.

COMBO
$2^1/_2$ oz. Dry Vermouth
1 tsp. Brandy
$^1/_2$ tsp. Triple Sec
$^1/_2$ tsp. Powdered Sugar
1 dash Bitters
Shake with ice and strain into old-fashioned glass over ice cubes.

COMMODORE COCKTAIL
Juice of $^1/_2$ Lime or $^1/_4$ Lemon
1 tsp. Powdered Sugar
2 dashes Orange Bitters
$1^1/_2$ oz. Blended Whiskey
Shake with ice and strain into cocktail glass.

CONTINENTAL
$1^3/_4$ oz. Light Rum
1 tbsp. Lime Juice
$1^1/_2$ tsps. Crème de Menthe (Green)
$^1/_2$ tsp. Powdered Sugar
Shake with ice and strain into cocktail glass. Add a twist of lemon peel.

COOLERS
See Index on page 258 for complete list of Cooler recipes.

COOPERSTOWN COCKTAIL
$^1/_2$ oz. Dry Vermouth
$^1/_2$ oz. Sweet Vermouth
1 oz. Gin
Shake with ice and strain into cocktail glass. Add a sprig of mint.

CORKSCREW
$1^1/_2$ oz. Light Rum
$^1/_2$ oz. Dry Vermouth
$^1/_2$ oz. Peach-Flavored Brandy
Shake with ice and strain into cocktail glass. Garnish with a lime slice.

*Cole's Restaurant, Buffalo, New York

a) Creme de menthe b) Creme de cacao
c) Amaretto

CORNELL COCKTAIL
$1/2$ tsp.　Lemon Juice
1 tsp　Maraschino
1 Egg White
$1^1/2$ oz.　Gin
Shake with ice and strain
into cocktail glass.

CORONATION COCKTAIL
$3/4$ oz.　Gin
$3/4$ oz.　Dubonnet®
$3/4$ oz.　Dry Vermouth
Stir with ice and strain into
cocktail glass.

COUNT CURREY
$1^1/2$ oz.　Gin
1 tsp.　Powdered
Sugar
Chilled Champagne
Shake with ice and strain
into champagne flute over
ice cubes.

COUNTRY CLUB COOLER ●
$1/2$ tsp. Grenadine
2 oz.　Carbonated Water
2 oz.　Dry Vermouth
Into collins glass, put
grenadine and carbonated
water and stir. Add ice
cubes and dry vermouth.
Fill with carbonated water
or ginger ale and stir again.
Insert a spiral of orange or
lemon peel (or both) and
dangle end over rim of
glass.

COWBOY COCKTAIL
$1^1/2$ oz.　Blended
Whiskey
1 tbsp.　Light Cream
Shake with ice and strain
into cocktail glass.

CREAM FIZZ
Juice of $1/2$ Lemon
1 tsp.　Powdered Sugar
2 oz.　Gin
1 tsp.　Light Cream
Shake with ice and strain
into highball glass over two
ice cubes. Fill with
carbonated water and stir.

CREAM PUFF
2 oz.　Light Rum
1 oz.　Light Cream
$1/2$ tsp.　Powdered
Sugar
Shake with ice and strain
into highball glass over two
ice cubes. Fill with
carbonated water and stir.

CREAMSICLE
$1^1/2$ oz.　Vanilla Liqueur
$1^1/2$ oz.　Milk
3 oz.　Orange Juice
Fill a tall glass with ice, add
the above ingredients, and
stir.

CREAMY ORANGE
1 oz.　Orange Juice
1 oz.　Cream Sherry
$3/4$ oz.　Brandy
1 tbsp.　Light Cream
Shake with ice and strain
into cocktail glass.

CREAMY SCREWDRIVER
2 oz. Vodka
1 Egg Yolk
6 oz. Orange Juice
1 tsp. Sugar
Combine all ingredients with a half-cup of crushed ice in an electric blender. Blend at low speed and pour into collins glass.

CRÈME DE CAFÉ
1 oz. Coffee-Flavored Brandy
$^1/_2$ oz. Rum
$^1/_2$ oz. Anisette
1 oz. Light Cream
Shake with ice and strain into old-fashioned glass.

CRÈME DE GIN COCKTAIL
$1^1/_2$ oz. Gin
$^1/_2$ oz. Crème de Menthe (White)
1 Egg White
2 tsps. Lemon Juice
2 tsps. Orange Juice
Shake with ice and strain into cocktail glass.

CRÈME DE MENTHE FRAPPÉ
Fill cocktail glass up to brim with shaved ice. Add Crème de Menthe (Green). Serve with two short straws.

CREOLE
$1^1/_2$ oz. Light Rum
1 dash Tabasco Sauce
1 tsp. Lemon Juice
Salt and Pepper
Beef Bouillon
Shake with ice and strain into old-fashioned glass over ice cubes.

CREOLE LADY
$1^1/_2$ oz. Bourbon
$1^1/_2$ oz. Madeira
1 tsp. Grenadine
Stir with ice and strain into cocktail glass. Serve with one green and one red cherry.

CRIMSON COCKTAIL
$1^1/_2$ oz. Gin
2 tsps. Lemon Juice
1 tsp. Grenadine
$^3/_4$ oz. Port
Shake with ice and strain into cocktail glass, leaving enough room on top to float port.

CRYSTAL SLIPPER COCKTAIL
$^1/_2$ oz. Blue Curaçao
2 dashes Orange Bitters
$1^1/_2$ oz. Gin
Stir with ice and strain into cocktail glass.

CUBA LIBRE
Juice of $^1/_2$ Lime
2 oz. Light Rum
Cola
Put lime juice and rind in highball glass, and add rum. Fill with cola and ice cubes.

CUBAN COCKTAIL NO. 1
Juice of $^1/_2$ Lime
$^1/_2$ tsp. Powdered
Sugar
2 oz. Light Rum
Shake with ice and strain
into cocktail glass.

CUBAN COCKTAIL NO. 2
Juice of $^1/_2$ Lime or $^1/_4$
Lemon
$^1/_2$ oz. Apricot-Flavored
Brandy
$1^1/_2$ oz. Brandy
1 tsp. Light Rum
Shake with ice and strain
into cocktail glass.

CUBAN SPECIAL
1 tbsp. Pineapple Juice
Juice of $^1/_2$ Lime
1 oz. Light Rum
$^1/_2$ tsp. Triple Sec
Shake with ice and strain
into cocktail glass. Decorate
with a slice of pineapple
and a cherry.

CUPS
See Index on page 259 for
complete list of Cup
recipes.

D

DAIQUIRI
Juice of 1 Lime
1 tsp. Powdered Sugar
1½ oz. Light Rum
Shake with ice and strain into cocktail glass.

DAISIES
Index on page 259 for complete list of Daisy recipes.

DAMN-THE-WEATHER COCKTAIL
1 tsp. Triple Sec
1 tbsp. Orange Juice
1 tbsp. Sweet Vermouth
1 oz. Gin
Shake with ice and strain into cocktail glass.

DARB COCKTAIL
1 tsp. Lemon Juice
¾ oz. Dry Vermouth
¾ oz. Gin
¾ oz. Apricot-Flavored Brandy
Shake with ice and strain into cocktail glass.

DEAUVILLE COCKTAIL
Juice of ¼ Lemon
½ oz. Brandy
½ oz. Apple Brandy
½ oz. Triple Sec
Shake with ice and strain into cocktail glass.

DEEP SEA COCKTAIL
1 oz. Dry Vermouth
¼ tsp. Anis
1 dash Orange Bitters
1 oz. Gin
Stir with ice and strain into cocktail glass.

DELMONICO NO. 1
¾ oz. Gin
½ oz. Dry Vermouth
½ oz. Sweet Vermouth
½ oz. Brandy
Stir with ice and strain into cocktail glass. Add a twist of lemon peel.

DELMONICO NO. 2
1 dash Orange Bitters
1 oz. Dry Vermouth
1½ oz. Gin
Stir with ice and strain into cocktail glass. Add a twist of lemon peel.

DEMPSEY COCKTAIL
1 oz.   Gin
1 oz.   Apple Brandy
1/2 tsp.   Anis
1/2 tsp.   Grenadine
Stir with ice and strain into
cocktail glass.

DEPTH BOMB
1 oz.   Apple Brandy
1 oz.   Brandy
1 dash Lemon Juice
1 dash Grenadine
Shake with ice and strain
into old-fashioned glass
over ice cubes.

DEPTH CHARGE
Shot of any flavor of
Schnapps in a glass of beer.

DERBY DAIQUIRI
1 1/2 oz.   Light Rum
1 oz.   Orange Juice
1 tbsp.   Lime Juice
1 tsp.   Sugar
Combine all ingredients
with a half-cup of shaved
ice in an electric blender.
Blend at low speed. Pour
into champagne flute.

DERBY FIZZ
Juice of 1/2 Lemon
1 tsp.   Powdered Sugar
1 Whole Egg
2 oz.   Scotch
1 tsp.   Triple Sec
Shake with ice and strain
into highball glass over two
ice cubes. Fill with
carbonated water and stir.

DEVIL'S COCKTAIL
1/2 tsp.   Lemon Juice
1 1/2 oz.   Port
1 1/2 oz.   Dry Vermouth
Stir with ice and strain into
cocktail glass.

DEVIL'S TAIL
1 1/2 oz.   Light Rum
1 oz.   Vodka
1 tbsp.   Lime Juice
1 1/2 tsp.   Grenadine
1 1/2 tsp. Apricot-Flavored
    Brandy
Combine all ingredients
with a half-cup of crushed
ice in an electric blender.
Blend at low speed and
pour into champagne flute.
Add a twist of lime peel.

DIAMOND FIZZ
Juice of 1/2 Lemon
1 tsp.   Powdered Sugar
2 oz.   Gin
Shake with ice and strain
into highball glass over two
cubes of ice. Fill with
champagne and stir.

DIANA COCKTAIL
Crème de Menthe
    (White)
Brandy
Fill cocktail glass with ice,
then fill 3/4 full with crème
de menthe and float brandy
on top.

DILLATINI
A Martini substituting a
dilly bean in place of the
olive. See Martini on
page 130.

DINAH COCKTAIL
Juice of $^1/_4$ Lemon
$^1/_2$ tsp. Powdered
Sugar
$1^1/_2$ oz. Blended
Whiskey
Shake well with ice and
strain into cocktail glass.
Serve with a mint leaf.

DIPLOMAT
$1^1/_2$ oz. Dry Vermouth
$^1/_2$ oz. Sweet
Vermouth
2 dashes Bitters
$^1/_2$ tsp. Maraschino
Stir with ice and strain into
cocktail glass. Serve with a
half slice of lemon and a
cherry.

DIXIE COCKTAIL
Juice of $^1/_4$ Orange
1 tbsp. Anis
$^1/_2$ oz. Dry Vermouth
1 oz. Gin
Shake with ice and strain
into cocktail glass.

DIXIE JULEP
Into a collins glass put:
1 tsp. Powdered
Sugar
$2^1/_2$ oz. Bourbon
Fill with ice and stir gently
until glass is frosted.
Decorate with sprigs of
mint. Serve with straws.

DIXIE WHISKEY COCKTAIL
$^1/_2$ tsp. Powdered Sugar
1 dash Bitters
$^1/_4$ tsp. Triple Sec
$^1/_2$ tsp. Crème de
Menthe (White)
2 oz. Bourbon
Shake with ice and strain
into cocktail glass.

DOCTOR COOK
$^3/_4$ oz. Gin
1 tbsp. Lemon Juice
1 dash Maraschino
1 Egg White
Shake with ice and strain
into wine glass.

DOUBLE STANDARD SOUR
Juice of $^1/_2$ Lemon or
1 Lime
$^1/_2$ tsp. Powdered
Sugar
$^3/_4$ oz. Blended
Whiskey
$^3/_4$ oz. Gin
$^1/_2$ tsp. Grenadine
Shake with ice and strain
into sour glass. Decorate
with a half-slice of lemon
and a cherry.

DREAM COCKTAIL
$^3/_4$ oz. Triple Sec
$1^1/_2$ oz. Brandy
$^1/_4$ tsp. Anisette
Shake with ice and strain
into cocktail glass.

DRY MARTINI Y (5-to-1)

1²/₃ oz. Gin
¹/₃ oz. Dry Vermouth

Stir vermouth and gin over ice cubes in a mixing glass. Strain into cocktail glass. Serve with a twist of lemon peel or olive, if desired.

DU BARRY COCKTAIL

1 dash Bitters
³/₄ oz. Dry Vermouth
¹/₂ tsp. Anis
1¹/₂ oz. Gin

Stir with ice and strain into cocktail glass. Add a slice of orange.

DUBONNET® COCKTAIL

1¹/₂ oz. Dubonnet®
³/₄ oz. Gin
1 dash Orange Bitters (if desired)

Stir with ice and strain into cocktail glass. Add a twist of lemon peel.

DUBONNET® FIZZ

Juice of ¹/₂ Orange
Juice of ¹/₄ Lemon
1 tsp. Cherry-Flavored Brandy
2 oz. Dubonnet®

Shake with ice and strain into highball glass over two ice cubes. Fill with carbonated water and stir.

DUBONNET® HIGHBALL ●

Put 2 oz. Dubonnet® in highball glass with two ice cubes and fill with ginger ale or carbonated water. Add a twist of lemon peel, if desired, and stir.

DUCHESS

1¹/₂ oz. Anis
¹/₂ oz. Dry Vermouth
¹/₂ oz. Sweet Vermouth

Shake with ice and strain into cocktail glass.

DUKE COCKTAIL ●

¹/₂ oz. Triple Sec
1 tsp. Orange Juice
2 tsp. Lemon Juice
¹/₂ tsp. Maraschino
1 Whole Egg
Chilled champagne to top

Add first five ingredients, shake with ice, and strain into champagne flute. Fill with chilled champagne and stir.

E

EAST INDIA COCKTAIL NO. 1

$1^1/_2$ oz.   Brandy
$^1/_2$ tsp.   Pineapple Juice
$^1/_2$ tsp.   Triple Sec
1 tsp.   Jamaica Rum
1 dash   Bitters

Shake with ice and strain into cocktail glass. Add a twist of lemon peel and a cherry.

EAST INDIA COCKTAIL NO. 2 🅛

$1^1/_2$ oz.   Dry Vermouth
$1^1/_2$ oz.   Dry Sherry
1 dash   Orange Bitters

Stir with ice and strain into cocktail glass.

ECLIPSE COCKTAIL 🅛

Grenadine
1 oz.   Gin
2 oz.   Sloe Gin
$^1/_2$ tsp.   Lemon Juice

Put enough grenadine into cocktail glass to cover a ripe olive. Mix the above ingredients in ice and pour onto the grenadine so that they do not mix.

EGG SOUR

1 Whole Egg
1 tsp.   Powdered Sugar
Juice of $^1/_2$ Lemon
2 oz.   Brandy
$^1/_4$ tsp.   Triple Sec

Shake with ice and strain into old-fashioned glass.

EGGNOG SUPREME

1 dozen Medium Eggs
1 cup   Sugar
$1^1/_2$ quarts Whole Milk
1 pint Heavy Cream, Whipped
1 750-ml bottle Cognac
Powdered Nutmeg

Separate eggs; beat yolks in large serving bowl, adding sugar while beating. Stir in milk and cream. Slowly add cognac and refrigerate for 1 hour. Before serving, whip egg whites stiff. Mix into eggnog, dust with nutmeg.

EGGNOGS

See Index on page 259 for additional Eggnog recipes.

🅛 indicates lower alcohol content

ELK'S OWN COCKTAIL
1 Egg White
1½ oz. Blended Whiskey
¾ oz. Port
Juice of ¼ Lemon
1 tsp. Powdered Sugar
Shake with ice and strain into cocktail glass. Add a strip of pineapple.

EL PRESIDENTE COCKTAIL NO. 1
Juice of 1 Lime
1 tsp. Pineapple Juice
1 tsp. Grenadine
1½ oz. Light Rum
Shake with ice and strain into cocktail glass.

EL PRESIDENTE COCKTAIL NO. 2
¾ oz. Dry Vermouth
1½ oz. Light Rum
1 dash Bitters
Stir with ice and strain into cocktail glass.

EMERALD ISLE COCKTAIL
2 oz. Gin
1 tsp. Crème de Menthe (Green)
3 dashes Bitters
Stir with ice and strain into cocktail glass.

EMERSON
1½ oz. Gin
1 oz. Sweet Vermouth
Juice of ½ Lime
1 tsp. Maraschino
Shake with ice and strain into cocktail glass.

ENGLISH HIGHBALL
¾ oz. Gin
¾ oz. Brandy
¾ oz. Sweet Vermouth
Pour into highball glass over ice cubes and fill with ginger ale or carbonated water. Add a twist of lemon peel, if desired, and stir.

ENGLISH ROSE COCKTAIL
1½ oz. Gin
¾ oz. Apricot-Flavored Brandy
¾ oz. Dry Vermouth
1 tsp. Grenadine
¼ tsp. Lemon Juice
Prepare rim of glass by rubbing with lemon and dipping in sugar. Shake all ingredients with ice and strain into cocktail glass. Serve with a cherry.

ETHEL DUFFY COCKTAIL
¾ oz. Apricot-Flavored Brandy
¾ oz. Crème de Menthe (White)
¾ oz. Triple Sec
Shake with ice and strain into cocktail glass.

EVERYBODY'S IRISH COCKTAIL
1 tsp. Crème de Menthe (Green)
1 tsp. Chartreuse (Green)
2 oz. Irish Whiskey
Stir with ice and strain into cocktail glass. Serve with a green olive.

EYE-OPENER
- 1 Egg Yolk
- 1/2 tsp. Powdered Sugar
- 1 tsp. Anis
- 1 tsp. Triple Sec
- 1 tsp. Crème de Cacao (White)
- 2 oz. Light Rum

Shake with ice and strain into sour glass.

F

FAIR-AND-WARMER COCKTAIL

$^3/_4$ oz.   Sweet Vermouth
$1^1/_2$ oz. Light Rum
$^1/_2$ tsp. Triple Sec

Stir with ice and strain into cocktail glass.

FAIRY BELLE COCKTAIL

1 Egg White
1 tsp.   Grenadine
$^3/_4$ oz.   Apricot-Flavored Brandy
$1^1/_2$ oz. Gin

Shake with ice and strain into cocktail glass.

FALLEN ANGEL

Juice of 1 Lime or
   $^1/_2$ Lemon
$1^1/_2$ oz. Gin
1 dash Bitters
$^1/_2$ tsp. Crème de Menthe (White)

Shake with ice and strain into cocktail glass. Serve with a cherry.

FANCY BRANDY

2 oz.   Brandy
1 dash Bitters
$^1/_4$ tsp.   Triple Sec
$^1/_4$ tsp.   Powdered Sugar

Shake with ice and strain into cocktail glass. Add a twist of lemon peel.

FANCY GIN

Same as Fancy Brandy but made with 2 oz. Gin.

FANCY WHISKEY

Same as Fancy Brandy but made with 2 oz. Blended Whiskey.

FANTASIO COCKTAIL

1 tsp. Crème de Menthe (White)
1 tsp. Maraschino
1 oz.   Brandy
$^3/_4$ oz. Dry Vermouth

Stir with ice and strain into cocktail glass.

FARE THEE WELL

$1^1/_2$ oz. Gin
$^1/_2$ oz.   Dry Vermouth
1 dash Sweet Vermouth
1 dash Triple Sec

Shake with ice and strain into cocktail glass.

FARMER'S COCKTAIL
1 oz.   Gin
1/2 oz.   Dry Vermouth
1/2 oz.   Sweet
Vermouth
2 dashes Bitters
Stir with ice and strain into cocktail glass.

FAVORITE COCKTAIL
3/4 oz.   Apricot-Flavored
Brandy
3/4 oz.   Dry Vermouth
3/4 oz.   Gin
1/4 tsp. Lemon Juice
Shake with ice and strain into cocktail glass.

FERRARI
1 oz.   Amaretto
2 oz.   Dry Vermouth
Mix in an old-fashioned glass on the rocks and add a lemon twist.

FIFTH AVENUE
1/2 oz.   Crème de Cacao
(Brown)
1/2 oz.   Apricot-Flavored
Brandy
1 tbsp. Light Cream
Pour carefully, in order given, into parfait glass, so that each ingredient floats on preceding one.

FIFTY-FIFTY COCKTAIL
1 1/2 oz. Gin
1 1/2 oz. Dry Vermouth
Stir with ice and strain into cocktail glass.

FINE-AND-DANDY COCKTAIL
Juice of 1/4 Lemon
1/2 oz.   Triple Sec
1 1/2 oz. Gin
1 dash   Bitters
Shake with ice and strain into cocktail glass. Serve with a cherry.

FINO MARTINI
2 oz.   Gin
2 tsp.   Fino Sherry
Stir gin and sherry over ice cubes in a mixing glass. Strain into cocktail glass. Serve with a twist of lemon peel.

FIREMAN'S SOUR
Juice of 2 Limes
1/2 tsp. Powdered
Sugar
1 tbsp. Grenadine
2 oz.   Light Rum
Shake with ice and strain into sour glass. Fill with carbonated water, if desired. Decorate with a half-slice of lemon and a cherry.

FISH HOUSE PUNCH
Juice of 1 dozen Lemons
Add enough powdered
sugar to sweeten. Pour over
large block of ice in punch
bowl and stir well. Then
add:
  1½ liters Brandy
  1 liter Peach-Flavored
    Brandy
  16 oz. Light Rum
  32 oz. Carbonated Water
  16 oz. Strong Tea
    (optional)
Stir well and decorate with
fruits in season. Serve in
punch glasses.

FIXES
See Index on page 260 for
complete list of Fix recipes.

FIZZES
See Index on page 260 for
complete list of Fizz
recipes.

FLAMINGO COCKTAIL
Juice of ½ Lime
  ½ oz. Apricot-Flavored
    Brandy
  1½ oz. Gin
  1 tsp. Grenadine
Shake with ice and strain
into cocktail glass.

FLIPS
See Index on page 260 for
complete list of Flip
recipes.

FLORADORA COOLER
Into collins glass put:
Juice of 1 Lime
  ½ tsp. Powdered Sugar
  1 tbsp. Grenadine
  2 oz. Carbonated
    Water
Stir. Fill glass with ice and
add 2 oz. Dry Gin. Fill with
carbonated water or ginger
ale and stir again.

FLORIDA
  ½ oz. Gin
  1½ tsp. Kirschwasser
  1½ tsp. Triple Sec
  1 oz. Orange Juice
  1 tsp. Lemon Juice
Shake with ice and strain
into cocktail glass.

FLYING DUTCHMAN
  2 oz. Gin
  1 dash Triple Sec
Shake with ice and strain
into old-fashioned glass
over ice cubes.

FLYING GRASSHOPPER
  ¾ oz. Crème de Menthe
    (Green)
  ¾ oz. Crème de Cacao
    (White)
  ¾ oz. Vodka
Stir with ice and strain into
cocktail glass.

FLYING SCOTCHMAN
  1 oz. Sweet Vermouth
  1 oz. Scotch
  1 dash Bitters
  ¼ tsp. Sugar Syrup
Stir with ice and strain into
cocktail glass.

FOG CUTTER

- 1 1/2 oz.   Light Rum
- 1/2 oz.   Brandy
- 1/2 oz.   Gin
- 1 oz.   Orange Juice
- 3 tbsp.   Lemon Juice
- 1 1/2 tsp.   Orgeat Syrup

Shake all ingredients and strain into collins glass over ice cubes. Top with a teaspoon of sweet sherry.

FOG HORN

- Juice of 1/2 Lime
- 1 1/2 oz.   Gin

Pour into highball glass over ice cubes. Fill with ginger ale. Stir. Add a slice of lime.

FONTAINEBLEAU SPECIAL

- 1 oz.   Brandy
- 1 oz.   Anisette
- 1/2 oz.   Dry Vermouth

Shake with ice and strain into cocktail glass.

FORT LAUDERDALE

- 1 1/2 oz.   Light Rum
- 1/2 oz.   Sweet Vermouth
- Juice of 1/4 Orange
- Juice of 1/4 Lime

Shake with ice and strain into old-fashioned glass over ice cubes. Add a slice of orange.

FOX RIVER COCKTAIL

- 1 tbsp.   Crème de Cacao (Brown)
- 2 oz.   Blended Whiskey
- 4 dashes Bitters

Stir with ice and strain into cocktail glass.

FRANKENJACK COCKTAIL

- 1 oz.   Gin
- 3/4 oz.   Dry Vermouth
- 1/2 oz.   Apricot-Flavored Brandy
- 1 tsp.   Triple Sec

Stir with ice and strain into cocktail glass. Serve with a cherry.

FREE SILVER

- Juice of 1/4 Lemon
- 1/2 tsp.   Powdered Sugar
- 1 1/2 oz.   Gin
- 1/2 oz.   Dark Rum
- 1 tbsp.   Milk

Shake with ice and strain into collins glass over ice cubes. Add carbonated water.

FREEZE or FRAPPE

Use any flavor **Liqueur**. Pour over crushed ice in a champagne flute.

FRENCH CONNECTION

- 1 1/2 oz.   Cognac
- 3/4 oz.   Amaretto

Serve in an old-fashioned glass over ice.

Strawberry Margarita

FRENCH "75"
Juice of 1 Lemon
2 tsp. Powdered Sugar
2 oz. Gin

Stir in collins glass. Then add ice cubes; fill with champagne and stir. Decorate with a slice of lemon or orange and a cherry. Serve with straws.

FRISCO SOUR
Juice of $^1/_4$ Lemon
Juice of $^1/_2$ Lime
$^1/_2$ oz. Benedictine
2 oz. Blended Whiskey

Shake with ice and strain into sour glass. Decorate with slices of lemon and lime.

FROTH BLOWER COCKTAIL
1 Egg White
1 tsp. Grenadine
2 oz. Gin

Shake with ice and strain into cocktail glass.

FROUPE COCKTAIL
$1^1/_2$ oz. Sweet Vermouth
$1^1/_2$ oz. Brandy
1 tsp. Benedictine

Stir with ice and strain into cocktail glass.

FROZEN APPLE
$1^1/_2$ oz. Applejack
1 tbsp. Lime Juice
1 tsp. Sugar
$^1/_2$ Egg White

Combine ingredients with a cup of crushed ice in an electric blender and blend at low speed. Pour into old-fashioned glass.

FROZEN BERKELEY
$1^1/_2$ oz. Light Rum
$^1/_2$ oz. Brandy
1 tbsp. Passion Fruit Syrup
1 tbsp. Lemon Juice

Combine ingredients with a half-cup of crushed ice in an electric blender and blend at low speed. Pour into champagne flute.

FROZEN BRANDY AND RUM
$1^1/_2$ oz. Brandy
1 oz. Light Rum
1 tbsp. Lemon Juice
1 Egg Yolk
1 tsp. Powdered Sugar

Combine ingredients with a cup of crushed ice in an electric blender and blend at low speed. Pour into old-fashioned glass.

FROZEN DAIQUIRI

1½ oz.   Light Rum
1 tbsp.   Triple Sec
1½ oz.   Lime Juice
1 tsp.   Sugar
1 cup   Crushed Ice

Combine ingredients in an electric blender and blend at low speed for five seconds. Then blend at high speed until firm. Pour into champagne flute. Top with a cherry.

FROZEN MARGARITA

1½ oz.   Tequila
½ oz.   Triple Sec
1 oz.   Lemon or
    Lime Juice

Combine ingredients with a cup of crushed ice in a blender at low speed for five seconds. Then blend at high speed until firm. Pour into cocktail glass. Garnish with a slice of lemon or lime.

FROZEN MATADOR

1½ oz.   Tequila
2 oz.   Pineapple Juice
1 tbsp.   Lime Juice

Combine all ingredients with a cup of crushed ice in an electric blender. Blend at low speed and pour into old-fashioned glass. Add a pineapple stick.

FROZEN MINT DAIQUIRI

2 oz.   Light Rum
1 tbsp.   Lime Juice
6   Mint Leaves
1 tsp.   Sugar

Combine all ingredients with a cup of crushed ice in an electric blender and blend at low speed. Pour into old-fashioned glass.

FROZEN PINEAPPLE DAIQUIRI

1½ oz.   Light Rum
4 Pineapple Chunks
1 tbsp.   Lime Juice
½ tsp.   Sugar

Combine all ingredients with a cup of crushed ice in an electric blender. Blend at low speed and pour into champagne flute.

FUZZY NAVEL

3 oz.   Peach Schnapps
3 oz.   Orange Juice

Combine orange juice and schnapps and pour over ice in tall glass. Garnish with orange slice.

G

GABLES COLLINS

- 1½ oz. Vodka
- 1 oz. Crème de Noyaux
- 1 tbsp. Lemon Juice
- 1 tbsp. Pineapple Juice

Shake with ice and strain into collins glass over ice cubes. Add carbonated water. Decorate with a slice of lemon and a pineapple chunk.

GAUGUIN

- 2 oz. Light Rum
- 1 tbsp. Passion Fruit Syrup
- 1 tbsp. Lemon Juice
- 1 tbsp. Lime Juice

Combine ingredients with a cup of crushed ice in an electric blender and blend at low speed. Serve in an old-fashioned glass. Top with a cherry.

GENERAL HARRISON'S EGGNOG

- 1 Whole Egg
- 1 tsp. Powdered Sugar
  Red wine

Shake with ice and strain into collins glass. Fill glass with red wine and stir. Sprinkle nutmeg on top.

GENTLE BEN

- 1 oz. Vodka
- 1 oz. Gin
- 1 oz. Tequila

Shake all ingredients with ice and pour into collins glass over ice cubes. Fill with orange juice and stir. Decorate with an orange slice and a cherry.

GEORGIA MINT JULEP

- 2 sprigs Mint Leaves
- 1 tsp. Powdered Sugar
- 1½ oz. Brandy
- 1 oz. Peach-Flavored Brandy

Place mint leaves in collins glass with ice. Add 1 teaspoon sugar and a little water. Muddle, then fill with brandy and peach liqueur. Decorate with mint leaves.

GIBSON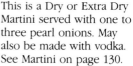

This is a Dry or Extra Dry Martini served with one to three pearl onions. May also be made with vodka. See Martini on page 130.

Gin Highball

GILROY COCKTAIL

Juice of $1/4$ Lemon
1 tbsp.   Dry Vermouth
$3/4$ oz.   Cherry-Flavored Brandy
$3/4$ oz.   Gin
1 dash   Orange Bitters

Shake with ice and strain into cocktail glass.

GIMLET

1 oz.   Lime Juice
1 tsp.   Powdered Sugar
$1^1/_2$ oz.   Gin

Shake with ice and strain into cocktail glass.

GIN ALOHA

$1^1/_2$ oz.   Gin
$1^1/_2$ oz.   Triple Sec
1 tbsp.   Unsweetened Pineapple Juice
1 dash   Orange Bitters

Shake with ice and strain into cocktail glass.

GIN AND BITTERS

$1/2$ tsp.   Bitters
Gin

Put bitters into cocktail glass and revolve glass until it is entirely coated with the bitters. Then fill with gin. (No ice is used in this drink.)

GIN BUCK

Juice of $1/2$ Lemon
$1^1/_2$ oz.   Gin
Ginger Ale

Pour ingredients into old-fashioned glass over ice cubes and stir.

GIN COBBLER

1 tsp.   Powdered Sugar
2 oz.   Carbonated Water
2 oz.   Gin

Dissolve powdered sugar in carbonated water, then fill goblet with ice and add gin. Stir and decorate with fruits in season. Serve with straws.

GIN COCKTAIL

2 oz.   Gin
2 dashes Bitters

Stir with ice and strain into cocktail glass. Serve with a twist of lemon peel.

GIN COOLER

$1/2$ tsp. Powdered Sugar
Carbonated Water
2 oz.   Gin

Into a collins glass stir powdered sugar with 2 oz. carbonated water. Fill glass with ice and add gin. Fill with carbonated water or ginger ale and stir again. Insert a spiral of orange or lemon peel (or both) and dangle end over rim of glass.

GIN DAISY

Juice of $1/2$ Lemon
$1/2$ tsp.   Powdered Sugar
1 tsp.   Grenadine
2 oz.   Gin

Shake with ice and strain into stein or metal cup. Add ice cubes and decorate with fruit.

GIN FIX
Juice of $1/2$ Lemon
1 tsp.   Powdered Sugar
1 tsp.   Water
$2^1/2$ oz. Gin

Mix lemon juice, powdered sugar, and water in a highball glass. Stir and fill glass with ice. Add gin. Stir, add a slice of lemon. Serve with straws.

GIN FIZZ
Juice of $1/2$ Lemon
1 tsp. Powdered Sugar
2 oz.   Gin

Shake with ice and strain into highball glass with two ice cubes. Fill with carbonated water and stir.

GIN HIGHBALL
2 oz. Gin

Pour into highball glass over ice cubes and fill with ginger ale or carbonated water. Add a twist of lemon peel, if desired, and stir.

GIN AND IT
2 oz.   Gin
1 oz.   Sweet Vermouth

Stir ingredients in cocktail glass. (No ice is used in this drink.)

GIN MILK PUNCH
1 tsp. Powdered Sugar
2 oz.   Gin
1 cup Milk

Shake with ice, strain into collins glass, and sprinkle nutmeg on top.

GIN RICKEY
Juice of $1/2$ Lime
$1^1/2$ oz. Gin

Pour ingredients into highball glass over ice cubes and fill with carbonated water. Stir. Add a wedge of lime.

GIN SANGAREE
$1/2$ tsp. Powdered Sugar
1 tsp.   Water
2 oz.   Gin
Carbonated Water
1 tbsp. Port

Dissolve powdered sugar in water and add gin. Pour into highball glass over ice cubes. Fill with carbonated water and stir. Float port on top and sprinkle lightly with nutmeg.

GIN AND SIN
1 oz.   Gin
1 oz.   Lemon Juice
1 tbsp. Orange Juice
1 dash Grenadine

Shake with ice and strain into cocktail glass.

GIN SLING
1 tsp. Powdered Sugar
1 tsp. Water
Juice of $1/2$ Lemon
2 oz.   Gin

Dissolve powdered sugar in water and lemon. Add gin. Pour into old-fashioned glass over ice cubes and stir. Add a twist of orange peel.

GIN SMASH
1 lump Sugar
1 oz.   Carbonated Water
4 sprigs Mint
2 oz.   Gin

Muddle sugar with carbonated water and mint in old-fashioned glass. Add gin and one ice cube. Stir, and decorate with a slice of orange and a cherry. Add a twist of lemon peel.

GIN SOUR
Juice of 1/2 Lemon
1/2 tsp. Powdered Sugar
2 oz.   Gin

Shake with ice and strain into sour glass. Decorate with half-slice of lemon and a cherry.

GIN SQUIRT
1 1/2 oz. Gin
1 tbsp. Powdered Sugar
1 tsp.   Grenadine

Stir with ice and strain into highball glass over ice cubes. Fill with carbonated water and stir. Decorate with cubes of pineapple and strawberries.

GIN SWIZZLE
Into collins glass put:
Juice of 1 Lime
1 tsp. Powdered Sugar
2 oz.   Carbonated Water

Fill glass with ice and stir. Then add:
2 dashes Bitters
2 oz.   Gin

Fill with carbonated water and serve with swizzle stick.

GIN THING
1 1/2 oz. Gin
Juice of 1/2 Lime

Pour gin and lime juice in highball glass over ice cubes and fill with ginger ale.

GIN TODDY
1/2 tsp.   Powdered Sugar
2 tsp.   Water
2 oz.   Gin

In an old-fashioned glass, mix powdered sugar and water. Add gin and one ice cube. Stir and add a twist of lemon peel.

GIN TODDY (HOT)
1 lump Sugar
Boiling Water
2 oz.   Gin

Put sugar into punch cup and fill two-thirds with boiling water. Add gin. Stir and decorate with a slice of lemon. Sprinkle nutmeg on top.

GIN AND TONIC
2 oz. Gin
Tonic

Pour gin into highball glass over ice cubes and fill with tonic water. Stir.

GLÖGG ◡
Pour the following into a kettle:

2 750-ml bottles Wine (Port, Cream Sherry, Claret, Burgundy, or Madeira)

Insert cheesecloth bag containing:

2 oz. Dried Orange Peel
2 oz. Cinnamon Sticks
20 Cardamom Seeds
25 Cloves

and boil slowly for 15 minutes, stirring occasionally. Add 1 lb. each blanched almonds and seedless raisins and continue to boil for additional 15 minutes. Remove kettle from stove and place wire grill containing 1 lb. lump sugar over opening. Pour one 750-ml Brandy over sugar, making sure to saturate all of it. Then light sugar with match and let it flame. After sugar has melted, replace kettle cover to extinguish flame. Stir again and remove spice bag. Serve hot in punch cups with a few almonds and raisins.

GLOOM LIFTER
1 oz. Blended Whiskey
$^1/_2$ oz. Brandy
Juice of $^1/_2$ Lemon
1 tbsp. Raspberry Syrup
$^1/_2$ tsp. Sugar
$^1/_2$ Egg White

Shake with ice and strain into highball glass with ice cubes.

GODCHILD
1 oz. Amaretto
1 oz. Vodka
1 oz. Heavy Cream

Shake well with cracked ice. Strain and serve in a champagne flute.

GODFATHER
$1^1/_2$ oz. Scotch
$^3/_4$ oz. Amaretto

Serve in an old-fashioned glass over ice. (Bourbon may be used instead of Scotch.)

GODMOTHER
$1^1/_2$ oz. Vodka
$^3/_4$ oz. Amaretto

Serve in an old-fashioned glass over ice.

GOLDEN CADILLAC
1 oz. Galliano
2 oz. Crème de Cacao
(White)
1 oz. Light Cream
Combine with half-cup of crushed ice in an electric blender at low speed for ten seconds. Strain into champagne flute.

GOLDEN DAWN
1 oz. Apple Brandy
$^1/_2$ oz. Apricot-Flavored Brandy
$^1/_2$ oz. Gin
1 oz. Orange Juice
1 tsp. Grenadine
Shake with ice and strain into old-fashioned glass filled with ice cubes. Add grenadine.

GOLDEN DAZE
$1^1/_2$ oz. Gin
$^1/_2$ oz. Peach-Flavored Brandy
1 oz. Orange Juice
Shake with ice and strain into cocktail glass.

GOLDEN DREAM
1 tbsp. Orange Juice
$^1/_2$ oz. Triple Sec
1 oz. Galliano
1 tbsp. Light Cream
Shake with ice and strain into cocktail glass.

GOLDEN FIZZ
Juice of $^1/_2$ Lemon
$^1/_2$ tbsp. Powdered Sugar
$1^1/_2$ oz. Gin
1 Egg Yolk
Shake with ice and strain into highball glass. Fill with carbonated water.

GOLDEN FRAPPE
1 cup Orange Juice
2 tbsp. Lemon Juice
1 tsp. Sugar
1 cup Port
Stir orange juice, lemon juice, and sugar in collins glass. Add crushed ice and port.

GOLDEN FRIENDSHIP
Equal Parts:
Amaretto
Sweet Vermouth
Light Rum
Mix in a collins glass over ice and fill with ginger ale. Garnish with an orange spiral and a cherry.

GOLDEN SLIPPER
$^3/_4$ oz. Chartreuse (Yellow)
2 oz. Apricot-Flavored Brandy
Stir with ice and strain into cocktail glass. Float an unbroken egg yolk on top.

GOLF COCKTAIL
$1^1/_2$ oz. Gin
$^3/_4$ oz. Dry Vermouth
2 dashes Bitters
Stir with ice and strain into cocktail glass.

a) Mulled Claret b) Tropical Heat

GRAND ROYAL FIZZ
Juice of 1/4 Orange
Juice of 1/2 Lemon
1 tsp.   Powdered
Sugar
2 oz.   Gin
1/2 tsp.   Maraschino
2 tsp.   Light Cream
Shake with ice and strain
into highball glass over two
ice cubes. Fill with
carbonated water and stir.

GRAPEFRUIT COCKTAIL
1 oz.   Grapefruit Juice
1 oz.   Gin
1 tsp. Maraschino
Shake with ice and strain
into cocktail glass. Serve
with a cherry.

GRAPEFRUIT NOG
1 1/2 oz.   Brandy
1/2 cup   Grapefruit Juice
1 oz.   Lemon Juice
1 tbsp. Honey
1 Whole Egg
Blend all ingredients with a
cup of crushed ice at low
speed and pour into collins
glass over ice cubes.

GRAPE VODKA FROTH
1 1/2 oz.   Vodka
1 oz.   Grape Juice
1 Egg White
1 oz.   Lemon Juice
Shake with ice and strain
into old-fashioned glass
over ice cubes.

GRASSHOPPER
3/4 oz.   Crème de Menthe
(Green)
3/4 oz.   Crème de Cacao
(White)
3/4 oz.   Light Cream
Shake with ice and strain
into cocktail glass.

GREENBACK
1 1/2 oz.   Gin
1 oz.   Crème de
Menthe (Green)
1 oz.   Lemon Juice
Shake with ice and strain
into old-fashioned glass
over ice cubes.

GREEN DEMON
1 oz.   Vodka
1 oz.   Rum
1 oz.   Melon Liqueur
Lemonade
Shake 1st three ingredients
and pour over ice in a
highball glass. Fill with
lemonade. Garnish with a
cherry.

GREEN DEVIL
1 1/2 oz.   Gin
1 1/2 oz.   Crème de
Menthe (Green)
1 tbsp.   Lime Juice
Shake with ice and strain
into old-fashioned glass
over ice cubes. Decorate
with mint leaves.

GREEN DRAGON

Juice of $^1/_2$ Lemon
$^1/_2$ oz. Kümmel
$^1/_2$ oz. Crème de
   Menthe (Green)
$1^1/_2$ oz. Gin
4 dashes Orange Bitters

Shake with ice and strain
into cocktail glass.

GREEN FIZZ

1 tsp. Powdered Sugar
1 Egg White
Juice of $^1/_2$ Lemon
2 oz. Gin
1 tsp. Crème de Menthe
   (Green)

Shake with ice and strain
into highball glass over two
cubes of ice. Fill with
carbonated water and stir.

GREEN HORNET (DRY)

2 oz. Lime Vodka
Lemon-Lime Soda

Pour lime vodka over ice
cubes in a collins glass. Fill
with lemon-lime soda, stir,
and add a half-slice of lime.

GREEN OPAL

$^1/_2$ oz. Gin
$^1/_2$ oz. Anisette
1 oz. Anis

Shake with ice and strain
into cocktail glass.

GREEN SWIZZLE

Make same as Gin Swizzle
on page 99 and add **1
tablespoon Crème de
Menthe (Green)**. If
desired, rum, brandy, or
whiskey may be substituted
for the gin.

GREYHOUND

See Salty Dog recipe on
page 163. Do not add the
salt.

GYPSY COCKTAIL

$1^1/_2$ oz. Sweet
   Vermouth
$1^1/_2$ oz. Gin

Stir with ice and strain into
cocktail glass. Serve with a
cherry.

H

HAIR RAISER
1 1/2 oz.   100-Proof
   Vodka
1/2 oz.   Rock and Rye
1 tbsp.   Lemon Juice
Shake with ice and strain
into cocktail glass.

HARLEM COCKTAIL
3/4 oz.   Pineapple Juice
1 1/2 oz.   Gin
1/2 tsp.   Maraschino
Shake with ice and strain
into cocktail glass. Decorate
with two pineapple chunks.

HARVARD COCKTAIL
1 1/2 oz.   Brandy
3/4 oz.   Sweet
   Vermouth
1 dash   Bitters
1 tsp.   Grenadine
2 tsp.   Lemon Juice
Shake with ice and strain
into cocktail glass.

HARVARD COOLER
1/2 tsp.   Powdered
   Sugar
2 oz.   Carbonated
   Water
2 oz.   Apple Brandy
Into collins glass put
powdered sugar and
carbonated water. Stir.
Then add ice cubes and
apple brandy. Fill with
carbonated water or ginger
ale and stir again. Insert a
spiral of orange or lemon
peel (or both) and dangle
end over rim of glass.

HARVEY WALLBANGER
1 oz.   Vodka
4 oz.   Orange Juice
1/2 oz.   Galliano
Pour vodka and orange
juice into collins glass over
ice cubes. Stir. Float
Galliano on top.

HASTY COCKTAIL
3/4 oz.   Dry Vermouth
1 1/2 oz.   Gin
1/4 tsp.   Anis
1 tsp.   Grenadine
Stir with ice and strain into
cocktail glass.

HAVANA COCKTAIL

$1^1/_2$ oz.   Pineapple Juice
$^1/_2$ tsp.   Lemon Juice
$^3/_4$ oz.   Light Rum

Shake with ice and strain into cocktail glass.

HAWAIIAN COCKTAIL

2 oz.   Gin
1 tbsp.   Pineapple Juice
$^1/_2$ oz.   Triple Sec

Shake with ice and strain into cocktail glass.

HEADLESS HORSEMAN

2 oz.   Vodka
3 dashes Bitters

Pour into collins glass and add several ice cubes. Fill with ginger ale and stir. Decorate with a slice of orange.

HIGHBALLS

See Index on page 262 for complete list of Highball recipes.

HIGHLAND COOLER

$^1/_2$ tsp.   Powdered Sugar
2 oz.   Carbonated Water
2 oz.   Scotch

Into collins glass, put powdered sugar and carbonated water. Stir. Then add ice cubes and scotch. Fill with carbonated water or ginger ale and stir again. Insert a spiral of orange or lemon peel (or both) and dangle end over rim of glass.

HIGHLAND FLING COCKTAIL

$^3/_4$ oz.   Sweet Vermouth
$1^1/_2$ oz.   Scotch
2 dashes Orange Bitters

Stir with ice and strain into cocktail glass. Serve with an olive.

HOFFMAN HOUSE COCKTAIL

$^3/_4$ oz.   Dry Vermouth
$1^1/_2$ oz.   Gin
2 dashes Orange Bitters

Stir with ice and strain into cocktail glass. Serve with an olive.

HOKKAIDO COCKTAIL

$1^1/_2$ oz.   Gin
1 oz.   Sake
$^1/_2$ oz.   Triple Sec

Shake with ice and strain into cocktail glass.

HOLE-IN-ONE

$1^3/_4$ oz.   Scotch
$^3/_4$ oz.   Vermouth
$^1/_4$ tsp.   Lemon Juice
1 dash   Orange Bitters

Shake with ice and strain into cocktail glass.

HOMESTEAD COCKTAIL

$1^1/_2$ oz.   Gin
$^3/_4$ oz.   Sweet Vermouth

Stir with ice and strain into cocktail glass and serve with a slice of orange.

HONEYMOON COCKTAIL
Y ³/₄ oz. Benedictine
   ³/₄ oz. Apple Brandy
   Juice of ¹/₂ Lemon
   1 tsp. Triple Sec
Shake with ice and strain
into cocktail glass.

HONOLULU COCKTAIL NO. 1
Y 1 dash Bitters
   ¹/₄ tsp. Orange Juice
   ¹/₄ tsp. Pineapple Juice
   ¹/₄ tsp. Lemon Juice
   ¹/₂ tsp. Powdered
      Sugar
   1¹/₂ oz. Gin
Shake with ice and strain
into cocktail glass.

HONOLULU COCKTAIL NO. 2
Y ³/₄ oz. Gin
   ³/₄ oz. Maraschino
   ³/₄ oz. Benedictine
Stir with ice and strain into
cocktail glass.

HOOT MON COCKTAIL
Y ³/₄ oz. Sweet
   Vermouth
   1¹/₂ oz. Scotch
   1 tsp. Benedictine
Stir with ice and strain into
cocktail glass. Twist a
lemon peel and drop in
glass.

HOP TOAD
Y Juice of ¹/₂ Lime
   ³/₄ oz. Apricot-Flavored
      Brandy
   ³/₄ oz. Light Rum
Stir with ice and strain into
cocktail glass.

HORSE'S NECK (WITH A KICK)
2 oz. Blended Whiskey
Ginger Ale
Peel rind of whole lemon
in spiral fashion and put in
collins glass with one end
hanging over the rim. Fill
glass with ice cubes. Add
blended whiskey. Then fill
with ginger ale and stir
well.

HOT BRANDY FLIP
1 Whole Egg
   1 tsp. Powdered
      Sugar
   1¹/₂ oz. Brandy
   Hot Milk
Beat egg, sugar, and
brandy; pour into mug and
fill with hot milk. Stir.
Sprinkle nutmeg on top.

HOT BRICK TODDY
Into punch cup, put:
1 tsp. Butter
   1 tsp. Powdered Sugar
   3 pinches Cinnamon
   1 oz. Hot Water
Dissolve thoroughly. Then
add 1¹/₂ oz. Blended
Whiskey.
Fill with boiling water and
stir.

HOT BUTTERED RUM
1 tsp. Brown Sugar
Boiling Water
Square of Butter
2 oz. Dark Rum

Put lump of sugar into
punch cup and fill two-
thirds with boiling water.
Add square of butter and
rum. Stir and sprinkle
nutmeg on top.

HOT BUTTERED WINE
For each serving, heat $\frac{1}{2}$
cup muscatel and $\frac{1}{4}$ cup
water just to simmering; do
not boil. Preheat mug or
cup with boiling water.
Pour heated wine mixture
into mug and add 1
teaspoon butter and 2
teaspoons maple syrup. Stir
and sprinkle nutmeg on
top. Serve at once.

HOTEL PLAZA COCKTAIL
$\frac{3}{4}$ oz. Sweet Vermouth
$\frac{3}{4}$ oz. Dry Vermouth
$\frac{3}{4}$ oz. Gin

Stir with ice and strain into
cocktail glass. Decorate
with a crushed slice of
pineapple.

HOT GOLD
6 oz. Very Warm
Orange Juice
3 oz. Amaretto

Pour orange juice into a
stemmed wine glass or
mug. Add Amaretto and
garnish with a cinnamon
stick as stirrer.

HOT PANTS
$1\frac{1}{2}$ oz. Tequila
$\frac{1}{2}$ oz. Peppermint
Schnapps
1 tbsp. Grapefruit Juice
1 tsp. Powdered
Sugar

Shake with ice cubes and
pour into old-fashioned
glass rimmed with salt.

HOT SHOT MARGARITA
2 oz. Tequila
1 oz. Hot Shot Tropical
Fruit Liqueur
$1\frac{1}{2}$ oz. Lemon or Lime
Juice

Rub rim of cocktail glass
with rind of lemon or lime,
dip rim in salt. Shake
ingredients with ice and
strain into the salt-rimmed
glass.

HOT SPRINGS COCKTAIL ●
$1\frac{1}{2}$ oz. White Wine
1 tbsp. Pineapple Juice
$\frac{1}{2}$ tsp. Maraschino
1 dash Orange Bitters

Shake with ice and strain
into cocktail glass.

H.P.W. COCKTAIL
$1\frac{1}{2}$ tsp. Dry Vermouth
$1\frac{1}{2}$ tsp. Sweet
Vermouth
$1\frac{1}{2}$ oz. Gin

Stir with ice and strain into
cocktail glass. Add a twist of
orange peel.

● indicates lower alcohol content

HUDSON BAY

1 oz.   Gin
1/2 oz.   Cherry-Flavored Brandy
1 1/2 tsp.   151-Proof Rum
1 tbsp.   Orange Juice
1 1/2 tsp.   Lime Juice

Shake with ice and strain into cocktail glass.

HULA-HULA COCKTAIL

3/4 oz.   Orange Juice
1 1/2 oz.   Gin
1/4 tsp.   Powdered Sugar

Shake with ice and strain into cocktail glass.

HUMMER

1 oz.   Coffee Liqueur
1 oz.   Light Rum
2 large scoops Vanilla Ice Cream

Blend briefly and serve in highball glass.

HUNTSMAN COCKTAIL

1 1/2 oz.   Vodka
1/2 oz.   Jamaica Rum
Juice of 1/2 Lime
Powdered Sugar to taste

Shake with ice and strain into cocktail glass.

HURRICANE

1 oz.   Dark Rum
1 oz.   Light Rum
1 tbsp.   Passion Fruit Syrup
2 tsp.   Lime Juice

Shake with ice and strain into cocktail glass.

HYATT'S JAMAICAN BANANA*

1/2 oz. Light Rum
1/2 oz. Crème de Cacao (White)
1/2 oz. Crème de Banana
2 scoops Vanilla Ice Cream
1 oz. Half-and-Half
1 Whole Banana

Blend, then garnish with 2 slices banana, strawberry, and nutmeg, and serve in a large brandy snifter.

*Hyatt Regency Hotel, Dallas, Texas

ICE CREAM FLIP
1 Whole Egg
1 oz.   Maraschino
1 oz.   Triple Sec
1 small scoop Vanilla Ice
Cream

Shake with ice and strain into sour glass. Sprinkle a little nutmeg on top.

IDEAL COCKTAIL
1 oz.   Dry Vermouth
1 oz.   Gin
1/4 tsp.   Maraschino
1/2 tsp.   Grapefruit or
Lemon Juice

Shake with ice and strain into cocktail glass. Serve with a cherry.

IMPERIAL COCKTAIL
1 1/2 oz.   Dry Vermouth
1 1/2 oz.   Gin
1/2 tsp.   Maraschino
1 dash   Bitters

Stir with ice and strain into cocktail glass. Serve with a cherry.

IMPERIAL EGGNOG
32 oz. Prepared Dairy
Eggnog
10 oz. Brandy
2 oz.   Apricot-Flavored
Brandy

Combine in large punch bowl and serve. Sprinkle nutmeg on top of each serving.

IMPERIAL FIZZ
Juice of 1/2 Lemon
1/2 oz.   Light Rum
1 1/2 oz.   Blended
Whiskey
1 tsp.   Powdered
Sugar

Shake with ice and strain into highball glass. Add two ice cubes. Fill with carbonated water and stir.

INCIDER COCKTAIL
1 1/2 oz.   Blended
Whiskey
Apple Cider

Mix blended whiskey with a generous helping of apple cider. Serve over ice in old-fashioned glass and garnish with a slice of apple.

INCOME TAX COCKTAIL
1½ tsp. Dry Vermouth
1½ tsp. Sweet
    Vermouth
1 oz.   Gin
1 dash Bitters
Juice of ¼ Orange
Shake with ice and strain into cocktail glass.

INDIAN SUMMER
Wet sour glass edge and rim and then dip in cinnamon. Add **2 ounces Apple Schnapps.** Top off with hot apple cider. Add cinnamon stick if desired.

IRISH COFFEE
1½ oz. Irish Whiskey
Hot Black Coffee
Sugar
Whipped cream
Into a stemmed glass or cup rimmed with sugar, pour Irish whiskey. Fill to within ½ inch of top with coffee. Cover surface to brim with chilled whipped cream.

IRISH RICKEY
Juice of ½ Lime
Carbonated Water
1½ oz. Irish Whiskey
Pour into highball glass over ice cubes. Stir. Add a piece of lime.

IRISH SHILLELAGH
Juice of ½ Lemon
1 tsp. Powdered Sugar
1½ oz. Irish Whiskey
1 tbsp. Sloe Gin
1 tbsp. Light Rum
Shake with ice and strain into punch glass. Decorate with fresh raspberries, strawberries, a cherry, and two peach slices.

IRISH WHISKEY
½ tsp. Triple Sec
½ tsp. Anis
¼ tsp. Maraschino
1 dash Bitters
2 oz.   Irish Whiskey
Stir with ice and strain into cocktail glass. Serve with an olive.

IRISH WHISKEY HIGHBALL
2 oz. Irish Whiskey
Ginger Ale
Pour Irish whiskey into highball glass over ice cubes and fill with ginger ale or carbonated water. Add a twist of lemon peel, if desired, and stir.

ITALIAN COFFEE
1½ oz. Amaretto
Hot Coffee
1½ tbsp. Coffee Ice
    Cream
Ground Coriander

Pour Amaretto into a heat-resistant stemmed glass or mug. Fill with hot coffee. Top with coffee ice cream. Sprinkle with coriander.

ITALIAN SOMBRERO
1½ oz. Amaretto
3 oz. Light Cream

Put in a blender or shake well. Serve over ice cubes or straight up in a champagne flute.

J

JACK-IN-THE-BOX
1 oz. Apple Brandy
1 oz. Pineapple Juice
1 dash Bitters
Shake with ice and strain
into cocktail glass.

JACK ROSE COCKTAIL
1½ oz. Apple Brandy
Juice of ½ Lime
1 tsp. Grenadine
Shake with ice and strain
into cocktail glass.

JADE
1½ oz. Light Rum
½ tsp. Crème de
Menthe (Green)
½ tsp. Triple Sec
1 tbsp. Lime Juice
1 tsp. Powdered
Sugar
Shake with ice and strain
into cocktail glass. Add a
lime slice.

JAMAICA COFFEE
1 oz. Coffee-Flavored
Brandy
¾ oz. Light Rum
Hot Coffee
Serve in mug, slightly
sweetened. Top with
whipped cream and
sprinkle with nutmeg.

JAMAICA GLOW
1 oz. Gin
1 tbsp. Claret
1 tbsp. Orange Juice
1 tsp. Jamaica Rum
Shake with ice and strain
into cocktail glass.

JAMAICA GRANITO
1 small scoop Lemon or
Orange Sherbet
1½ oz. Brandy
1 oz. Triple Sec
Carbonated Water
Combine in collins glass
and stir. Sprinkle nutmeg
on top.

a) Bellini b) Pineapple Cooler c) Adonis

JAMAICA HOP

1 oz. Coffee-Flavored
     Brandy
1 oz. Crème de Cacao
     (White)
1 oz. Light Cream
Shake well with ice and
strain into cocktail glass.

JAPANESE

2 oz. Brandy
1½ tsp. Orgeat Syrup
1 tbsp. Lime Juice
1 dash Bitters
Shake with ice and strain
into cocktail glass. Add
twist of lime peel.

JAPANESE FIZZ

Juice of ½ Lemon
1 tsp. Powdered
     Sugar
1½ oz. Blended
     Whiskey
1 tbsp. Port
1 Egg White
Shake with ice and strain
into highball glass over two
cubes of ice. Fill with
carbonated water and stir.
Serve with slice of
pineapple.

JEAN LAFITTE
COCKTAIL

1 oz. Gin
½ oz. Triple Sec
½ oz. Anis
1 tsp. Powdered
     Sugar
1 Egg Yolk
Shake with ice and strain
into cocktail glass.

JERSEY LIGHTNING

1½ oz. Apple Brandy
½ oz. Sweet
     Vermouth
Juice of 1 lime
Shake with ice and strain
into cocktail glass.

JEWEL COCKTAIL

¾ oz. Chartreuse
     (Green)
¾ oz. Sweet Vermouth
¾ oz. Gin
1 dash Orange Bitters
Stir with ice and strain into
cocktail glass. Serve with a
cherry.

JEYPLAK COCKTAIL

1½ oz. Gin
¾ oz. Sweet
     Vermouth
¼ tsp. Anis
Stir with ice and strain into
cocktail glass. Serve with a
cherry.

JOCKEY CLUB
COCKTAIL

1 dash Bitters
¼ tsp. Crème de
     Cacao (White)
Juice of ¼ Lemon
1½ oz. Gin
Shake with ice and strain
into cocktail glass.

JOCOSE JULEP

2¹/₂ oz. Bourbon
¹/₂ oz. Crème de
Menthe (Green)
1 oz. Lime Juice
1 tsp. Sugar
5 Chopped Mint Leaves

Combine all ingredients in an electric blender without ice. Pour into collins glass over ice cubes. Fill with carbonated water and decorate with a sprig of mint.

JOHN COLLINS

Juice of ¹/₂ Lemon
1 tsp. Powdered Sugar
2 oz. Blended Whiskey

Shake with ice and strain into collins glass. Add several cubes of ice, fill with carbonated water, and stir. Decorate with slices of orange and lemon, and a cherry. Serve with straws.

JOHNNIE COCKTAIL

³/₄ oz. Triple Sec
1¹/₂ oz. Sloe Gin
1 tsp. Anisette

Shake with ice and strain into cocktail glass.

JOULOUVILLE

1 oz. Gin
¹/₂ oz. Apple Brandy
1¹/₂ tsp. Sweet
Vermouth
1 tbsp. Lemon Juice
2 dashes Grenadine

Shake with ice and strain into cocktail glass.

JOURNALIST COCKTAIL

1¹/₂ tsp. Dry Vermouth
1¹/₂ tsp. Sweet
Vermouth
1¹/₂ oz. Gin
¹/₂ tsp. Lemon Juice
¹/₂ tsp. Triple Sec
1 dash Bitters

Shake with ice and strain into cocktail glass.

JUDGE JR. COCKTAIL

³/₄ oz. Gin
³/₄ oz. Light Rum
Juice of ¹/₄ Lemon
¹/₂ tsp. Powdered
Sugar
¹/₄ tsp. Grenadine

Shake with ice and strain into cocktail glass.

JUDGETTE COCKTAIL

³/₄ oz. Peach-Flavored
Brandy
³/₄ oz. Gin
³/₄ oz. Dry Vermouth
Juice of ¹/₄ Lime

Shake with ice and strain into cocktail glass. Serve with a cherry.

JULEPS

See Index on page 263 for complete list of Julep recipes.

K

KAMIKAZE
1 oz. Lime Juice
1 oz. Triple Sec
1 oz. Vodka
Shake and serve over ice in old-fashioned glass.

KANGAROO COCKTAIL
$1^1/_2$ oz. Vodka
$^3/_4$ oz. Dry Vermouth
Shake with ice and strain into cocktail glass. Serve with a twist of lemon peel.

K.G.B. COCKTAIL
$^1/_2$ oz. Kümmel
$1^1/_2$ oz. Gin
$^1/_4$ tsp. Apricot-Flavored Brandy
$^1/_4$ tsp. Lemon Juice
Shake with ice and strain into cocktail glass. Add a twist of lemon peel.

KENTUCKY COCKTAIL
$^3/_4$ oz. Pineapple Juice
$1^1/_2$ oz. Bourbon
Shake with ice and strain into cocktail glass.

KENTUCKY COLONEL COCKTAIL
$^1/_2$ oz. Benedictine
$1^1/_2$ oz. Bourbon
Stir with ice and strain into cocktail glass. Add a twist of lemon peel.

KING COLE COCKTAIL
1 slice Orange
1 slice Pineapple
$^1/_2$ tsp. Powdered Sugar
Muddle well in old-fashioned glass and add:
2 oz. Blended Whiskey
2 Ice Cubes
Stir well.

KIR 🅛
3 oz. White Wine
Splash of Crème de Cassis
Pour wine over ice in an old-fashioned glass. Add crème de cassis, a twist of lemon, and stir.

🅛 indicates lower alcohol content

KIR ROYALE
6 oz.   Champagne
Splash of Crème de
Cassis
Serve in a large champagne
or wine glass.

KISS-IN-THE-DARK
³/₄ oz. Gin
³/₄ oz. Cherry-Flavored
Brandy
³/₄ oz. Dry Vermouth
Stir with ice and strain into
cocktail glass.

KISS THE BOYS
GOODBYE
³/₄ oz. Sloe Gin
³/₄ oz. Brandy
¹/₂ Egg White
Juice of 1 Lemon
Shake with ice and strain
into cocktail glass.

KLONDIKE COOLER
¹/₂ tsp. Powdered
Sugar
2 oz.   Carbonated
Water
2 oz.   Blended
Whiskey
Ginger Ale
Into collins glass, mix
powdered sugar and
carbonated water. Fill glass
with ice and add blended
whiskey. Fill with
carbonated water or ginger
ale and stir again. Insert a
spiral of orange or lemon
peel (or both) and dangle
end over rim of glass.

KNICKERBOCKER
COCKTAIL
¹/₄ tsp. Sweet
Vermouth
³/₄ oz. Dry Vermouth
1¹/₂ oz. Gin
Stir with ice and strain into
cocktail glass. Add a twist of
lemon peel.

KNICKERBOCKER
SPECIAL COCKTAIL
1 tsp. Raspberry
Syrup
1 tsp. Lemon Juice
1 tsp. Orange Juice
2 oz.   Light Rum
¹/₂ tsp. Triple Sec
Shake with ice and strain
into cocktail glass. Decorate
with a small slice of
pineapple.

KNOCK-OUT COCKTAIL
¹/₂ oz. Anis
³/₄ oz. Gin
³/₄ oz. Dry Vermouth
1 tsp. Crème de Menthe
(White)
Stir with ice and strain into
cocktail glass. Serve with a
cherry.

Kir

KRETCHMA COCKTAIL

1 oz.   Vodka
1 oz.   Crème de
    Cacao (White)
1 tbsp. Lemon Juice
1 dash   Grenadine

Shake with ice and strain
into cocktail glass.

KUP'S INDISPENSABLE
COCKTAIL

$^{1}/_{2}$ oz.   Light Vermouth
$^{1}/_{2}$ oz.   Dry Vermouth
$1^{1}/_{2}$ oz. Gin
1 dash Bitters

Stir with ice and strain into
cocktail glass.

L

LADIES COCKTAIL
1¾ oz. Blended Whiskey
½ tsp. Anisette
2 dashes Bitters

Stir with ice and strain into cocktail glass. Serve with a pineapple stick on top.

LADY BE GOOD
1½ oz. Brandy
½ oz. Crème de Menthe (White)
½ oz. Sweet Vermouth

Shake with ice and strain into cocktail glass.

LADY FINGER
1 oz. Gin
½ oz. Kirschwasser
1 oz. Cherry-Flavored Brandy

Shake with ice and strain into cocktail glass.

LADY LOVE FIZZ
1 tsp. Powdered Sugar
Juice of ½ Lemon
1 Egg White
2 oz. Gin
2 tsp. Light Cream

Shake with ice and strain into cocktail glass over two ice cubes. Fill with carbonated water and stir.

LA JOLLA
1½ oz. Brandy
½ oz. Crème de Banana
1 tsp. Orange Juice
2 tsp. Lemon Juice

Shake with ice and strain into cocktail glass.

LASKY COCKTAIL
¾ oz. Grape Juice
¾ oz. Swedish Punch
¾ oz. Gin

Shake with ice and strain into cocktail glass.

LAWHILL COCKTAIL
Y 3/4 oz. Dry Vermouth
1 1/2 oz. Blended
    Whiskey
  1/4 tsp. Anis
  1/4 tsp. Maraschino
  1 dash Bitters
Stir with ice and strain into
cocktail glass.

LEAP FROG HIGHBALL
Juice of 1/2 Lemon
2 oz. Gin
Pour into highball glass
over ice cubes and fill with
ginger ale. Stir.

LEAP YEAR COCKTAIL
Y 1 1/4 oz. Gin
  1/2 oz. Orange-
    Flavored Gin
  1/2 oz. Sweet
    Vermouth
  1/4 tsp. Lemon Juice
Shake with ice and strain
into cocktail glass.

LEAVE-IT-TO-ME
COCKTAIL NO. 1
Y 1/2 oz. Apricot-
    Flavored Brandy
  1/2 oz. Dry Vermouth
  1 oz. Gin
  1/4 tsp. Lemon Juice
  1/4 tsp. Grenadine
Shake with ice and strain
into cocktail glass.

LEAVE-IT-TO-ME
COCKTAIL NO. 2
Y 1 tsp. Raspberry
    Syrup
  1 tsp. Lemon Juice
  1/4 tsp. Maraschino
  1 1/2 oz. Gin
Stir with ice and strain into
cocktail glass.

LEMONADE (CLARET)
2 tsp. Powdered Sugar
Juice of 1 Lemon
  2 oz. Claret or Red
    Wine
Dissolve sugar and lemon
in collins glass, then add
ice and enough water to fill
glass, leaving room to float
wine. Decorate with slices
of orange and lemon, and a
cherry. Serve with straws.

LEMONADE (MODERN)
1 Lemon
2 tsp. Powdered
    Sugar
  1 1/2 oz. Dry Sherry
  1 oz. Sloe Gin
Cut lemon into quarters
and muddle well with
sugar. Add sherry and sloe
gin. Shake with ice and
strain into collins glass. Fill
glass with carbonated
water.

LIBERTY COCKTAIL
$^3/_4$ oz.   Light Rum
1$^1/_2$ oz.   Apple Brandy
$^1/_4$ tsp.   Sugar Syrup
Stir with ice and strain into cocktail glass.

LIL NAUE
1 oz.   Brandy
$^1/_2$ oz. Port
$^1/_2$ oz.   Apricot-Flavored Brandy
1 tsp.   Powdered Sugar
1 Egg Yolk
Shake with ice and strain into wine glass. Sprinkle cinnamon on top.

LIME GIANT
2 oz.   Lime Vodka
Lemon/Lime Soda
Put ice cubes in collins glass and add lime vodka. Fill with lemon and lime soda. Decorate with a slice of lime.

LIMESTONE
1$^1/_2$ oz.   Yellowstone Bourbon
Collins Mix
Lime Juice
In ice-filled highball glass, pour bourbon, fill glass with collins mix, and add lime juice to taste.

LIMEY
1 oz.   Light Rum
1 oz.   Lime Liqueur
$^1/_2$ oz.   Triple Sec
2 tsp.   Lime Juice
Combine ingredients and a half-cup of crushed ice in an electric blender. Blend at low speed and pour into champagne flute. Add a twist of lime peel.

LINSTEAD COCKTAIL
1 oz.   Blended Whiskey
1 oz.   Pineapple Juice
$^1/_2$ tsp.   Powdered Sugar
$^1/_4$ tsp.   Anis
$^1/_4$ tsp.   Lemon Juice
Shake with ice and strain into cocktail glass.

LITTLE DEVIL COCKTAIL
Juice of $^1/_4$ Lemon
1$^1/_2$ tsp.   Triple Sec
$^3/_4$ oz.   Light Rum
$^3/_4$ oz.   Gin
Shake with ice and strain into cocktail glass.

LITTLE PRINCESS COCKTAIL
1$^1/_2$ oz.   Sweet Vermouth
1$^1/_2$ oz.   Light Rum
Stir with ice and strain into cocktail glass.

LONDON BUCK
2 oz. Gin
Juice of $\frac{1}{2}$ Lemon
Ginger Ale
Pour over ice cubes in
highball glass and stir.

LONDON COCKTAIL
2 oz. Gin
2 dashes Orange Bitters
$\frac{1}{2}$ tsp. Sugar Syrup
$\frac{1}{2}$ tsp. Maraschino
Stir with ice and strain into
cocktail glass. Add a twist of
lemon peel.

LONDON SPECIAL
Put a large twist of orange
peel into champagne flute.
Add 1 lump sugar and 2
dashes bitters. Fill with
well-chilled champagne and
stir.

LONE TREE COCKTAIL
$\frac{3}{4}$ oz. Sweet
Vermouth
$1\frac{1}{2}$ oz. Gin
Stir with ice and strain into
cocktail glass.

LONE TREE COOLER
Into collins glass, put:
$\frac{1}{2}$ tsp. Powdered
Sugar
2 oz. Carbonated
Water
Stir and fill glass with ice
and add:
2 oz. Gin
1 tbsp. Dry Vermouth
Fill with carbonated water
or ginger ale and stir again.
Insert a spiral of orange or
lemon peel (or both) and
dangle end over rim of
glass.

LONG ISLAND TEA
$\frac{1}{2}$ oz. Vodka
$\frac{1}{2}$ oz. Gin
$\frac{1}{2}$ oz. Light Rum
$\frac{1}{2}$ oz. Tequila
Juice of $\frac{1}{2}$ Lemon
Cola
Combine ingredients and
pour over ice in tall glass.
Add a dash of cola for
color. Garnish with slice of
lemon.

LOOK OUT BELOW
$1^1/_2$ oz. 151-Proof Rum
Juice of $^1/_4$ Lime
1 tsp. Grenadine
Shake with ice and strain
into old-fashioned glass
over ice cubes.

LOS ANGELES COCKTAIL
Juice of $^1/_2$ Lemon
1 tsp. Powdered Sugar
1 Whole Egg
$^1/_4$ tsp. Sweet
Vermouth
$1^1/_2$ oz. Blended
Whiskey
Shake with ice and strain
into sour glass.

LOVE COCKTAIL
2 oz. Sloe Gin
1 Egg White
$^1/_2$ tsp. Lemon Juice
$^1/_2$ tsp. Raspberry Juice
Shake with ice and strain
into cocktail glass.

LOVING CUP
4 tsp. Powdered Sugar
6 oz. Carbonated Water
1 oz. Triple Sec
2 oz. Brandy
16 oz. Claret
Fill large glass pitcher with
ice and stir in the
ingredients above. Decorate
with fruits in season and
also rind of cucumber
inserted on each side of
pitcher. Top with a small
bunch of mint sprigs.

LUGGER
1 oz. Brandy
1 oz. Apple Brandy
1 dash Apricot-
Flavored Brandy
Shake with ice and strain
into cocktail glass.

LUXURY COCKTAIL
3 oz. Brandy
2 dashes Orange Bitters
3 oz. Well-Chilled
Champagne
Stir and pour into
champagne flute.

Mexican Coffee

Martini

M

MADRAS
1½ oz. Vodka
4 oz. Cranberry Juice
1 oz. Orange Juice
Pour into highball glass over ice. Garnish with wedge of lime.

MAIDEN'S BLUSH COCKTAIL
¼ tsp. Lemon Juice
1 tsp. Triple Sec
1 tsp. Grenadine
1½ oz. Gin
Shake with ice and strain into cocktail glass.

MAIDEN'S PRAYER
1½ oz. Gin
½ oz. Triple Sec
1 oz. Lemon Juice
Shake with ice and strain into cocktail glass.

MAI-TAI
½ tsp. Powdered Sugar
2 oz. Light Rum
1 oz. Triple Sec
1 tbsp. Orgeat or Almond-Flavored Syrup
1 tbsp. Grenadine
1 tbsp. Lime Juice
Shake with ice and strain into large old-fashioned glass about 1/3 full with crushed ice. Decorate with a maraschino cherry speared to a wedge of fresh pineapple. For a hair raiser, top with a dash of 151-proof rum; for a true Hawaiian effect, float an orchid on each drink. Serve with straws.

MAJOR BAILEY

$1^1/_2$ tsp. Lime Juice
$1^1/_2$ tsp. Lemon Juice
$^1/_2$ tsp. Powdered
Sugar
12 Mint Leaves
2 oz. Gin

Muddle first four
ingredients well, pour into
collins glass filled with ice,
and add gin. Stir until glass
is frosted. Decorate with
sprig of mint and serve
with straws.

MALMAISON

Juice of $^1/_2$ Lemon
1 oz. Light Rum
$^1/_2$ oz. Cream Sherry

Shake with ice and strain
into cocktail glass rimmed
with Anisette.

MAMIE GILROY

Juice of $^1/_2$ Lime
2 oz. Scotch
Ginger Ale

Fill in a collins glass with
ice. Stir.

MAMIE'S SISTER

Juice of 1 Lime
2 oz. Gin
Ginger Ale

Add the juice of one lime
and rind in collins glass,
and add gin. Fill glass with
ginger ale and ice. Stir.

MANDEVILLE

$1^1/_2$ oz. Light Rum
1 oz. Dark Rum
1 tsp. Anis
1 tbsp. Lemon Juice
1 tbsp. Cola
$^1/_4$ tsp. Grenadine

Shake with ice and strain
into old-fashioned glass
over ice cubes.

MANHASSET

$1^1/_2$ oz. Blended
Whiskey
$1^1/_2$ tsp. Dry Vermouth
$1^1/_2$ tsp. Sweet
Vermouth
1 tbsp. Lemon Juice

Shake with ice and strain
into cocktail glass.

MANHATTAN

$^3/_4$ oz. Sweet
Vermouth
$1^1/_2$ oz. Blended
Whiskey

Stir with ice and strain into
cocktail glass. Serve with a
cherry.

MANHATTAN (DRY)

$^3/_4$ oz. Dry Vermouth
$1^1/_2$ oz. Blended
Whiskey

Stir with ice and strain into
cocktail glass. Serve with an
olive.

MANILA FIZZ
2 oz. Gin
1 Whole Egg
1 tsp. Powdered Sugar
2 oz. Root Beer
Juice of 1 Lime or ¹/₂
    Lemon

Shake with ice and strain into highball glass over two ice cubes.

MARGARITA
1¹/₂ oz. Tequila
¹/₂ oz. Triple Sec
1 oz. Lemon or Lime Juice

Rub rim of cocktail glass with rind of lemon or lime, dip rim in salt. Shake ingredients with ice and strain into the salt-rimmed glass.

MARIPOSA
1 oz. Light Rum
¹/₂ oz. Brandy
1 tbsp. Lemon Juice
1 tbsp. Orange Juice
1 dash Grenadine

Shake with ice and strain into cocktail glass.

MARMALADE
1¹/₂ oz. Curacao
Tonic Water

Pour Curacao over ice in a highball glass and fill with tonic. Garnish with an orange slice.

MARTINEZ COCKTAIL
1 dash Orange Bitters
1 oz. Dry Vermouth
¹/₄ tsp. Triple Sec
1 oz. Gin

Stir with ice and strain into cocktail glass. Serve with a cherry.

MARTINI
(Traditional 2-to-1)
1¹/₂ oz. Gin
³/₄ oz. Dry Vermouth

Stir vermouth and gin over ice cubes in a mixing glass. Strain into cocktail glass. Serve with a twist of lemon peel or olive, if desired.

MARTINI (DRY)
(5-to-1)
1²/₃ oz. Gin
¹/₃ oz. Dry Vermouth

Follow directions for Martini preparation.

MARTINI (EXTRA DRY)
(8-to-1)
2 oz. Gin
¹/₄ oz. Dry Vermouth

Follow directions for Martini preparation.

MARTINI (MEDIUM)
1¹/₂ oz. Gin
¹/₂ oz. Dry Vermouth
¹/₂ oz. Sweet Vermouth

Follow directions for Martini preparation.

MARTINI (SWEET)
1 oz. Gin
1 oz. Sweet Vermouth

Follow directions for Martini preparation.

MARY GARDEN COCKTAIL

Y 1½ oz.   Dubonnet®
   ¾ oz.   Dry Vermouth
Stir with ice and strain into
cocktail glass.

MARY PICKFORD COCKTAIL

Y 1 oz.   Light Rum
  1 oz.   Pineapple Juice
  ¼ tsp.   Grenadine
  ¼ tsp.   Maraschino
Shake with ice and strain
into cocktail glass.

MAURICE COCKTAIL

Y Juice of ¼ Orange
  ½ oz.   Sweet Vermouth
  ½ oz.   Dry Vermouth
  1 oz.   Gin
  1 dash   Bitters
Shake with ice and strain
into cocktail glass.

MAXIM

Y 1½ oz.   Gin
  1 oz.   Dry Vermouth
  1 dash   Crème de
       Cacao (White)
Shake with ice and strain
into cocktail glass.

MAY BLOSSOM FIZZ

U 1 tsp.   Grenadine
   Juice of ½ Lemon
  2 oz.   Swedish Punch
Shake with ice and strain
into highball glass over two
ice cubes. Fill with
carbonated water and stir.

McCLELLAND COCKTAIL

Y ¾ oz.   Triple Sec
  1½ oz.   Sloe Gin
  1 dash   Orange Bitters
Shake with ice and strain
into cocktail glass.

MELON BALL

U 1 oz.   Melon Liqueur
  1 oz.   Vodka
  2 oz.   Pineapple Juice
Pour over ice in a highball
glass and garnish with an
orange, pineapple, or
watermelon slice.

MELON COCKTAIL

Y 2 oz.   Gin
  ¼ tsp.   Lemon Juice
  ¼ tsp.   Maraschino
Shake with ice and strain
into cocktail glass. Serve
with a cherry.

MERRY WIDOW COCKTAIL NO. 1

Y 1¼ oz.   Gin
  1¼ oz.   Dry Vermouth
  ½ tsp.   Benedictine
  ½ tsp.   Anis
  1 dash Orange Bitters
Stir with ice and strain into
cocktail glass. Add a twist of
lemon peel.

MERRY WIDOW COCKTAIL NO. 2

Y 1¼ oz.   Maraschino
  1¼ oz.   Cherry-Flavored
       Brandy
Stir with ice and strain into
cocktail glass. Serve with a
cherry.

MERRY WIDOW FIZZ
Juice of ½ Orange
Juice of ½ Lemon
1 Egg White
1 tsp. Powdered Sugar
1½ oz. Sloe Gin
Shake with ice and strain into highball glass with two ice cubes. Fill with carbonated water and stir.

METROPOLITAN COCKTAIL
1¼ oz. Brandy
1¼ oz. Sweet Vermouth
½ tsp. Sugar Syrup
1 dash Bitters
Stir with ice and strain into cocktail glass.

MEXICANA
1½ oz. Tequila
1 oz. Lemon Juice
1 tbsp. Pineapple Juice
1 tsp. Grenadine
Shake with ice and strain into cocktail glass.

MEXICAN COFFEE
1 oz. Coffee Liqueur
½ oz. Tequila
5 oz. Very Hot Black Coffee
Whipped Cream
Stir coffee liqueur and tequila in coffee cup, add coffee, and top with whipped cream.

MEXICOLA
2 oz. Tequila
Juice of ½ Lime
Cola
Fill collins glass with ice cubes. Add tequila and lime juice, fill with cola, and stir.

MIAMI
1½ oz. Light Rum
½ oz. Crème de Menthe (White)
1 dash Lemon Juice
Shake with ice and strain into cocktail glass.

MIAMI BEACH COCKTAIL
¾ oz. Scotch
¾ oz. Dry Vermouth
¾ oz. Grapefruit Juice
Shake with ice and strain into cocktail glass.

MIDNIGHT COCKTAIL
1 oz. Apricot-Flavored Brandy
½ oz. Triple Sec
1 tbsp. Lemon Juice
Shake with ice and strain into cocktail glass.

MIKADO COCKTAIL
1 oz. Brandy
1 dash Triple Sec
1 dash Grenadine
1 dash Crème de Noyaux
1 dash Bitters
Stir in old-fashioned glass over ice cubes.

MILK PUNCH

1 tsp. Powdered Sugar
2 oz. Blended Whiskey
1 cup Milk

Shake with ice and strain into collins glass. Sprinkle nutmeg on top.

MILLIONAIRE COCKTAIL

1 Egg White
1/4 tsp. Grenadine
1/2 oz. Triple Sec
1 1/2 oz. Blended Whiskey

Shake with ice and strain into cocktail glass.

MILLION-DOLLAR COCKTAIL

2 tsp. Pineapple Juice
1 tsp. Grenadine
1 Egg White
3/4 oz. Sweet Vermouth
1 1/2 oz. Gin

Shake with ice and strain into cocktail glass.

MIMOSA 🅛

Equal Parts:
Chilled Champagne
Orange Juice

Serve chilled in a stemmed goblet.

MINT COLLINS

Juice of 1/2 Lemon
2 oz. Mint-Flavored Gin

Shake with ice and strain into collins glass. Add several ice cubes, fill with carbonated water, and stir. Decorate with slices of lemon and orange, and a cherry. Serve with straws.

MINT GIN COCKTAIL 🅛

1 oz. Mint-Flavored Gin
1 oz. White Port
1 1/2 tsp. Dry Vermouth

Stir with ice and strain into cocktail glass.

MINT HIGHBALL

2 oz. Crème de Menthe (Green)
Ginger Ale or Carbonated Water

Pour into highball glass over ice cubes and fill with ginger ale or carbonated water. Add a twist of lemon peel, if desired, and stir.

MINT JULEP

4 sprigs Mint
1 tsp. Powdered Sugar
2 tsp. Water
2 1/2 oz. Bourbon

In a silver julep cup, silver mug, or collins glass, muddle mint leaves, powdered sugar, and water. Fill glass or mug with shaved or crushed ice and add bourbon. Top with more ice and garnish with a mint sprig and straws.

🅛 indicates lower alcohol content

MINT JULEP (SOUTHERN STYLE)

Into a silver mug or collins glass, dissolve one teaspoon powdered sugar with two teaspoons of water. Then fill with finely shaved ice and add 2¹/₂ oz. **Bourbon.** Stir until glass is heavily frosted, adding more ice if necessary. (Do not hold glass with hand while stirring.) Decorate with five or six sprigs of fresh mint so that the tops are about two inches above rim of mug or glass. Use short straws so that it will be necessary to bury nose in mint. The mint is intended for scent rather than taste.

MINT ON ROCKS

Pour 2 oz. **Crème de Menthe (Green)** over ice cubes in old-fashioned glass.

MISSISSIPPI PLANTERS PUNCH

1 tbsp. Powdered Sugar
Juice of 1 Lemon
¹/₂ oz. **Light Rum**
¹/₂ oz. **Bourbon**
1 oz. **Brandy**

Shake all ingredients with ice and strain into collins glass with cubed ice. Fill with carbonated water and stir.

MR. MANHATTAN COCKTAIL

Muddle lump of sugar with:
4 sprigs Mint
¹/₄ tsp. **Lemon Juice**
1 tsp. **Orange Juice**
1¹/₂ oz. **Gin**

Shake with ice and strain into cocktail glass.

MOCHA MINT

³/₄ oz. **Coffee-Flavored Brandy**
³/₄ oz. **Crème de Cacao (White)**
³/₄ oz. **Crème de Menthe (White)**

Shake with ice and strain into cocktail glass.

MODERN COCKTAIL

1¹/₂ oz. **Scotch**
¹/₂ tsp. **Lemon Juice**
¹/₄ tsp. **Anis**
¹/₂ tsp. **Jamaica Rum**
1 dash **Orange Bitters**

Shake with ice and strain into cocktail glass. Serve with a cherry.

MONTANA

1¹/₂ oz. **Brandy**
1 oz. **Port**
¹/₂ oz. **Dry Vermouth**

Stir in old-fashioned glass on the rocks.

a) Bourbon Straight-Up b) Mint Julep
c) Bourbon on Rocks

MONTE CARLO IMPERIAL HIGHBALL
2 oz. Gin
$^1/_2$ oz. Crème de Menthe (White)
Juice of $^1/_4$ Lemon
Shake with ice and strain into highball glass over ice cubes. Fill glass with champagne and stir.

MONTEZUMA
$1^1/_2$ oz. Tequila
1 oz. Madeira
1 Egg Yolk
$^1/_2$ cup Crushed Ice
Mix in blender at low speed and serve in champagne flute.

MONTMARTRE COCKTAIL
$1^1/_4$ oz. Dry Gin
$^1/_2$ oz. Sweet Vermouth
$^1/_2$ oz. Triple Sec
Stir with ice and strain into cocktail glass. Serve with a cherry.

MONTREAL CLUB BOUNCER
$1^1/_2$ oz. Gin
$^1/_2$ oz. Anis
Pour into old-fashioned glass over ice cubes. Stir.

MONTREAL GIN SOUR
1 oz. Gin
1 oz. Lemon Juice
$^1/_2$ Egg White
1 tsp. Powdered Sugar
Shake with ice and strain into sour glass. Add a slice of lemon.

MOONLIGHT
2 oz. Apple Brandy
Juice of 1 Lemon
1 tsp. Powdered Sugar
Shake with ice and strain into old-fashioned glass over ice cubes.

MOON QUAKE SHAKE
$1^1/_2$ oz. Dark Rum
1 oz. Coffee-Flavored Brandy
1 tbsp. Lemon Juice
Shake with ice and strain into cocktail glass.

MORNING COCKTAIL
1 oz. Brandy
1 oz. Dry Vermouth
$^1/_4$ tsp. Triple Sec
$^1/_4$ tsp. Maraschino
$^1/_4$ tsp. Anis
2 dashes Orange Bitters
Stir with ice and strain into cocktail glass. Serve with a cherry.

MORNING GLORY FIZZ
Juice of ¹/₂ Lemon or 1 Lime
1 tsp. Powdered Sugar
1 Egg White
¹/₂ tsp. Anis
2 oz. Scotch

Shake with ice and strain into highball glass over two ice cubes. Fill with carbonated water and stir.

MORRO
1 oz. Gin
¹/₂ oz. Dark Rum
1 tbsp. Pineapple Juice
1 tbsp. Lime Juice
¹/₂ tsp. Powdered Sugar

Shake with ice and strain into sugar rimmed old-fashioned glass over ice cubes.

MOSCOW MULE
Into a copper mug, pour:
1¹/₂ oz. Vodka
Juice of ¹/₂ Lime

Add ice cubes and fill with ginger beer. Drop lime wedge in mug for decoration.

MOULIN ROUGE
1¹/₂ oz. Sloe Gin
³/₄ oz. Sweet Vermouth
1 dash Bitters

Stir with ice and strain into cocktail glass.

MOUNTAIN COCKTAIL
1 Egg White
¹/₄ tsp. Lemon Juice
¹/₄ tsp. Dry Vermouth
¹/₄ tsp. Sweet Vermouth
1¹/₂ oz. Blended Whiskey

Shake with ice and strain into cocktail glass.

MULLED CLARET
Into a metal mug, put:
1 lump Sugar
Juice of ¹/₂ Lemon
1 dash Bitters
1 tsp. Mixed Cinnamon and Nutmeg
5 oz. Claret or Red Wine

Heat poker red hot and hold in liquid until boiling and serve; or warm on a stove.

N

NAPOLEON
2 oz.   Gin
$^1/_2$ tsp. Curaçao
$^1/_2$ tsp. Dubonnet®
Stir with ice and strain into cocktail glass.

NARRAGANSETT
1$^1/_2$ oz. Bourbon
1 oz.   Sweet Vermouth
1 dash Anisette
Stir in old-fashioned glass with ice cubes. Add a twist of lemon peel.

NASHVILLE EGGNOG
32 oz. Prepared Dairy
        Eggnog
6 oz.   Bourbon
3 oz.   Brandy
3 oz.   Jamaica Rum
Combine in large punch bowl and serve. Sprinkle nutmeg on top of each serving.

NEGRONI
$^3/_4$ oz. Gin
$^3/_4$ oz. Campari
$^3/_4$ oz. Sweet or Dry
        Vermouth
Stir with ice and strain into cocktail glass, or into old-fashioned glass over ice cubes, with or without a splash of carbonated water. Add a twist of lemon peel.

NETHERLAND
1 oz.   Brandy
1 oz.   Triple Sec
1 dash Orange Bitters
Stir in old-fashioned glass with ice cubes.

NEVADA COCKTAIL
1$^1/_2$ oz. Light Rum
1 oz.   Grapefruit Juice
Juice of 1 Lime
1 dash Bitters
3 tsp.   Powdered
        Sugar
Shake with ice and strain into cocktail glass.

NEVINS

1½ oz. Bourbon
1½ tsp. Apricot-
Flavored Brandy
1 tbsp. Grapefruit Juice
1½ tsp. Lemon Juice
1 dash Bitters
Shake with ice and strain into cocktail glass.

NEW ORLEANS BUCK

1½ oz. Light Rum
1 oz. Orange Juice
½ oz. Lemon Juice
Shake all ingredients with ice and strain into collins glass over ice cubes. Fill with ginger ale and stir.

NEW ORLEANS GIN FIZZ

Juice of ½ Lemon
Juice of ½ Lime
(optional)
1 tsp. Powdered
Sugar
1 Egg White
2 oz. Gin
1 tbsp. Light Cream
½ tsp. Triple Sec
Shake with ice and strain into highball glass with two ice cubes. Fill with carbonated water and stir.

NEW YORK COCKTAIL

Juice of 1 Lime or ½
Lemon
1 tsp. Powdered
Sugar
1½ oz. Blended
Whiskey
½ tsp. Grenadine
Shake with ice and strain into cocktail glass. Add a twist of lemon peel.

NEW YORK SOUR

Juice of ½ Lemon
1 tsp. Powdered Sugar
2 oz. Blended Whiskey
Claret
Shake first three ingredients with ice and strain into sour glass, leaving about half-inch on which to float claret. Decorate with a half-slice of lemon and a cherry.

NIGHT CAP

2 oz. Light Rum
1 tsp. Powdered Sugar
Add enough warm milk to fill a mug and stir. Sprinkle a little nutmeg on top.

NIGHTMARE

1½ oz. Gin
½ oz. Madeira
½ oz. Cherry-Flavored
Brandy
1 tsp. Orange Juice
Shake with ice and strain into cocktail glass.

NINOTCHKA COCKTAIL

1 1/2 oz. Vodka
1/2 oz. Crème de
Cacao (White)
1 tbsp. Lemon Juice

Shake with ice and strain
into cocktail glass.

NORTH POLE COCKTAIL

1 Egg White
1/2 oz. Lemon Juice
1/2 oz. Maraschino
1 oz. Gin

Shake with ice and strain
into cocktail glass. Top with
whipped cream.

NUTTY COLADA

3 oz. Amaretto
3 tbsp. Coconut Milk
3 tbsp. Crushed
Pineapple

Put in electric blender with
2 cups of crushed ice and
blend at high speed for a
short time. Pour into a
collins glass and serve with
a straw.

O

OLD-FASHIONED
Into an old-fashioned glass, put a small cube of sugar, a dash of bitters, a teaspoon of water, and muddle well. Add **2 oz. Blended Whiskey**. Stir. Add a twist of lemon peel and ice cubes. Decorate with slices of orange, lemon, and a cherry. Serve with a swizzle stick.

OLD PAL COCKTAIL
$^1/_2$ oz.   Grenadine
$^1/_2$ oz.   Sweet Vermouth
$1^1/_4$ oz. Blended Whiskey
Stir with ice and strain into cocktail glass.

OLYMPIC COCKTAIL
$^3/_4$ oz.   Orange Juice
$^3/_4$ oz.   Triple Sec
$^3/_4$ oz.   Brandy
Shake with ice and strain into cocktail glass.

OPAL COCKTAIL
1 oz.   Gin
$^1/_2$ oz.   Triple Sec
1 tbsp.   Orange Juice
$^1/_4$ tbsp. Powdered Sugar
Shake with ice and strain into cocktail glass.

OPENING COCKTAIL
$^1/_2$ oz.   Grenadine
$^1/_2$ oz.   Sweet Vermouth
$1^1/_2$ oz. Blended Whiskey
Stir with ice and strain into cocktail glass.

OPERA COCKTAIL
1 tbsp.   Maraschino
$^1/_2$ oz.   Dubonnet®
$1^1/_2$ oz. Gin
Stir with ice and strain into cocktail glass.

ORANGE BLOSSOM
1 oz.   Gin
1 oz.   Orange Juice
$^1/_4$ tsp. Powdered Sugar
Shake with ice and strain into cocktail glass.

ORANGE BUCK
1½ oz. Gin
1 oz. Orange Juice
1 tbsp. Lime Juice
Shake with ice and strain into highball glass over ice cubes. Fill with ginger ale and stir.

ORANGE OASIS
1½ oz. Gin
½ oz. Cherry-Flavored Brandy
4 oz. Orange Juice
Shake with ice and strain into highball glass over ice cubes. Fill with ginger ale and stir.

ORIENTAL COCKTAIL
1 oz. Blended Whiskey
½ oz. Sweet Vermouth
½ oz. Triple Sec
Juice of ½ Lime
Shake with ice and strain into cocktail glass.

OUTRIGGER
1 oz. Peach-Flavored Brandy
1 oz. Lime Vodka
1 oz. Pineapple Juice
Shake with ice and strain into old-fashioned glass over ice cubes.

P

PADDY COCKTAIL
1½ oz. Irish Whiskey
1½ oz. Sweet
Vermouth
1 dash Bitters
Stir with ice and strain into cocktail glass.

PAISLEY MARTINI
2 oz. Gin
½ oz. Dry Vermouth
1 tsp. Scotch
Stir in old-fashioned glass over ice cubes. Add a twist of lemon peel.

PALL MALL
1½ oz. Gin
½ oz. Sweet
Vermouth
½ oz. Dry Vermouth
½ oz. Crème de
Menthe (White)
Stir in old-fashioned glass over ice cubes.

PALM BEACH COCKTAIL
1½ oz. Gin
1½ tsp. Sweet
Vermouth
1½ tsp. Grapefruit Juice
Shake with ice and strain into cocktail glass.

PALMER COCKTAIL
2 oz. Blended
Whiskey
1 dash Bitters
½ tsp. Lemon Juice
Stir with ice and strain in cocktail glass.

PALMETTO COCKTAIL
1½ oz. Light Rum
1½ oz. Dry Vermouth
2 dashes Bitters
Stir with ice and strain into cocktail glass.

PANAMA COCKTAIL
1 oz. Crème de Cacao
(White)
1 oz. Light Cream
1 oz. Brandy
Shake with ice and strain into cocktail glass.

PAPAYA SLING
1½ oz. Gin
1 dash Bitters
Juice of 1 Lime
1 tbsp. Papaya Syrup
Shake with ice and strain into collins glass over ice cubes. Fill with carbonated water and stir. Add a pineapple stick.

Pousse Café

PARADISE COCKTAIL

1 oz.   Apricot-Flavored
    Brandy
³/₄ oz. Gin
Juice of ¹/₄ Orange
Shake with ice and strain
into cocktail glass.

PARISIAN

1 oz.   Gin
1 oz.   Dry Vermouth
¹/₄ oz. Crème de Cassis
Shake with ice and strain
into cocktail glass.

PARISIAN BLONDE

³/₄ oz. Light Cream
³/₄ oz. Triple Sec
³/₄ oz. Jamaica Rum
Shake with ice and strain
into cocktail glass.

PARK AVENUE

1¹/₂ oz. Gin
³/₄ oz. Sweet
    Vermouth
1 tbsp. Pineapple Juice
Stir with ice and strain into
cocktail glass.

PASSION DAIQUIRI

1¹/₂ oz. Light Rum
Juice of 1 Lime
1 tsp.   Powdered
    Sugar
1 tbsp. Passion Fruit
    Juice
Shake with ice and strain
into cocktail glass.

PASSION MIMOSA🅛

2 oz.   Chilled Passion
    Fruit Juice
Chilled Champagne
Pour chilled juice into
champagne flute, fill with
chilled champagne. Garnish
with strawberry.

PEACH BLOSSOM

1 tsp.   Lemon Juice
¹/₂ tsp. Powdered
    Sugar
2 oz.   Gin
¹/₂ Peach
Shake with ice and strain
into highball glass over ice
cubes. Fill with carbonated
water and stir.

PEACH BLOW FIZZ

Juice of ¹/₂ Lemon
¹/₂ tsp. Powdered
    Sugar
1 oz.   Light Cream
2 oz.   Gin
¹/₄ Peach
Shake with ice and strain
into highball glass over ice
cubes. Fill with carbonated
water and stir.

PEACH BUNNY

³/₄ oz. Peach-Flavored
    Brandy
³/₄ oz. Crème de Cacao
    (White)
³/₄ oz. Light Cream
Shake well with ice and
strain into cocktail glass.

🅛 indicates lower alcohol content

PEACH SANGAREE

2 oz.   Peach-Flavored
    Brandy
Carbonated Water
1 tsp.   Port

Put brandy into highball glass with ice cubes. Fill glass with carbonated water. Stir and float port on top. Sprinkle lightly with nutmeg.

PEGGY COCKTAIL

$^3/_4$ oz.   Dry Vermouth
$1^1/_2$ oz.   Gin
$^1/_4$ tsp.   Anis
$^1/_4$ tsp.   Dubonnet®

Stir with ice and strain into cocktail glass.

PENDENNIS TODDY

Muddle a lump of sugar with one teaspoon of water, in sour glass. Fill with ice, add **2 oz. Bourbon**, and stir. Decorate with two slices of lemon.

PEPPERMINT ICEBERG

Pour **2 oz. Peppermint Schnapps** into old-fashioned glass over ice cubes. Stir and serve with a peppermint-candy swizzle stick.

PEPPERMINT PATTIE

1 oz.   Crème de Cacao
    (White)
1 oz.   Crème de Menthe
    (White)

Shake with ice and strain into old-fashioned glass over ice cubes.

L indicates lower alcohol content

PEPPERMINT STICK

1 oz.   Peppermint
    Schnapps
$1^1/_2$ oz.   Crème de
    Cacao (White)
1 oz.   Light Cream

Shake with ice and strain into champagne flute.

PERFECT COCKTAIL

$1^1/_2$ tsp.   Dry Vermouth
$1^1/_2$ tsp.   Sweet
    Vermouth
$1^1/_2$ oz.   Gin
1 dash   Bitters

Stir with ice and strain into cocktail glass.

PETER PAN COCKTAIL

2 dashes Bitters
$^3/_4$ oz. Orange Juice
$^3/_4$ oz. Dry Vermouth
$^3/_4$ oz. Gin

Shake with ice and strain into cocktail glass.

PHOEBE SNOW

$1^1/_2$ oz.   Dubonnet®
$1^1/_2$ oz.   Brandy
$^1/_2$ tsp.   Anis

Stir with ice and strain into cocktail glass.

PICCADILLY COCKTAIL

$^3/_4$ oz.   Dry Vermouth
$1^1/_2$ oz.   Gin
$^1/_4$ tsp.   Anis
$^1/_4$ tsp.   Grenadine

Stir with ice and strain into cocktail glass.

PICON COCKTAIL

See Amer Picon Cocktail on **page 41**.

PIÑA COLADA

3 oz. Light Rum
3 tbsp. Coconut Milk
3 tbsp. Crushed
Pineapple

Place in an electric blender
with two cups of crushed
ice and blend at high speed
for a short time. Strain into
collins glass and serve with
straw.

PINEAPPLE COCKTAIL

³/₄ oz. Pineapple Juice
1¹/₂ oz. Light Rum
¹/₂ tsp. Lemon Juice

Shake with ice and strain
into cocktail glass.

PINEAPPLE COOLER 🄻

Into collins glass, put:
2 oz. Pineapple Juice
¹/₂ tsp. Powdered
Sugar
2 oz. Carbonated
Water
2 oz. White Wine

Stir. Add ice cubes. Fill
with carbonated water and
stir again. Insert a spiral of
orange or lemon peel (or
both) and dangle end over
rim of glass.

PINEAPPLE FIZZ

1 oz. Pineapple Juice
¹/₂ tsp. Powdered
Sugar
2 oz. Light Rum

Shake with ice and strain
into highball glass over two
ice cubes. Fill with
carbonated water and stir.

PING-PONG COCKTAIL

Juice of ¹/₄ Lemon
1 Egg White
2 oz. Sloe Gin

Shake with ice and strain
into cocktail glass.

PINK CREOLE

1¹/₂ oz. Light Rum
1 tbsp. Lime Juice
1 tsp. Grenadine
1 tsp. Light Cream

Shake with ice and strain
into cocktail glass. Add a
black cherry soaked in
rum.

PINK GIN

See Gin and Bitters recipe
on page 97.

PINK LADY

1 Egg White
1 tsp. Grenadine
1 tsp. Light Cream
1¹/₂ oz. Gin

Shake with ice and strain
into cocktail glass.

PINK PUSSY CAT

Into a highball glass almost
filled with ice, put 1¹/₂ oz.
Vodka or **Gin**. Fill balance
of glass with pineapple or
grapefruit juice. Add a dash
of grenadine for color and
stir.

🄻 indicates lower alcohol content

PINK ROSE FIZZ
Juice of $1/2$ Lemon
1 tsp. Powdered Sugar
1 Egg White
2 tsp. Light Cream
2 oz. Gin

Shake with ice and strain into highball glass over two ice cubes. Fill with carbonated water and stir.

PINK SQUIRREL
1 oz. Crème de Noyaux
1 tbsp. Crème de Cacao (White)
1 tbsp. Light Cream

Shake with ice and strain into cocktail glass.

PLAIN VERMOUTH COCKTAIL
See Vermouth Cocktail on page 189.

PLANTER'S COCKTAIL
Juice of $1/4$ Lemon
$1/2$ tsp. Powdered Sugar
$1^1/2$ oz. Jamaica Rum

Shake with ice and strain into cocktail glass.

PLANTER'S PUNCH NO. 1
Juice of 2 Limes
2 tsp. Powdered Sugar
2 oz. Carbonated Water

Mix in a collins glass, add ice cubes and stir until glass is frosted. Add two dashes bitters and $2^1/2$ oz. **Light Rum**. Stir and top with a **dash of grenadine**. Decorate with slices of lemon, orange, pineapple, and a cherry. Serve with a straw.

PLANTER'S PUNCH NO. 2
Juice of 1 Lime
Juice of $1/2$ Lemon
Juice of $1/2$ Orange
1 tsp. Pineapple Juice
2 oz. Light Rum

Pour into collins glass, filled well with ice. Stir until glass is frosted. Then add 1 oz. **Jamaica Rum**, stir, and top with **2 dashes Triple Sec and a dash of grenadine**. Decorate with slices of orange, lemon, pineapple, a cherry, and a sprig of mint dipped in powdered sugar. Serve with a straw.

PLAZA COCKTAIL
$3/4$ oz. Sweet Vermouth
$3/4$ oz. Dry Vermouth
$3/4$ oz. Gin

Shake with ice and strain into cocktail glass. Add a strip of pineapple.

POKER COCKTAIL

1½ oz. Sweet Vermouth
1½ oz. Light Rum

Stir with ice and strain into cocktail glass.

POLLYANNA

Muddle 3 slices of orange and 3 slices of pineapple with:

2 oz. Gin
½ oz. Sweet Vermouth
½ tsp. Grenadine

Shake with ice and strain into cocktail glass.

POLO COCKTAIL

1 tbsp. Lemon Juice
1 tbsp. Orange Juice
1 oz. Gin

Shake with ice and strain into cocktail glass.

POLONAISE

1½ oz. Brandy
1 tbsp. Blackberry-Flavored Brandy
½ oz. Dry Sherry
1 dash Lemon Juice

Shake with ice and strain into old-fashioned glass over ice cubes.

POLYNESIAN COCKTAIL

1½ oz. Vodka
¾ oz. Cherry-Flavored Brandy
Juice of 1 Lime

Rub rim of cocktail glass with lime and dip into powdered sugar. Shake above ingredients with ice and strain into prepared glass.

POMPANO

1 oz. Gin
½ oz. Dry Vermouth
1 oz. Grapefruit Juice

Shake with ice and strain into cocktail glass.

POOP DECK COCKTAIL

1 oz. Brandy
1 oz. Port
1 tbsp. Blackberry-Flavored Brandy

Shake with ice and strain into cocktail glass.

POPPY COCKTAIL

¾ oz. Crème de Cacao (White)
1½ oz. Gin

Shake with ice and strain into cocktail glass.

PORT AND STARBOARD
- 1 tbsp. Grenadine
- 1/2 oz. Crème de Menthe (Green)

Pour carefully into pousse-café glass, so that crème de menthe floats on grenadine.

PORT MILK PUNCH ●
- 1 tsp. Powdered Sugar
- 2 oz. Port
- 1 cup Milk

Shake with ice and strain into collins glass. Sprinkle nutmeg on top.

PORT WINE COBBLER
Dissolve 1 teaspoon powdered sugar in 2 oz. carbonated water; then fill goblet with shaved ice and add 3 oz. port. Stir and decorate with fruits in season. Serve with straws.

PORT WINE COCKTAIL
- 2 1/2 oz. Port
- 1/2 tsp. Brandy

Stir with ice and strain into cocktail glass.

PORT WINE EGGNOG
- 1 Whole Egg
- 1 tsp. Powdered Sugar
- 3 oz. Port
- 6 oz. Milk

Shake well with ice and strain into collins glass. Sprinkle nutmeg on top.

PORT WINE FLIP ●
- 1 Whole Egg
- 1 tsp. Powdered Sugar
- 1 1/2 oz. Port
- 2 tsp. Light Cream (if desired)

Shake with ice and strain into sour glass. Sprinkle a little nutmeg on top.

PORT WINE NEGUS ●
- 1/2 lump Sugar
- 2 oz. Port

Pour into punch cup, fill with hot water, and stir. Sprinkle nutmeg on top.

PORT WINE SANGAREE
Dissolve 1/2 teaspoon powdered sugar in 1 teaspoon water in highball glass. Add 2 oz. port and ice cubes. Fill with carbonated water, leaving enough room on which to float a tablespoon of **Brandy**. Stir. Float brandy on top. Sprinkle with nutmeg.

● indicates lower alcohol content

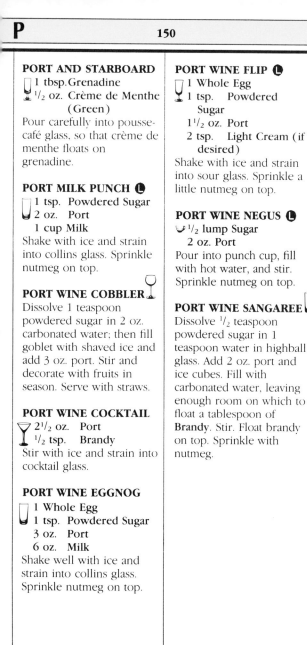

POUSSE CAFÉ
Equal parts:
Grenadine
Chartreuse (Yellow)
Crème de Cassis
Crème de Menthe
    (White)
Chartreuse (Green)
Brandy

Pour carefully, in order given, into pousse café glass so that each ingredient floats on preceding one. (For other Pousse Café recipes, see Index on page 264.)

POUSSE L'AMOUR
1 tbsp. Maraschino
1 Egg Yolk
$^1/_2$ oz. Benedictine
$^1/_2$ oz. Brandy

Pour carefully, in order given, into 2-oz. sherry glass, so that each ingredient floats on preceding one.

PRADO
$1^1/_2$ oz. Tequila
$^3/_4$ oz. Lemon Juice
1 tbsp. Maraschino
$^1/_2$ Egg White
1 tsp. Grenadine

Shake with ice and strain into sour glass. Add a slice of lime and a cherry.

PRAIRIE CHICKEN
1 oz. Gin
1 Whole Egg
Pepper and Salt

Open egg without breaking the yolk and put in wine glass. Pour gin on top. Add pepper and salt.

PRAIRIE OYSTER
1 oz. Brandy
1 tbsp. Worcestershire
    Sauce
1 tsp. Catsup
1 tbsp. Vinegar
1 pinch Pepper

Shake with ice and strain into old-fashioned glass over two ice cubes. Place an egg yolk on top without breaking it. Add a dash of cayenne pepper.

PREAKNESS COCKTAIL
$^3/_4$ oz. Sweet
    Vermouth
$1^1/_2$ oz. Blended
    Whiskey
1 dash Bitters
$^1/_2$ tsp. Benedictine

Stir with ice and strain into cocktail glass. Add a twist of lemon peel.

PRESTO COCKTAIL
1 tbsp. Orange Juice
½ oz. Sweet Vermouth
1½ oz. Brandy
¼ tsp. Anis

Shake with ice and strain into cocktail glass.

PRINCE'S SMILE
½ oz. Apricot-Flavored Brandy
½ oz. Apple Brandy
1 oz. Gin
¼ tsp. Lemon Juice

Shake with ice and strain into cocktail glass.

PRINCESS POUSSE CAFÉ
¾ oz. Apricot-Flavored Brandy
1½ tsp. Light Cream

Pour cream carefully on top of brandy, so that it does not mix. Use pousse-café glass.

PRINCETON COCKTAIL
1 oz. Gin
1 oz. Dry Vermouth
Juice of ½ Lime

Stir with ice and strain into cocktail glass.

PUERTO APPLE
1½ oz. Applejack
¾ oz. Light Rum
1 tbsp. Lime Juice
1 oz. Orgeat Syrup

Shake with ice and strain into old-fashioned glass over ice cubes. Decorate with a slice of lime.

PUNCHES
See Index on page 264 for complete list of Punch recipes.

PURPLE MASK
1 oz. Vodka
1 oz. Grape Juice
½ oz. Crème de Cacao (White)

Shake with ice and strain into cocktail glass.

PURPLE PASSION
1½ oz. Vodka
3 oz. Grapefruit Juice
3 oz. Grape Juice

Chill, stir, add sugar to taste, and serve in a collins glass.

Q

QUAKER'S COCKTAIL
3/4 oz. Light Rum
3/4 oz. Brandy
Juice of 1/4 Lemon
2 tsp. Raspberry Syrup
Shake with ice and strain into cocktail glass.

QUARTER DECK COCKTAIL
1/3 oz. Cream Sherry
1 1/2 oz. Light Rum
Juice of 1/2 Lime
Stir with ice and strain into cocktail glass.

QUEBEC
1 1/2 oz. Canadian Whisky
1/2 oz. Dry Vermouth
1 1/2 tsp. Amer Picon
1 1/2 tsp. Maraschino
Shake with ice and strain into cocktail glass rimmed with sugar.

QUEEN BEE
1 1/2 oz. Lime Vodka
1 oz. Coffee-Flavored Brandy
1/2 oz. Cream Sherry
Shake with ice and strain into cocktail glass.

QUEEN CHARLOTTE **L**
2 oz. Claret or Red Wine
1 oz. Grenadine
Lemon Soda
Pour into collins glass over ice cubes. Stir.

QUEEN ELIZABETH
1 1/2 oz. Gin
1/2 oz. Dry Vermouth
1 1/2 tsp. Benedictine
Stir with ice and strain into cocktail glass.

L indicates lower alcohol content

a) Rum Fix b) Planter's Punch
c) Rum Daisy

R

RACQUET CLUB COCKTAIL

$1^1/_2$ oz.   Gin
$^3/_4$ oz.   Dry Vermouth
1 dash   Orange Bitters

Stir with ice and strain into cocktail glass.

RAMOS FIZZ

Juice of $^1/_2$ Lemon
1 Egg White
1 tsp.   Powdered Sugar
2 oz.   Gin
1 tbsp.   Light Cream
$^1/_2$ tsp.   Triple Sec

Shake with ice and strain into highball glass over two ice cubes. Fill with carbonated water and stir.

RATTLESNAKE COCKTAIL

$1^1/_2$ oz.   Blended Whiskey
1 Egg White
1 tsp.   Lemon Juice
$^1/_2$ tsp.   Powdered Sugar
$^1/_4$ tsp.   Anis

Shake with ice and strain into cocktail glass.

REBEL CHARGE

1 oz.   Bourbon
$^1/_2$ oz.   Triple Sec
1 tbsp.   Orange Juice
1 tbsp.   Lemon Juice
$^1/_2$ Egg White

Shake with ice and strain into old-fashioned glass over ice cubes. Add orange slice.

RED APPLE

1 oz.   100-Proof Vodka
1 oz.   Apple Juice
1 tbsp.   Lemon Juice
1 tsp.   Grenadine

Shake with ice and strain into cocktail glass.

RED CLOUD

$1^1/_2$ oz.   Gin
$^1/_2$ oz.   Apricot-Flavored Brandy
1 tbsp.   Lemon Juice
1 tsp.   Grenadine

Shake with ice and strain into cocktail glass.

RED RAIDER

1 oz. Bourbon
$^1/_2$ oz. Triple Sec
1 oz. Lemon Juice
1 dash Grenadine

Shake with ice and strain into cocktail glass.

RED SWIZZLE

Make the same as Gin Swizzle (see page 99) and add one tablespoon of grenadine. If desired, rum, brandy, or whiskey may be substituted for the gin.

REFORM COCKTAIL ⓛ

$^3/_4$ oz. Dry Vermouth
$1^1/_2$ oz. Dry Sherry
1 dash Orange Bitters

Stir with ice and strain into cocktail glass. Serve with a cherry.

REMSEN COOLER

$^1/_2$ tsp. Powdered Sugar
Carbonated Water
2 oz. Gin

Into collins glass, put powdered sugar and 2 oz. carbonated water. Stir. Add ice cubes and gin. Fill with carbonated water or ginger ale and stir again. Insert a spiral of orange or lemon peel (or both) and dangle end over rim of glass.

RENAISSANCE COCKTAIL

$1^1/_2$ oz. Gin
$^1/_2$ oz. Dry Sherry
1 tbsp. Light Cream

Shake with ice and strain into cocktail glass. Sprinkle with nutmeg.

RESOLUTE COCKTAIL

Juice of $^1/_4$ Lemon
$^1/_2$ oz. Apricot-Flavored Brandy
1 oz. Gin

Shake with ice and strain into cocktail glass.

RHINE WINE CUP

4 tsp. Powdered Sugar
6 oz. Carbonated Water
1 oz. Triple Sec
2 oz. Brandy
16 oz. White Wine

Mix ingredients and pour into large glass pitcher over cubes of ice. Stir and decorate with fruits in season. Insert rind of cucumber on each side of pitcher. Top with mint sprigs. Serve in red-wine glasses.

RICKEYS

See Index on page 265 for complete list of Rickey recipes.

a) Royal Purple Punch b) Brandy Punch c) Banana Punch

RITZ FIZZ

Chilled Champagne
1 dash lemon juice
1 dash Blue Curacao
1 dash Amaretto

Fill champagne flute with Chilled Champagne. Add remaining ingredients and stir. Garnish with a lemon twist.

ROAD RUNNER

1 oz. Vodka
$^1/_2$ oz. Amaretto
$^1/_2$ oz. Coconut Cream

Mix in blender with $^1/_2$ scoop of crushed ice for 15 seconds. Rim edge of a chilled champagne flute with a slice of orange. Dip rim in a sugar and nutmeg mixture. Pour cocktail into the prepared glass. Top with a dash of nutmeg.

ROBERT E. LEE COOLER

Into collins glass, put:

Juice of $^1/_2$ Lime
$^1/_2$ tsp. Powdered Sugar
2 oz. Carbonated Water

Stir. Add ice cubes and:

$^1/_4$ tsp. Anis
2 oz. Gin

Fill with ginger ale and stir again. Add a spiral of orange or lemon peel (or both) and dangle end over rim of glass.

ROBIN'S NEST

1 oz. Vodka
1 oz. Cranberry Juice
$^1/_2$ oz. Crème de Cacao (White)

Shake with ice and strain into cocktail glass.

ROB ROY

$^3/_4$ oz. Sweet Vermouth
$1^1/_2$ oz. Scotch

Stir with ice and strain into cocktail glass.

ROBSON COCKTAIL

2 tsp. Lemon Juice
1 tbsp. Orange Juice
$1^1/_2$ tsp. Grenadine
1 oz. Jamaica Rum

Shake with ice and strain into cocktail glass.

ROCK & RYE COCKTAIL

1 oz. Rock & Rye
1 oz. White Port
$1^1/_2$ tsp. Dry Vermouth

Stir with ice and strain into cocktail glass.

ROCK & RYE COOLER

1 oz. Rock & Rye
$1^1/_2$ oz. Vodka
1 tbsp. Lime Juice
Bitter Lemon Soda

Shake with ice and strain into collins glass over ice.

ROCOCO

1 oz. Cherry Vodka
1 oz. Orange Juice
$^1/_2$ oz. Triple Sec

Shake with ice and strain into cocktail glass.

ROLLS-ROYCE

Y ½ oz. Dry Vermouth
½ oz. Sweet
Vermouth
1½ oz. Gin
¼ tsp. Benedictine
Stir with ice and strain into
cocktail glass.

RORY O'MORE

Y ¾ oz. Sweet
Vermouth
1½ oz. Irish Whiskey
1 dash Orange Bitters
Stir with ice and strain into
cocktail glass.

ROSE COCKTAIL
(ENGLISH)

Y ½ oz. Apricot-
Flavored Brandy
½ oz. Dry Vermouth
1 oz. Gin
½ tsp. Lemon Juice
1 tsp. Grenadine
Moisten rim of cocktail
glass with lemon juice and
dip into powdered sugar.
Shake ingredients above
with ice and strain into
prepared glass.

ROSE COCKTAIL
(FRENCH)

Y ½ oz. Cherry-Flavored
Brandy
½ oz. Dry Vermouth
1½ oz. Gin
Stir with ice and strain into
cocktail glass.

ROSELYN COCKTAIL

Y ¾ oz. Dry Vermouth
1½ oz. Gin
½ tsp. Grenadine
Stir with ice and strain into
cocktail glass. Add a twist of
lemon peel.

ROSITA

1 oz. Tequila
½ oz. Dry Vermouth
½ oz. Sweet Vermouth
1 oz. Campari
Stir in old-fashioned glass
with cracked ice. Add a
twist of lemon peel and
serve with short straws.

ROYAL CLOVER CLUB
COCKTAIL

Juice of 1 Lime
1 tbsp. Grenadine
1 Egg Yolk
1½ oz. Gin
Shake with ice and strain
into sour glass.

ROYAL COCKTAIL

1 Whole Egg
Juice of ½ Lemon
½ tsp. Powdered
Sugar
1½ oz. Gin
Shake with ice and strain
into sour glass.

ROYAL GIN FIZZ

Juice of ½ Lemon
1 tsp. Powdered Sugar
2 oz. Gin
1 Whole Egg
Shake with ice and strain
into highball glass with two
ice cubes. Fill with
carbonated water and stir.

ROYAL PURPLE PUNCH ⌣ ❶

Pour two bottles (750-ml size) claret or red wine and two large bottles ginger ale over ice cubes in punch bowl. Stir well. Float thin slices of lemon studded with cloves on top. Serve in punch glasses.

ROYAL SMILE COCKTAIL

Juice of ¹/₄ Lemon
1 tsp. Grenadine
¹/₂ oz. Gin
1 oz. Apple Brandy

Stir with ice and strain into cocktail glass.

RUBY FIZZ

Juice of ¹/₂ Lemon
1 tsp. Powdered Sugar
1 Egg White
1 tsp. Grenadine
2 oz. Sloe Gin

Shake with ice and strain into highball glass over two ice cubes. Fill with carbonated water and stir.

RUM COBBLER

In a goblet, dissolve 1 teaspoon powdered sugar in 2 oz. carbonated water. Fill goblet with shaved ice, and add 2 oz. Light Rum. Stir and decorate with fruits in season. Serve with a straw.

RUM COLA

See Cuba Libre recipe on **page 79**.

RUM COLLINS

Juice of 1 Lime
1 tsp. Powdered Sugar
2 oz. Light Rum

Shake with ice and strain into collins glass. Add several ice cubes, fill with carbonated water, and stir. Decorate with a slice of lemon and a cherry. Serve with a straw.

RUM COOLER

In collins glass, dissolve ¹/₂ teaspoon powdered sugar in 2 oz. carbonated water. Stir. Fill glass with ice and add 2 oz. Light Rum. Fill with carbonated water or ginger ale and stir again. Insert a spiral of orange or lemon peel (or both) and dangle end over rim of glass.

RUM DAISY

Juice of ¹/₂ Lemon
¹/₂ tsp. Powdered Sugar
1 tsp. Grenadine
2 oz. Light Rum

Shake with ice and strain into stein or metal cup. Add one ice cube and decorate with fruit.

RUM DUBONNET®

1¹/₂ oz. Light Rum
1¹/₂ tsp. Dubonnet®
1 tsp. Lemon Juice

Shake with ice and strain into cocktail glass.

❶ indicates lower alcohol content

RUM EGGNOG
1 Whole Egg
1 tsp. Powdered Sugar
2 oz. Light or Dark Rum
6 oz. Milk

Shake with ice and strain into collins glass. Sprinkle nutmeg on top.

RUM FIX
Juice of $1/2$ Lemon or 1 Lime
1 tsp. Powdered Sugar
1 tsp. Water

Stir together in a highball glass and fill glass with ice. Add $2^1/2$ oz. **Light Rum**. Stir and add slice of lemon. Serve with a straw.

RUM HIGHBALL
Pour 2 oz. **Light or Dark Rum** in highball glass over ice cubes and fill with ginger ale or carbonated water. Add a twist of lemon peel, if desired, and stir.

RUM OLD FASHIONED
$1/2$ tsp. Powdered Sugar
1 dash Bitters
1 tsp. Water
$1^1/2$ oz. Light Rum
1 tsp. 151-Proof Light Rum

Stir sugar, bitters, and water in old-fashioned glass. When sugar is dissolved, add ice cubes and light rum. Add a twist of lime peel and float the 151-proof rum on top.

RUM MARTINI
4 to 5 parts Light Rum
Dash Dry Vermouth

Serve on the rocks in a cocktail glass with a twist of lemon.

RUM MILK PUNCH
1 tsp. Powdered Sugar
2 oz. Light Rum
1 cup Milk

Shake with ice, strain into collins glass, and sprinkle nutmeg on top.

RUM RICKEY
Juice of $1/2$ Lime
$1^1/2$ oz. Light Rum

Pour into highball glass over ice cubes and fill with carbonated water and ice cubes. Stir. Add a wedge of lime.

RUM RUNNER
$1^1/2$ oz. Gin
Juice of 1 Lime
1 oz. Pineapple Juice
1 tsp. Sugar
1 dash Bitters

Shake with ice and strain over ice cubes in an old-fashioned glass rimmed with salt.

RUM SCREWDRIVER
$1^1/2$ oz. Light Rum
5 oz. Orange Juice

Combine ingredients in highball glass with ice cubes.

RUM SOUR

Juice of $^1/_2$ Lemon
$^1/_2$ tsp. Powdered
   Sugar
2 oz.   Light Rum

Shake with ice and strain
into sour glass. Decorate
with a half-slice of lemon
and a cherry.

RUM SWIZZLE

Made same as Gin Swizzle
(see page 99) substituting **2
oz. Light or Dark Rum** for
gin.

RUM TODDY

In old-fashioned glass,
dissolve $^1/_2$ teaspoon
powdered sugar in 2
teaspoons water. Stir and
add **2 oz. Light or Dark
Rum** and a cube of ice. Stir
again and add a twist of
lemon peel.

RUM TODDY (HOT)

Put lump of sugar into Irish
coffee cup and fill $^2/_3$ with
boiling water. Add **2 oz.
Light or Dark Rum**. Stir
and decorate with a slice of
lemon. Sprinkle nutmeg on
top.

RUSSIAN BEAR
COCKTAIL

1 oz.   Vodka
$^1/_2$ oz.   Crème de
   Cacao (White)
1 tbsp. Light Cream

Stir with ice and strain into
cocktail glass.

RUSSIAN COCKTAIL

$^3/_4$ oz. Crème de Cacao
   (White)
$^3/_4$ oz. Gin
$^3/_4$ oz. Vodka

Shake with ice and strain
into cocktail glass.

RUSTY NAIL

$^3/_4$ oz. Scotch
$^1/_4$ oz. Drambuie

Serve in old-fashioned glass
with ice cubes. Float
Drambuie on top.

RYE HIGHBALL

Put **2 oz. Rye Whiskey** in
highball glass over ice
cubes and fill with ginger
ale or carbonated water
and ice cubes. Add a twist
of lemon peel, if desired,
and stir.

RYE WHISKEY
COCKTAIL

1 dash Bitters
1 tsp. Powdered Sugar
2 oz.   Rye Whiskey

Shake with ice and strain
into cocktail glass. Serve
with a cherry.

S

ST. CHARLES PUNCH
1 oz. Brandy
½ oz. Triple Sec
3 oz. Port
Juice of 1 Lemon
1 tsp. Sugar

Shake all ingredients with ice except port. Strain into collins glass with ice. Top with port. Add a slice of lemon and a cherry.

ST. PATRICK'S DAY
¾ oz. Crème de Menthe (Green)
¾ oz. Chartreuse (Green)
¾ oz. Irish Whiskey
1 dash Bitters

Stir with ice and strain into cocktail glass.

SAKE MARTINI (SAKINI)
1 part Sake
3 parts Gin

Stir with ice, strain into 3- or 4-oz. cocktail glass and serve with an olive.

SALTY DOG
1½ oz. Gin
5 oz. Grapefruit Juice
¼ tsp. Salt

Pour into highball glass over ice cubes. Stir well. Vodka may be substituted for the gin.

SAND-MARTIN COCKTAIL
1 tsp. Chartreuse (Green)
1½ oz. Sweet Vermouth
1½ oz. Gin

Stir with ice and strain into cocktail glass.

SAN FRANCISCO COCKTAIL
¾ oz. Sloe Gin
¾ oz. Sweet Vermouth
¾ oz. Dry Vermouth
1 dash Bitters
1 dash Orange Bitters

Shake with ice and strain into cocktail glass. Serve with a cherry.

SANGAREES
See Index on page 266 for complete list of Sangaree recipes.

SANGRIA ●

- ¼ cup Sugar (or to taste)
- 1 cup Water
- 1 Thinly Sliced Orange
- 1 Thinly Sliced Lime
- 1 750-ml bottle Red or Rosé Wine
- 6 oz. Sparkling Water
- Other fruit as desired (i.e., bananas, strawberry)

Dissolve sugar in water in large pitcher. Add fruit and wine and 12 or more ice cubes. Stir until cold. Add sparkling water. Serve in red-wine glasses, putting some fruit in each glass.

SAN SEBASTIAN

- 1 oz. Gin
- 1½ tsp. Light Rum
- 1 tbsp. Grapefruit Juice
- 1½ tsp. Triple Sec
- 1 tbsp. Lemon Juice

Shake with ice and strain into cocktail glass.

SANTIAGO COCKTAIL

- ½ tsp. Powdered Sugar
- ¼ tsp. Grenadine
- Juice of 1 Lime
- 1½ oz. Light Rum

Shake with ice and strain into cocktail glass.

SANTINI'S POUSSE CAFÉ

- ½ oz. Brandy
- 1 tbsp. Maraschino
- ½ oz. Triple Sec
- ½ oz. Rum

Pour in order given into pousse-café glass.

SARATOGA COCKTAIL

- 2 oz. Brandy
- 2 dashes Bitters
- 1 tsp. Lemon Juice
- 1 tsp. Pineapple Juice
- ½ tsp. Maraschino

Shake with ice and strain into cocktail glass.

SAUCY SUE COCKTAIL

- ½ tsp. Apricot-Flavored Brandy
- ½ tsp. Pernod
- 2 oz. Apple Brandy

Stir with ice and strain into cocktail glass.

SAUTERNE CUP

- 4 tsp. Powdered Sugar
- 6 oz. Carbonated Water
- 1 tbsp. Triple Sec
- 1 tbsp. Curacao
- 2 oz. Brandy
- 16 oz. Sauterne

Put all ingredients in a large glass pitcher with ice. Stir and decorate with fruits in season and also rind of cucumber inserted on each side of pitcher. Top with a small bunch of mint sprigs. Serve in white-wine glass.

SAVANNAH

- Juice of ½ Orange
- 1 oz. Gin
- 1 dash Crème de Cacao (White)
- 1 Egg White

Shake with ice and strain into cocktail glass.

● indicates lower alcohol content

SAXON COCKTAIL
Juice of $1/2$ Lime
$1/2$ tsp. Grenadine
$1^3/4$ oz. Light Rum
Shake with ice and strain into cocktail glass. Serve with a twist of orange peel.

SCOOTER
1 oz.   Amaretto
1 oz.   Brandy
1 oz.   Light Cream
Combine in an electric blender or shake well with cracked ice. Strain into cocktail glass.

SCOTCH BIRD FLYER
$1^1/2$ oz. Scotch
1 Egg Yolk
$1/2$ oz. Triple Sec
$1/2$ tsp. Powdered Sugar
1 oz.   Light Cream
Shake with ice and strain into champagne flute.

SCOTCH BISHOP COCKTAIL
1 oz.   Scotch
1 tbsp. Orange Juice
$1/2$ oz. Dry Vermouth
$1/2$ tsp. Triple Sec
$1/4$ tsp. Powdered Sugar
Shake with ice and strain into cocktail glass. Add a twist of lemon peel.

SCOTCH COBBLER
2 oz.   Scotch
4 dashes Curaçao
4 dashes Brandy
Pour ingredients over ice in old fashioned glass. Garnish with slice of orange and mint sprig.

SCOTCH COOLER
2 oz.   Scotch
3 dashes Crème de Menthe (White)
Pour into highball glass over ice cubes. Fill with chilled carbonated water and stir.

SCOTCH HIGHBALL
Put 2 oz. Scotch in highball glass with ice cubes and fill with ginger ale or carbonated water. Add a twist of lemon peel, if desired, and stir.

SCOTCH HOLIDAY SOUR
$1^1/2$ oz. Scotch
1 oz.   Cherry-Flavored Brandy
$1/2$ oz. Sweet Vermouth
1 oz.   Lemon Juice
Shake with ice and strain into old-fashioned glass over ice cubes. Add a slice of lemon.

SCOTCH MILK PUNCH
2 oz.   Scotch
6 oz.   Milk
1 tsp. Powdered Sugar
Shake with ice and strain into collins glass. Sprinkle with nutmeg.

SCOTCH MIST
Pack old-fashioned glass with crushed ice. Pour in 2 oz. Scotch. Add a twist of lemon peel. Serve with short straw.

a) Scotch Mist b) Scotch Bishop

SCOTCH OLD-FASHIONED
Make same as Old-Fashioned (see page 141), but substitute Scotch.

SCOTCH RICKEY
Juice of ¹/₂ Lime
1¹/₂ oz.   Scotch
Pour into highball glass over ice and fill with carbonated water. Add a rind of lime. Stir.

SCOTCH SOUR
1¹/₂ oz.   Scotch
Juice of ¹/₂ Lime
¹/₂ tsp.   Powdered Sugar
Shake with ice and strain into sour glass. Decorate with a half-slice of lemon and a cherry.

SCOTCH STINGER
Make same as Stinger on page 175, but substitute Scotch for brandy.

SCREWDRIVER
1¹/₂ oz.   Vodka
5 oz.   Orange Juice
Pour into highball glass over ice cubes. Stir well.

SEABOARD
1 oz.   Blended Whiskey
1 oz.   Gin
1 tbsp.   Lemon Juice
1 tsp.   Powdered Sugar
Shake with ice and strain into old-fashioned glass over ice cubes. Decorate with mint leaves.

SEABREEZE
1¹/₂ oz. Vodka
4 oz.   Cranberry Juice
1 oz.   Grapefruit Juice
Pour into highball glass over ice cubes. Garnish with wedge of lime.

SENSATION COCKTAIL
Juice of ¹/₄ Lemon
1¹/₂ oz.   Gin
1 tsp.   Maraschino
Shake with ice and strain into cocktail glass. Add two sprigs of fresh mint.

SEPTEMBER MORN COCKTAIL
1 Egg White
1¹/₂ oz.   Light Rum
Juice of ¹/₂ Lime
1 tsp.   Grenadine
Shake with ice and strain into cocktail glass.

SEVENTH HEAVEN COCKTAIL
2 tsp.   Grapefruit Juice
1 tbsp.   Maraschino
1¹/₂ oz.   Gin
Shake with ice and strain into cocktail glass. Decorate with a sprig of fresh mint.

SEVILLA COCKTAIL
$^1/_2$ tsp. Powdered Sugar
1 Whole Egg
1 oz. Port
1 oz. Light Rum
Shake with ice and strain into sour glass.

SHADY GROVE
$1^1/_2$ oz. Gin
Juice of $^1/_2$ Lemon
1 tsp. Powdered Sugar
Shake with ice and strain into highball glass with ice cubes. Fill with ginger beer.

SHADY LADY
1 oz. Tequila
1 oz. Melon Liqueur
4 oz. grapefruit juice
Combine ingredients over ice in a highball glass. Garnish with a lime and a cherry.

SHALOM
$1^1/_2$ oz. 100-Proof Vodka
1 oz. Madeira
1 tbsp. Orange Juice
Shake with ice and strain into old-fashioned glass over ice cubes. Add an orange slice.

SHAMROCK
$1^1/_2$ oz. Irish Whiskey
$^1/_2$ oz. Dry Vermouth
1 tsp. Crème de Menthe (Green)
Stir with ice and strain into cocktail glass. Serve with an olive.

SHANDY GAFF ⓛ
5 oz. Beer
5 oz. Ginger Ale
Pour into collins glass and stir.

SHANGHAI COCKTAIL
Juice of $^1/_4$ Lemon
1 tsp. Anisette
1 oz. Jamaica Light Rum
$^1/_2$ tsp. Grenadine
Shake with ice and strain into cocktail glass.

SHAVETAIL
$1^1/_2$ oz. Peppermint Schnapps
1 oz. Pineapple Juice
1 oz. Light Cream
Shake with ice and strain into old-fashioned glass.

SHERRY-AND-EGG COCKTAIL ⓛ
Place an egg in a cocktail glass, being careful not to break the yolk. Add 2 oz. cream sherry.

SHERRY COBBLER ⓛ
1 tsp. Powdered Sugar
2 oz. Carbonated Water
2 oz. Sweet Sherry
In a red-wine glass, dissolve powdered sugar in carbonated water. Fill glass with ice and add sherry. Stir and decorate with fruits in season. Serve with straws.

ⓛ indicates lower alcohol content

SHERRY COCKTAIL ⓛ

2½ oz.   Cream Sherry
1 dash   Bitters

Stir with ice and strain into cocktail glass. Add a twist of orange peel.

SHERRY EGGNOG ⓛ

1 Whole Egg
1 tsp.   Powdered Sugar
2 oz.   Cream Sherry
  Milk

Shake above ingredients, except milk, with ice and strain into collins glass. Fill glass with milk and stir. Sprinkle nutmeg on top.

SHERRY FLIP ⓛ

1 Whole Egg
1 tsp.   Powdered Sugar
1½ oz.   Cream Sherry
2 tsp.   Light Cream (if desired)

Shake with ice and strain into sour glass. Sprinkle a little nutmeg on top.

SHERRY MILK PUNCH ⓛ

1 tsp.   Powdered Sugar
2 oz.   Cream Sherry
16 oz.   Milk

Shake with ice, strain into collins glass, and sprinkle nutmeg on top.

SHERRY SANGAREE

½ tsp.   Powdered Sugar
1 tsp.   Water
2 oz.   Cream Sherry
  Splash Carbonated Water
1 tbsp.   Port

In an old-fashioned glass, dissolve powdered sugar in water, add sherry, and stir. Add ice cubes and a splash of carbonated water, leaving enough room on which to float port. Add port. Sprinkle lightly with nutmeg.

SHERRY TWIST COCKTAIL

1 oz.   Cream Sherry
½ oz.   Brandy
½ oz.   Dry Vermouth
½ oz.   Triple Sec
½ tsp.   Lemon Juice

Shake with ice and strain into cocktail glass. Top with pinch of cinnamon and a twist of orange peel.

THE SHOOT

1 oz.   Scotch
1 oz.   Dry Sherry
1 tsp.   Orange Juice
1 tsp.   Lemon Juice
½ tsp.   Powdered Sugar

Shake with ice and strain into cocktail glass.

SHRINER COCKTAIL

1½ oz.   Brandy
1½ oz.   Sloe Gin
2 dashes Bitters
½ tsp.   Sugar Syrup

Stir with ice and strain into cocktail glass. Add a twist of lemon peel.

ⓛ indicates lower alcohol content

SIDECAR COCKTAIL
Juice of $^1/_4$ Lemon
$^1/_2$ oz. Triple Sec
1 oz. Brandy
Shake with ice and strain into cocktail glass.

SILK STOCKINGS
$1^1/_2$ oz. Tequila
1 oz. Creme de Cacao
$1^1/_2$ oz. cream
1 dash Grenadine
Shake ingredients with crushed ice. Strain into cocktail glass. Sprinkle cinnamon on top.

SILVER BULLET
1 oz. Gin
1 oz. Kümmel
1 tbsp. Lemon Juice
Shake with ice and strain into cocktail glass.

SILVER COCKTAIL
1 oz. Dry Vermouth
1 oz. Gin
2 dashes Orange Bitters
$^1/_4$ tsp. Sugar Syrup
$^1/_2$ tsp. Maraschino
Stir with ice and strain into cocktail glass. Add a twist of lemon peel.

SILVER FIZZ
Juice of $^1/_2$ Lemon
1 tsp. Powdered Sugar
2 oz. Gin
1 Egg White
Carbonated Water
Shake with ice and strain into highball glass over two ice cubes.

SILVER KING COCKTAIL
1 Egg White
Juice of $^1/_4$ Lemon
$1^1/_2$ oz. Gin
$^1/_2$ tsp. Powdered Sugar
2 dashes Orange Bitters
Shake with ice and strain into cocktail glass.

SILVER STALLION FIZZ
1 scoop Vanilla Ice Cream
2 oz. Gin
Carbonated Water
Shake gin and ice cream with ice and strain into highball glass. Fill with carbonated water and stir.

SILVER STREAK
$1^1/_2$ oz. Gin
1 oz. Kümmel
Shake with ice and strain into cocktail glass.

SINGAPORE SLING
Juice of $^1/_2$ Lemon
1 tsp. Powdered Sugar
2 oz. Gin
Carbonated Water
$^1/_2$ oz. Cherry-Flavored Brandy
Shake lemon, sugar, and gin with ice and strain into collins glass. Add ice cubes and fill with carbonated water. Float cherry-flavored brandy on top. Decorate with fruits in season and serve with straws.

SIR WALTER COCKTAIL
- ¾ oz. Rum
- ¾ oz. Brandy
- 1 tsp. Grenadine
- 1 tsp. Triple Sec
- 1 tsp. Lemon Juice

Shake with ice and strain into cocktail glass.

SLINGS
See Index on page 266 for complete list of Sling recipes.

SLOEBERRY COCKTAIL
- 1 dash Bitters
- 2 oz. Sloe Gin

Stir with ice and strain into cocktail glass.

SLOE DRIVER
- 1½ oz. Sloe Gin
- 5 oz. Orange Juice

Pour ingredients over ice in a highball glass and stir.

SLOE GIN COCKTAIL
- 2 oz. Sloe Gin
- 1 dash Orange Bitters
- ¼ tsp. Dry Vermouth

Stir with ice and strain into cocktail glass.

SLOE GIN COLLINS
- Juice of ½ Lemon
- 2 oz. Sloe Gin
  Carbonated Water

Shake lemon and sloe gin with ice and strain into collins glass. Add several ice cubes, fill with carbonated water, and stir. Decorate with slices of lemon, orange, and a cherry. Serve with straws.

SLOE GIN FIZZ
- Juice of ½ Lemon
- 1 tsp. Powdered Sugar
- 2 oz. Sloe Gin

Shake with ice and strain into highball glass with two ice cubes. Fill with carbonated water and stir. Decorate with a slice of lemon.

SLOE GIN FLIP
- 1 Whole Egg
- 1 tsp. Powdered Sugar
- 1 tbsp. Sloe Gin
- 2 tsp. Light Cream (if desired)

Shake with ice and strain into sour glass. Sprinkle a little nutmeg on top.

SLOE GIN RICKEY
- Juice of ½ Lime
- 2 oz. Sloe Gin
  Carbonated Water

Pour into highball glass over ice cubes. Stir. Drop a lime rind into glass.

SLOE TEQUILA

1 oz.   Tequila
$^1/_2$ oz.   Sloe Gin
1 tbsp.   Lime Juice

Combine ingredients with a half-cup of crushed ice in an electric blender. Blend at low speed and pour into old-fashioned glass. Add ice cubes and cucumber peel.

SLOE VERMOUTH

1 oz.   Sloe Gin
1 oz.   Dry Vermouth
1 tbsp.   Lemon Juice

Shake with ice and strain into cocktail glass.

SLOPPY JOE'S COCKTAIL NO. 1

Juice of 1 Lime
$^1/_4$ tsp.   Triple Sec
$^1/_4$ tsp.   Grenadine
$^3/_4$ oz.   Light Rum
$^3/_4$ oz.   Dry Vermouth

Shake with ice and strain into cocktail glass.

SLOPPY JOE'S COCKTAIL NO. 2

$^3/_4$ oz.   Pineapple Juice
$^3/_4$ oz.   Brandy
$^3/_4$ oz.   Port
$^1/_4$ tsp.   Triple Sec
$^1/_4$ tsp.   Grenadine

Shake with ice and strain into cocktail glass.

SMASHES

See Index on page 267 for complete list of Smash recipes.

SMILE COCKTAIL

1 oz.   Grenadine
1 oz.   Gin
$^1/_2$ tsp.   Lemon Juice

Shake with ice and strain into cocktail glass.

SMILER COCKTAIL

$^1/_2$ oz.   Sweet Vermouth
$^1/_2$ oz.   Dry Vermouth
1 oz.   Gin
1 dash   Bitters
$^1/_4$ tsp.   Orange Juice

Shake with ice and strain into cocktail glass.

SNOWBALL

$1^1/_2$ oz.   Gin
$^1/_2$ oz.   Anisette
1 tbsp.   Light Cream

Shake with ice and strain into cocktail glass.

SNYDER

$1^1/_2$ oz.   Gin
$^1/_2$ oz.   Dry Vermouth
$^1/_2$ oz.   Triple Sec

Shake with ice and strain into cocktail glass. Add a twist of lemon peel.

SOCIETY COCKTAIL

$1^1/_2$ oz.   Gin
$^3/_4$ oz.   Dry Vermouth
$^1/_4$ tsp.   Grenadine

Stir with ice and strain into cocktail glass.

SOMBRERO

$1^1/_2$ oz.   Coffee-Flavored Brandy
1 oz.   Light Cream

Pour brandy into old-fashioned glass over ice cubes. Float cream on top.

SOOTHER COCKTAIL
½ oz. Brandy
½ oz. Apple Brandy
½ oz. Triple Sec
Juice of ½ Lemon
1 tsp. Powdered Sugar
Shake with ice and strain into cocktail glass.

SOUL KISS COCKTAIL
1½ tsp. Orange Juice
1½ tsp. Dubonnet®
¾ oz. Dry Vermouth
¾ oz. Bourbon
Shake with ice and strain into cocktail glass.

SOURS
See Index on page 267 for complete list of Sour recipes.

SOUTH OF THE BORDER
1 oz. Tequila
¾ oz. Coffee-Flavored Brandy
Juice of ½ Lime
Shake with ice and strain into sour glass. Add a lime slice.

SOUTHERN BRIDE
1½ oz. Gin
1 oz. Grapefruit Juice
1 dash Maraschino
Shake with ice and strain into cocktail glass.

SOUTHERN GIN COCKTAIL
2 oz. Gin
2 dashes Orange Bitters
½ tsp. Triple Sec
Stir with ice and strain into cocktail glass. Add a twist of lemon peel.

SOUTH-SIDE COCKTAIL
Juice of ½ Lemon
1 tsp. Powdered Sugar
1½ oz. Gin
Shake with ice and strain into cocktail glass. Add two sprigs of fresh mint.

SOUTH-SIDE FIZZ
Juice of ½ Lemon
1 tsp. Powdered Sugar
2 oz. Gin
Shake with ice and strain into highball glass with ice cubes. Fill with carbonated water and stir. Add fresh mint leaves.

SOVIET
1½ oz. Vodka
½ oz. Amontillado Sherry
½ oz. Dry Vermouth
Shake with ice and strain into old-fashioned glass over ice cubes. Add a twist of lemon peel.

SPANISH COFFEE
1 oz. Spanish Brandy
Hot Coffee
Add coffee to brandy in a mug and top with whipped cream.

SPANISH TOWN COCKTAIL
2 oz.   Light Rum
1 tsp. Triple Sec
Stir with ice and strain into cocktail glass.

SPECIAL ROUGH COCKTAIL
1 1/2 oz.   Apple Brandy
1 1/2 oz.   Brandy
1/2 tsp.   Anis
Stir with ice and strain into cocktail glass.

SPENCER COCKTAIL
3/4 oz.   Apricot-
          Flavored Brandy
1 1/2 oz. Gin
1 dash   Bitters
1/4 tsp. Orange Juice
Shake with ice and strain into cocktail glass. Add a cherry and twist of orange peel.

SPHINX COCKTAIL
1 1/2 oz.   Gin
1 1/2 tsp. Sweet
            Vermouth
1 1/2 tsp. Dry Vermouth
Stir with ice and strain into cocktail glass. Serve with a slice of lemon.

SPRING FEELING COCKTAIL
1 tbsp. Lemon Juice
1/2 oz. Chartreuse
         (Green)
1 oz.   Gin
Shake with ice and strain into cocktail glass.

SPRITZER 🥛 Ⓛ
Pour 3 oz. chilled white wine into highball glass or wine glass with ice cubes. Fill balance with carbonated water and stir gently.

STANLEY COCKTAIL
Juice of 1/4 Lemon
1 tsp.   Grenadine
3/4 oz. Gin
1/4 oz. Light Rum
Shake with ice and strain into cocktail glass.

STAR COCKTAIL
1 oz.   Apple Brandy
1 oz.   Sweet Vermouth
1 dash Bitters
Stir with ice and strain into cocktail glass. Add a twist of lemon peel.

STAR DAISY 🍺
Juice of 1/2 Lemon
1/2 tsp.   Powdered
           Sugar
1 tsp.   Grenadine
1 oz.   Gin
1 oz.   Apple Brandy
Shake with ice and strain into stein or metal cup. Add an ice cube and decorate with fruit.

STARS AND STRIPES
1/3 Grenadine
1/3 Heavy Cream
1/3 Blue Curaçao
Pour carefully, in order given, into pousse-café glass, so that each ingredient floats on preceding one.

Ⓛ indicates lower alcohol content

STILETTO

Juice of $^1/_2$ Lemon
$1^1/_2$ tsp. Amaretto
$1^1/_2$ oz. Bourbon or
Blended Whiskey

Pour into an old-fashioned glass over ice cubes and stir.

STINGER

$^1/_2$ oz. Crème de Menthe (White)
$1^1/_2$ oz. Brandy

Shake with ice and strain into cocktail glass.

STIRRUP CUP

1 oz. Cherry-Flavored Brandy
1 oz. Brandy
Juice of $^1/_2$ Lemon
1 tsp. Sugar

Shake with ice and strain into old-fashioned glass over ice cubes.

STONE COCKTAIL

$^1/_2$ oz. Light Rum
$^1/_2$ oz. Sweet Vermouth
1 oz. Dry Sherry

Stir with ice and strain into cocktail glass.

STONE FENCE

2 dashes Bitters
2 oz. Scotch
Carbonated Water or Cider

Fill highball glass with ice cubes. Add scotch and bitters and fill with carbonated water or cider. Stir.

STRAIGHT LAW COCKTAIL

$^3/_4$ oz. Gin
$1^1/_2$ oz. Dry Sherry

Stir with ice and strain into cocktail glass.

STRAWBERRIES AND CREAM

1 oz. Strawberry Schnapps
$1^1/_2$ tbsp. Sugar
2 oz. Half-and-Half
2 Whole Strawberries

Place in an electric blender with 2 cups of crushed ice and blend at high speed. Add 2 whole strawberries and blend for 10 seconds. Pour in a parfait glass and serve with a straw. Garnish with a fresh strawberry.

STRAWBERRY DAIQUIRI

1 oz. Light Rum
$^1/_2$ oz. Strawberry Schnapps
1 oz. Lime Juice
1 tsp. Powdered Sugar
1 oz. Fresh or Frozen Strawberries

Shake with ice and strain into cocktail glass.

STRAWBERRY DAWN
1 oz.   Gin
1 oz.   Cream of
   Coconut
4 Fresh Strawberries or
   $^1/_3$ Cup Frozen
   Strawberries
Blend ingredients with one
cup ice in blender at high
speed. Pour in cocktail
glass. Garnish with a
strawberry slice and mint
spring.

STRAWBERRY FIELDS FOREVER
2 oz.   Strawberry
   Schnapps
$^1/_2$ oz. Brandy
Pour over ice in a highball
glass. Fill with carbonated
water. Garnish with a fresh
strawberry.

STRAWBERRY MARGARITA
1 oz.   Tequila
$^1/_2$ oz. Triple Sec
$^1/_2$ oz. Strawberry
   Schnapps
1 oz.   Lemon or Lime
   Juice
1 oz.   Fresh or Frozen
   Strawberries
If desired, rub rim of
cocktail glass with a rind of
lemon or lime, dip rim in
salt. Shake ingredients with
ice and strain into the glass.

STRAWBERRY SUNRISE
2 oz.   Strawberry
   Schnapps
$^1/_2$ oz. Grenadine
   Syrup
Pour over ice in a highball
glass. Fill with orange juice.
Garnish with a fresh
strawberry.

SUISSESSE COCKTAIL
2 oz.   Anisette
1 Egg White
Shake with ice and strain
into cocktail glass.

SUNBURN
2 oz.   Hot Shot Tropical
   Fruit Liqueur
2 oz.   Grapefruit Juice
Pour over ice in a highball
glass. Fill with club soda.
Add a dash of grenadine
for color.

SUNSHINE COCKTAIL
$^3/_4$ oz. Sweet
   Vermouth
$1^1/_2$ oz. Gin
1 dash   Bitters
Stir with ice and strain into
cocktail glass. Add a twist of
orange peel.

SUNTAN
2 oz.   Hot Shot Tropical
   Fruit Liqueur
2 oz.   Orange Juice
Pour over ice in a highball
glass. Fill with club soda.

SURF RIDER

3 oz. Vodka
1 oz. Sweet Vermouth
½ c. Orange Juice
Juice of ½ Lemon
½ tsp. Grenadine

Shake with ice and strain into cocktail glass. Garnish with an orange slice and cherry.

SUSIE TAYLOR

Juice of ½ Lime
2 oz. Light Rum

Pour into collins glass over ice cubes and fill with ginger ale. Stir.

SWEET MARIA

1 tbsp. Light Cream
½ oz. Amaretto
1 oz. Vodka

Shake with cracked ice. Strain into cocktail glass.

SWEET PATOOTIE COCKTAIL

1 oz. Gin
½ oz. Triple Sec
1 tbsp. Orange Juice

Shake with ice and strain into cocktail glass.

SWISS FAMILY COCKTAIL

½ tsp. Anis
2 dashes Bitters
¾ oz. Dry Vermouth
1½ oz. Blended Whiskey

Stir with ice and strain into cocktail glass.

SWIZZLES

See Index on page 267 for complete list of Swizzle recipes.

T

TAHITI CLUB

2 oz.   Light Rum
1 tbsp. Lemon Juice
1 tbsp. Lime Juice
1 tbsp. Pineapple Juice
$1/2$ tsp. Maraschino

Shake with ice and strain into old-fashioned glass over ice cubes. Add a slice of lemon.

TAHITIAN TEA

In a highball glass, mix $1/2$ oz. each of **Gin, Light Rum, Vodka,** and **Hot Shot Tropical Fruit Liqueur.** Add 1 oz. each of 7-Up, cranberry juice, and orange juice. Stir.

TAILSPIN COCKTAIL

3/4 oz. Gin
3/4 oz. Sweet
        Vermouth
3/4 oz. Chartreuse
        (Green)
1 dash Orange Bitters

Stir with ice and strain into cocktail glass. Add a twist of lemon peel and a cherry or olive.

TANGO COCKTAIL

1 tbsp. Orange Juice
$1/2$ oz. Dry Vermouth
$1/2$ oz. Sweet
        Vermouth
1 oz.   Gin
$1/2$ tsp. Triple Sec

Shake with ice and strain into a cocktail glass.

TCHOUPITOLAS STREET GUZZLE

1 oz. Light Rum
Ginger Beer

Pour rum into highball glass over ice cubes. Add ginger beer.

TEMPTATION COCKTAIL

$1 1/2$ oz. Blended
        Whiskey
$1/2$ tsp. Triple Sec
$1/2$ tsp. Anis
$1/2$ tsp. Dubonnet®

Shake with ice and strain into cocktail glass. Add twists of lemon and orange peel.

Chilled Vodka

TEMPTER COCKTAIL

1 oz.   Port
1 oz.   Apricot-Flavored
Brandy

Stir with ice and strain into cocktail glass.

TEQUILA COCKTAIL

2 oz.   Tequila
Juice of ½ lemon
4 dashes Grenadine
1 dash egg white

Shake ingredients with crushed ice and strain into a cocktail glass. Garnish with a lemon slice.

TEQUILA COLLINS

Make same as Tom Collins (see page 183) but use Tequila instead of gin.

TEQUILA FIZZ

2 oz.   Tequila
3/4 oz.   Grenadine
1 tbsp.   Lemon Juice
1 Egg White

Shake well with ice and strain into collins glass over ice cubes. Fill with ginger ale and stir.

TEQUILA MANHATTAN

2 oz.   Tequila
1 oz.   Sweet Vermouth
1 dash Lime Juice

Shake with ice and strain over ice cubes in old-fashioned glass. Add a cherry and an orange slice.

TEQUILA MATADOR

1½ oz.   Tequila
3 oz.   Pineapple Juice
Juice of ½ Lime

Shake with crushed ice and strain into champagne flute.

TEQUILA MOCKINGBIRD

1½ oz.   Tequila
3/4 oz.   Crème de
Menthe (Green)
Juice of 1 Lime

Shake with ice and strain into cocktail glass. Decorate with a lime slice.

TEQUILA OLD-FASHIONED

1½ oz.   Tequila
½ tsp.   Sugar
1 dash   Bitters
Splash Carbonated Water

Mix sugar, bitters, and a teaspoon of water in old-fashioned glass. Add tequila, ice, and a splash of carbonated water. Decorate with a pineapple stick.

TEQUILA PINK

1½ oz.   Tequila
1 oz.   Dry Vermouth
1 dash   Grenadine

Shake with ice and strain into cocktail glass.

TEQUILA PUNCH

1 liter Chilled Tequila
1 750-ml bottle Chilled
Champagne
4 750-ml bottles Chilled
Sauterne
64 oz. Fresh Fruits
(Cubes or Balls)

Sweeten to taste, chill thoroughly, and add ice cubes just before serving. Place in a large bowl and serve in 8 punch cups.

TEQUILA SOUR
Juice of $^1/_2$ Lemon
1 tsp. Powdered Sugar
2 oz. Tequila
Shake with ice and strain into sour glass. Decorate with a half-slice of lemon and a cherry.

TEQUILA STRAIGHT
$^1/_4$ Lemon
1 pinch Salt
$1^1/_2$ oz. Tequila
Put salt between thumb and index finger on back of left hand. Hold jigger of tequila in same hand and the lemon wedge in right hand. Taste salt, drink the tequila, and then suck the lemon.

TEQUILA SUNRISE
2 oz. Tequila
4 oz. Orange Juice
$^3/_4$ oz. Grenadine
Stir tequila and orange juice with ice and strain into highball glass. Add ice cubes. Pour in grenadine slowly and allow to settle. Before drinking, stir to complete your sunrise.

TEQUINI
$1^1/_2$ oz. Tequila
$^1/_2$ oz. Dry Vermouth
1 dash Bitters (if desired)
Stir with ice and strain into cocktail glass. Serve with a twist of lemon peel and an olive.

TEQUONIC
2 oz. Tequila
Juice of $^1/_2$ Lemon or Lime
Tonic
Pour tequila over ice cubes in old-fashioned glass. Add fruit juice, fill with tonic, and stir.

THANKSGIVING SPECIAL
$^3/_4$ oz. Apricot-Flavored Brandy
$^3/_4$ oz. Gin
$^3/_4$ oz. Dry Vermouth
$^1/_4$ tsp. Lemon Juice
Shake with ice and strain into cocktail glass. Serve with a cherry.

THIRD-DEGREE COCKTAIL
$1^1/_2$ oz. Gin
$^3/_4$ oz. Dry Vermouth
1 tsp. Anis
Stir with ice and strain into cocktail glass.

THIRD-RAIL COCKTAIL
$^3/_4$ oz. Light Rum
$^3/_4$ oz. Apple Brandy
$^3/_4$ oz. Brandy
$^1/_4$ tsp. Anis
Shake with ice and strain into cocktail glass.

THISTLE COCKTAIL
$1^1/_2$ oz. Sweet Vermouth
$1^1/_2$ oz. Scotch
2 dashes Bitters
Stir with ice and strain into cocktail glass.

THREE MILLER COCKTAIL

$1^1/_2$ oz. Light Rum
$^3/_4$ oz. Brandy
1 tsp. Grenadine
$^1/_4$ tsp. Lemon Juice
Shake with ice and strain
into cocktail glass.

THREE STRIPES COCKTAIL

1 oz. Gin
$^1/_2$ oz. Dry Vermouth
1 tbsp. Orange Juice
Shake with ice and strain
into cocktail glass.

THUNDER

1 tsp. Powdered Sugar
1 Egg Yolk
$1^1/_2$ oz. Brandy
1 pinch Cayenne Pepper
Shake with ice and strain
into cocktail glass.

THUNDER-AND-LIGHTNING

1 Egg Yolk
1 tsp. Powdered
Sugar
$1^1/_2$ oz. Brandy
Shake with ice and strain
into cocktail glass.

THUNDERCLAP

$^3/_4$ oz. Gin
$^3/_4$ oz. Blended Whiskey
$^3/_4$ oz. Brandy
Shake with ice and strain
into cocktail glass.

TIDBIT

1 oz. Gin
1 scoop Vanilla Ice
Cream
1 dash Dry Sherry
Blend at low speed and
pour into highball glass.

TIPPERARY COCKTAIL

$^3/_4$ oz. Irish Whiskey
$^3/_4$ oz. Chartreuse
(Green)
$^3/_4$ oz. Sweet Vermouth
Stir well with ice and strain
into cocktail glass.

T.N.T. NO. 1

$1^1/_2$ oz. Blended
Whiskey
$1^1/_2$ oz. Anis
Shake with ice and strain
into cocktail glass.

T.N.T. NO. 2

1 oz. Tequila
Tonic
Mix with ice in an old-
fashioned glass.

TOASTED ALMOND

$1^1/_2$ oz. Coffee Liqueur
1 oz. Amaretto
$1^1/_2$ oz. Cream or Milk
Add all ingredients over ice
in an old-fashioned glass.

TODDIES

See Index on page 267 for
complete list of Toddy
recipes.

TOM-AND-JERRY
One Egg Separated
Powdered Sugar
Baking Soda
1/4 oz. Light Rum

First prepare batter, using yolk and white of one egg, beating each separately and thoroughly. Then combine both, adding enough superfine powdered sugar to stiffen. Add to this one pinch of baking soda and rum to preserve the batter. Then add a little more sugar to stiffen.

Hot Milk
1 1/2 oz. Light Rum
1/2 oz. Brandy

To serve, use hot mug, using one tablespoon of above batter, dissolved in 3 tablespoons hot milk. Add rum. Then fill mug with hot milk within 1/4 inch of the top of the mug and stir. Then top with brandy and sprinkle a little nutmeg on top. The secret of a Tom-and-Jerry is to have a stiff batter and a warm mug.

TOMBOY ⬤
1/2 cup Chilled Tomato Juice
1/2 cup Cold Beer

Pour tomato juice into highball glass. Add beer.

TOM COLLINS
Juice of 1/2 Lemon
1 tsp. Powdered Sugar
2 oz. Gin

Shake with ice and strain into collins glass. Add several ice cubes, fill with carbonated water, and stir. Decorate with slices of lemon, orange, and a cherry. Serve with straw.

TOP BANANA
1 oz. Vodka
1 oz. Crème de Banana
Juice of 1/2 Orange

Shake with ice and strain into old-fashioned glass over ice cubes.

TOREADOR
1 1/2 oz. Tequila
1/2 oz. Crème de Cacao
1 tbsp. Light Cream

Shake with ice and strain into cocktail glass. Top with a little whipped cream and sprinkle lightly with cocoa.

TORRIDORA COCKTAIL
1 1/2 oz. Light Rum
1/2 oz. Coffee-Flavored Brandy
1 1/2 tsp. Light Cream
1 tsp. 151-Proof Rum

Shake with ice, strain into cocktail glass. Float rum on top.

⬤ indicates lower alcohol content

TOVARICH COCKTAIL

$1^1/_2$ oz. Vodka
$3/_4$ oz. Kümmel
Juice of $^1/_2$ Lime
Shake with ice and strain
into cocktail glass.

TRILBY COCKTAIL

$1^1/_2$ oz. Bourbon
$3/_4$ oz. Sweet
Vermouth
2 dashes Orange Bitters
Stir with ice and strain into
cocktail glass.

TRINITY COCKTAIL

$3/_4$ oz. Sweet Vermouth
$3/_4$ oz. Dry Vermouth
$3/_4$ oz. Gin
Stir with ice and strain into
cocktail glass.

TROIS RIVIÈRES

$1^1/_2$ oz. Canadian
Whisky
1 tbsp. Dubonnet®
$1^1/_2$ tsp. Triple Sec
Shake with ice and strain
into old-fashioned glass
over ice cubes. Add a twist
of orange peel.

TROPICAL COCKTAIL

$3/_4$ oz. Crème de Cacao
(White)
$3/_4$ oz. Maraschino
$3/_4$ oz. Dry Vermouth
1 dash Bitters
Stir with ice and strain into
cocktail glass.

TROPICAL HEART

1 oz. Hot Shot Tropical
Fruit Liqueur
Hot Apple Cider
Pour ingredients into Irish
coffee cup and stir. Garnish
with a cinnamon stick.

TULIP COCKTAIL

$1^1/_2$ tsp. Lemon Juice
$1^1/_2$ tsp. Apricot-
Flavored Brandy
$3/_4$ oz. Sweet
Vermouth
$3/_4$ oz. Apple Brandy
Shake with ice and strain
into cocktail glass.

TURF COCKTAIL

$^1/_4$ tsp. Anis
2 dashes Bitters
1 oz. Dry Vermouth
1 oz. Gin
Stir with ice and strain into
cocktail glass. Add a twist of
orange peel.

TUXEDO COCKTAIL

$1^1/_2$ oz. Gin
$1^1/_2$ oz. Dry Vermouth
$^1/_4$ tsp. Maraschino
$^1/_4$ tsp. Anis
2 dashes Orange Bitters
Stir with ice and strain into
cocktail glass. Serve with a
cherry.

TWIN HILLS

1½ oz.   Blended Whiskey
2 tsp.   Benedictine
1½ tsp.   Lemon Juice
1½ tsp.   Lime Juice
1 tsp.   Sugar

Shake with ice and strain into sour glass. Add a slice of lime and a slice of lemon.

TWIN SIX COCKTAIL

1 oz.   Gin
½ oz.   Sweet Vermouth
¼ tsp.   Grenadine
1 tbsp.   Orange Juice
1 Egg White

Shake with ice and strain into cocktail glass.

TWISTER

2 oz.   Vodka
Juice of ⅓ Lime
Lemon Soda

Pour vodka and lime into collins glass. Add several ice cubes and drop a lime rind into glass. Fill with lemon soda and stir.

TYPHOON

1 oz.   Gin
½ oz.   Anisette
1 oz.   Lime Juice
Chilled Champagne

Shake all ingredients, except champagne, with ice. Strain into collins glass with ice cubes. Fill glass with chilled champagne.

U

ULANDA COCKTAIL

- 1½ oz. Gin
- ¾ oz. Triple Sec
- ¼ tsp. Anis

Stir with ice and strain into cocktail glass.

UNION JACK COCKTAIL

- ¾ oz. Sloe Gin
- 1½ oz. Gin
- ½ tsp. Grenadine

Shake with ice and strain into cocktail glass.

V

VALENCIA COCKTAIL
1 tbsp.   Orange Juice
1½ oz.   Apricot-
Flavored Brandy
2 dashes Orange Bitters
Shake with ice and strain
into cocktail glass.

VANDERBILT COCKTAIL
¾ oz.   Cherry-Flavored
Brandy
1½ oz.   Brandy
1 tsp.   Sugar Syrup
2 dashes Bitters
Stir with ice and strain into
cocktail glass.

VAN VLEET
3 oz.   Light Rum
1 oz.   Maple Syrup
1 oz.   Lemon Juice
Shake well with ice and
strain into old-fashioned
glass over ice cubes.

VELVET HAMMER NO. 1
1½ oz.   Vodka
1 tbsp.   Crème de
Cacao
1 tbsp.   Light Cream
Shake with ice and strain
into cocktail glass.

a) Vermouth Cassis b) Vermouth Cocktail

VELVET HAMMER NO. 2
1 1/2 oz. Strega
1 oz. Crème de Cacao (White)
1 tbsp. Light Cream
Shake with ice and strain into cocktail glass.

VERBOTEN
1 1/2 oz. Gin
1 tbsp. Forbidden Fruit
1 tbsp. Orange Juice
1 tbsp. Lemon Juice
Shake with ice and strain into cocktail glass. Add brandied cherry.

VERMOUTH CASSIS
3/4 oz. Crème de Cassis
1 1/2 oz. Dry Vermouth
Stir in highball glass with ice cubes and fill with carbonated water. Stir again and serve.

VERMOUTH COCKTAIL 🅛
1 oz. Dry Vermouth
1 oz. Sweet Vermouth
1 dash Orange Bitters
Stir with ice and strain into cocktail glass. Serve with a cherry.

VESUVIO
1 oz. Light Rum
Juice of 1/2 Lemon
1 tsp. Powdered Sugar
1/2 Egg White
1/2 oz. Sweet Vermouth
Shake with ice and strain into old-fashioned glass over ice cubes.

VICTOR
1 1/2 oz. Gin
1/2 oz. Brandy
1/2 oz. Sweet Vermouth
Shake with ice and strain into cocktail glass.

VICTORY COLLINS
1 1/2 oz. Vodka
3 oz. Unsweetened Grape Juice
3 oz. Lemon Juice
1 tsp. Powdered Sugar
Shake with ice and strain into collins glass with ice cubes. Add a slice of orange.

VIRGIN
1 oz. Gin
1/2 oz. Crème de Menthe (White)
1 oz. Forbidden Fruit
Shake with ice and strain into cocktail glass.

VIVA VILLA
Juice of 1 Lime
1 tsp. Sugar
1¹/₂ oz. Tequila
Shake with ice and strain over ice cubes into old-fashioned glass, rimmed with salt.

VODKA AND APPLE JUICE
Put two or three cubes of ice into highball glass. Add 2 oz. Vodka. Fill balance of glass with apple juice and stir.

VODKA AND TONIC
Pour 2 oz. Vodka into highball glass over ice cubes. Add tonic and stir.

VODKA COLLINS
Make same as Tom Collins (see page 183) but use Vodka instead of gin.

VODKA COOLER
Make same as Gin Cooler (see page 97) but use Vodka instead of gin.

VODKA DAISY
Juice of ¹/₂ Lemon
¹/₂ tsp. Powdered Sugar
1 tsp. Grenadine
2 oz. Vodka
Shake with ice and strain into stein or metal cup. Add ice cubes and decorate with fruit.

VODKA GIMLET
Make same as Gimlet (see page 97) but use Vodka instead of gin.

VODKA GRASSHOPPER
3/4 oz. Vodka
3/4 oz. Crème de Menthe (Green)
3/4 oz. Crème de Cacao (White)
Shake with ice and strain into cocktail glass.

VODKA ON THE ROCKS
Put two or three cubes of ice in old-fashioned glass and add 2 oz. Vodka. Serve with a twist of lemon peel.

VODKA SALTY DOG
1¹/₂ oz. Vodka
5 oz. Grapefruit Juice
¹/₄ tsp. Salt
Pour into highball glass over ice cubes. Stir well.

VODKA "7"
2 oz. Vodka
Juice of ¹/₂ Lime
Carbonated Water
Pour lime and vodka into collins glass over ice cubes. Drop a lime rind in glass, fill balance with lemon soda, and stir.

VODKA SLING
Make same as Gin Sling (see page 98) but use Vodka instead of gin.

VODKA SOUR
Juice of $1/2$ Lemon
$1/2$ tsp. Powdered Sugar
2 oz. Vodka
Shake with ice and strain
into sour glass. Decorate
with a half-slice of lemon
and a cherry.

VODKA STINGER
1 oz. Vodka
1 oz. Crème de Menthe
(White)
Shake with ice and strain
into cocktail glass.

W

WAIKIKI BEACHCOMBER
¾ oz.   Gin
¾ oz.   Triple Sec
1 tbsp. Fresh Pineapple Juice
Shake with ice and strain into cocktail glass.

WALLICK COCKTAIL
1½ oz. Dry Vermouth
1½ oz. Gin
1 tsp.   Triple Sec
Stir with ice and strain into cocktail glass.

WALLIS BLUE COCKTAIL
1 oz.   Triple Sec
1 oz.   Gin
Juice of 1 Lime
Moisten rim of an old-fashioned glass with lime juice and dip into powdered sugar. Shake ingredients with ice and strain into prepared glass over ice cubes.

WALTERS
1½ oz.   Scotch
1 tbsp. Orange Juice
1 tbsp. Lemon Juice
Shake with ice and strain into cocktail glass.

WARD EIGHT
Juice of ½ Lemon
1 tsp. Powdered Sugar
1 tsp. Grenadine
2 oz.   Blended Whiskey
Shake with ice and strain into red-wine glass filled with cracked ice. Add slices of orange, lemon, and a cherry. Serve with straws.

WARSAW COCKTAIL
1½ oz.   Vodka
½ oz. Blackberry-Flavored Brandy
½ oz. Dry Vermouth
1 tsp. Lemon Juice
Shake with ice and strain into cocktail glass.

WASHINGTON COCKTAIL

🍸 1½ oz. Dry Vermouth
¾ oz. Brandy
2 dashes Bitters
½ tsp. Sugar Syrup

Stir with ice and strain into cocktail glass.

WASSAIL BOWL

🥣 2 cups Water
1 tsp. Freshly Ground Nutmeg
2 tsp. Ground Ginger
2 sticks of Cinnamon
6 whole Cloves
6 Allspice Berries
4 Coriander Seeds
4 Cardamom Seeds
2 750-ml bottles Cream Sherry
64 oz. Ale
4 cups Sugar
12 Eggs Separated
1 cup Brandy
12 Roasted Apple Slices or 12 Tiny Roasted Apples

Combine water and spices in a large saucepan and simmer for 10 minutes. Add sherry and ale and stir in sugar. Heat, but do not boil. Beat 12 egg yolks until they are pale and thick; fold in 12 stiffly beaten egg whites. Strain half the ale and sherry mixture over the eggs. Pour into a warmed punch bowl. Bring the remaining hot mixture to a boil and strain into punch bowl. Add brandy and apples.

WATERBURY COCKTAIL

$^1/_2$ tsp. Powdered Sugar
Juice of $^1/_4$ Lemon or
   $^1/_2$ Lime
1 Egg White
$1^1/_2$ oz. Brandy
$^1/_2$ tsp. Grenadine
Shake with ice and strain
into cocktail glass.

WATERLOO

1 oz. Light Rum
3 oz. Orange Juice
$^1/_2$ oz. Mandarine
   Napoleon Liqueur
Pour rum and orange juice
over ice in an old-
fashioned glass. Stir. Float
Mandarine Napoleon on
top.

WATERMELON

Equal Parts:
Vodka
Strawberry Liqueur
Sweet and Sour Mix
Orange Juice
Serve over ice in a collins
glass.

WEBSTER COCKTAIL

Juice of $^1/_2$ Lime
$1^1/_2$ tsp. Apricot-
   Flavored Brandy
$^1/_2$ oz. Dry Vermouth
1 oz. Gin
Shake with ice and strain
into cocktail glass.

WEDDING BELLE
COCKTAIL

$1^1/_2$ tsp. Orange Juice
$1^1/_2$ tsp. Cherry-Flavored
   Brandy
$^3/_4$ oz. Gin
$^3/_4$ oz. Dubonnet®
Shake with ice and strain
into cocktail glass.

WEEP-NO-MORE
COCKTAIL

Juice of $^1/_2$ Lime
$^3/_4$ oz. Dubonnet®
$^3/_4$ oz. Brandy
$^1/_4$ tsp. Maraschino
Shake with ice and strain
into cocktail glass.

WEMBLY COCKTAIL

$^3/_4$ oz. Dry Vermouth
$1^1/_2$ oz. Gin
$^1/_4$ tsp. Apricot-
   Flavored Brandy
$^1/_2$ tsp. Apple Brandy
Stir with ice and strain into
cocktail glass.

WEST INDIAN PUNCH
64 oz. Light Rum
1 750-ml Crème de Banana
32 oz. Pineapple Juice
32 oz. Orange Juice
32 oz. Lemon Juice
³/₄ cup Powdered Sugar
1 tsp. Grated Nutmeg
1 tsp. Cinnamon
¹/₂ tsp. Grated Cloves
6 oz. Carbonated Water

Dissolve sugar and spices in carbonated water. Pour into large punchbowl over a block of ice, and add other ingredients. Stir and decorate with sliced bananas.

WESTERN ROSE
¹/₂ oz. Apricot-Flavored Brandy
1 oz. Gin
¹/₂ oz. Dry Vermouth
¹/₄ tsp. Lemon Juice

Shake with ice and strain into cocktail glass.

WHAT THE HELL
1 oz. Gin
1 oz. Dry Vermouth
1 oz. Apricot-Flavored Brandy
1 dash Lemon Juice

Stir in old-fashioned glass over ice cubes.

WHIP COCKTAIL
¹/₂ oz. Dry Vermouth
¹/₂ oz. Sweet Vermouth
1¹/₂ oz. Brandy
¹/₄ tsp. Anis
1 tsp. Triple Sec

Stir with ice and strain into cocktail glass.

WHISKEY COBBLER
Dissolve one teaspoon powdered sugar in 2 oz. carbonated water in a red-wine glass. Fill with shaved ice and add **2 oz. Blended Whiskey**. Stir and decorate with fruits in season. Serve with straw.

WHISKEY COCKTAIL
1 dash Bitters
1 tsp. Sugar Syrup
2 oz. Blended Whiskey

Stir with ice and strain into cocktail glass. Serve with a cherry.

WHISKEY COLLINS
Juice of ¹/₂ Lemon
1 tsp. Powdered Sugar
2 oz. Blended Whiskey

Shake with ice and strain into collins glass. Add several ice cubes, fill with carbonated water, and stir. Decorate with slices of lemon, orange, and a cherry. Serve with straw.

Wine

WHISKEY DAISY

Juice of $^1/_2$ Lemon
$^1/_2$ tsp. Powdered Sugar
1 tsp. Grenadine
2 oz. Blended Whiskey

Shake with ice and strain into stein or metal cup. Add one ice cube and decorate with fruit.

WHISKEY EGGNOG

1 Whole Egg
1 tsp. Powdered Sugar
2 oz. Blended Whiskey

Shake ingredients with ice and strain into collins glass. Fill glass with milk. Sprinkle nutmeg on top.

WHISKEY FIX

Juice of $^1/_2$ Lemon
1 tsp. Powdered Sugar

Shake with ice and strain into highball glass. Fill glass with ice. Add $2^1/_2$ oz. Blended Whiskey. Stir and add a slice of lemon. Serve with straws.

WHISKEY FLIP

1 Whole Egg
1 tsp. Powdered Sugar
$1^1/_2$ oz. Blended Whiskey
2 tsp. Light Cream (if desired)

Shake with ice and strain into sour glass. Sprinkle a little nutmeg on top.

WHISKEY HIGHBALL

Pour 2 oz. Blended Whiskey into highball glass over ice cubes and fill with ginger ale or carbonated water. Add a twist of lemon peel, if desired, and stir.

WHISKEY MILK PUNCH

1 tsp. Powdered Sugar
2 oz. Blended Whiskey
8 oz. Milk

Shake with ice, strain into collins glass, and sprinkle nutmeg on top.

WHISKEY ORANGE

Juice of $^1/_2$ Orange
1 tsp. Powdered Sugar
$^1/_2$ tsp. Anis
$1^1/_2$ oz. Blended Whiskey

Shake with ice and strain into highball glass over ice cubes. Decorate with slices of orange and lemon.

WHISKEY RICKEY

Juice of $^1/_2$ Lime
$1^1/_2$ oz. Blended Whiskey

Pour into highball glass over ice cubes and fill with carbonated water. Stir. Drop the lime rind into glass.

WHISKEY SANGAREE
In an old-fashioned glass, dissolve $^1/_2$ teaspoon powdered sugar in 1 teaspoon of water and add **2 oz. Blended Whiskey**. Add ice cubes and a splash of carbonated water. Stir and float a tablespoon of port on top. Sprinkle lightly with nutmeg.

WHISKEY SKIN
Put lump of sugar into hot punch cup and fill two-thirds with boiling water. Add **2 oz. Blended Whiskey**. Stir, then add a twist of lemon peel.

WHISKEY SLING
In an old-fashioned glass, dissolve one teaspoon powdered sugar in one teaspoon of water and juice of $^1/_2$ lemon; add ice cubes and **2 oz. Blended Whiskey**. Stir and add a twist of lemon peel.

WHISKEY SMASH
Muddle one lump of sugar in an old-fashioned glass with 1 oz. carbonated water and 4 sprigs of mint. Add **2 oz. Blended Whiskey**, then ice cubes. Stir and decorate with a slice of orange and a cherry. Add a twist of lemon peel.

WHISKEY SOUR
Juice of $^1/_2$ Lemon
$^1/_2$ tsp.   Powdered Sugar
2 oz.   Blended Whiskey
Shake with ice and strain into sour glass. Decorate with a half-slice of lemon and a cherry.

WHISKEY SQUIRT
$1^1/_2$ oz.   Blended Whiskey
1 tbsp.   Powdered Sugar
1 tbsp.   Grenadine
Shake with ice and strain into highball glass and fill with carbonated water and ice cubes. Decorate with cubes of pineapple and strawberries.

WHISKEY SWIZZLE
Make same as Gin Swizzle (see page 99) using **2 oz. Blended Whiskey** instead of gin.

WHISKEY TODDY (COLD)
$^1/_2$ tsp.   Powdered Sugar
2 tsp. Water
2 oz.   Blended Whiskey
Stir sugar and water in a mug. Add ice cubes and whiskey, and stir. Add a twist of lemon peel.

WHISKEY TODDY (HOT)

Put lump of sugar into hot mug and fill two-thirds with boiling water. Add 2 oz. **Blended Whiskey**. Stir and decorate with a slice of lemon. Sprinkle nutmeg on top.

WHISPERS-OF-THE-FROST COCKTAIL

3/4 oz. Blended Whiskey
3/4 oz. Cream Sherry
3/4 oz. Port
1 tsp. Powdered Sugar

Stir with ice and strain into cocktail glass. Serve with slices of lemon and orange.

WHITE CARGO COCKTAIL

1 scoop Vanilla Ice Cream
1 oz. Gin

Shake until thoroughly mixed and add water or sauterne if the mixture is too thick. Serve in an old-fashioned glass.

WHITE ELEPHANT

1 1/2 oz. Gin
1 oz. Sweet Vermouth
1 Egg White

Shake with ice and strain into cocktail glass.

WHITE LADY

1 Egg White
1 tsp. Powdered Sugar
1 tsp. Light Cream
1 1/2 oz. Gin

Shake with ice and strain into cocktail glass.

WHITE LILY COCKTAIL

3/4 oz. Triple Sec
3/4 oz. Light Rum
3/4 oz. Gin
1/4 tsp. Anisette

Shake with ice and strain into cocktail glass.

WHITE LION COCKTAIL

Juice of 1/2 Lemon
1 tsp. Powdered Sugar
2 dashes Bitters
1/2 tsp. Grenadine
1 1/2 oz. Light Rum

Shake with ice and strain into cocktail glass.

WHITE PLUSH

2 oz. Blended Whiskey
1 cup Milk
1 tsp. Powdered Sugar

Shake with ice and strain into collins glass.

WHITE ROSE COCKTAIL

3/4 oz. Gin
1 tbsp. Orange Juice
Juice of 1 Lime
1/2 oz. Maraschino
1 Egg White

Shake with ice and strain into cocktail glass.

WHITE RUSSIAN

1 oz. Coffee Liqueur
2 oz. Vodka
Milk or Cream

Put coffee liqueur and vodka in an old-fashioned glass over ice cubes and fill with milk or cream.

WHITE WAY COCKTAIL
$3/4$ oz. Creme de Menthe (White)
$1^1/2$ oz. Gin
Shake with ice and strain into cocktail glass.

WHY NOT?
1 oz. Gin
1 oz. Apricot-Flavored Brandy
$1/2$ oz. Dry Vermouth
1 dash Lemon Juice
Shake with ice and strain into cocktail glass.

WIDOW'S DREAM
$1^1/2$ oz. Benedictine
1 Whole Egg
Shake with ice and strain into cocktail glass. Float one teaspoon of sweet cream on top.

WIDOW'S KISS
1 oz. Brandy
$1/2$ oz. Chartreuse (Yellow)
$1/2$ oz. Benedictine
1 dash Bitters
Shake with ice and strain into cocktail glass.

WILL ROGERS
$1^1/2$ oz. Gin
1 tbsp. Orange Juice
$1/2$ oz. Dry Vermouth
1 dash Triple Sec
Shake with ice and strain into cocktail glass.

WINDY CORNER COCKTAIL
Stir 2 oz. Blackberry-Flavored Brandy with ice and strain into cocktail glass. Sprinkle a little nutmeg on top.

WINE COOLER L
Pour 3 oz. red wine into wine glass with ice cubes. Fill balance with lemon-lime soda or, if preferred, clear carbonated soda, and stir.

WOO WOO
$1^1/2$ oz. Peach or Tropical-Fruit Schnapps
$1^1/2$ oz. Vodka
$3^1/2$ oz. Cranberry Juice
Pour ingredients over ice in a highball glass and stir.

WOODSTOCK
$1^1/2$ oz. Gin
1 oz. Lemon Juice
$1^1/2$ tsp. Maple Syrup
1 dash Orange Bitters
Shake with ice and strain into cocktail glass.

WOODWARD COCKTAIL
$1^1/2$ oz. Scotch
$1/2$ oz. Dry Vermouth
1 tbsp. Grapefruit Juice
Shake with ice and strain into cocktail glass.

L indicates lower alcohol content

X

XANTHIA COCKTAIL
¾ oz. Cherry-Flavored Brandy
¾ oz. Chartreuse (Yellow)
¾ oz. Gin
Stir with ice and strain into cocktail glass.

XERES COCKTAIL
1 dash Orange Bitters
2 oz. Dry Sherry
Stir with ice and strain into cocktail glass.

X.Y.Z. COCKTAIL
1 tbsp. Lemon Juice
½ oz. Triple Sec
1 oz. Light Rum
Shake with ice and strain into cocktail glass.

Y

YALE COCKTAIL
1 1/2 oz. Gin
1/2 oz. Dry Vermouth
1 dash Bitters
1 tsp. Blue Curaçao
Stir with ice and strain into cocktail glass.

YELLOW PARROT COCKTAIL
3/4 oz. Anisette
3/4 oz. Chartreuse (Yellow)
3/4 oz. Apricot-Flavored Brandy
Shake with ice and strain into cocktail glass.

YELLOW RATTLER
1 oz. Gin
1 tbsp. Orange Juice
1/2 oz. Dry Vermouth
1/2 oz. Sweet Vermouth
Shake with ice and strain into cocktail glass. Add a cocktail onion.

YOLANDA
1/2 oz. Brandy
1/2 oz. Gin
1/2 oz. Anisette
1 oz. Sweet Vermouth
1 dash Grenadine
Shake with ice and strain into cocktail glass. Add a twist of orange peel.

Z

ZAZA COCKTAIL
$1^1/_2$ oz. Gin
$^3/_4$ oz. Dubonnet®
Stir with ice and strain into cocktail glass. Add a twist of orange peel.

ZERO MIST
For each serving, chill 2 oz. Crème de Menthe (Green) mixed with 1 oz. water in freezer compartment of refrigerator for 2 hours or longer, if desired. (Does not have to be frozen solid.) Serve in cocktail glasses.

ZOMBIE
1 oz. Unsweetened Pineapple Juice
Juice of 1 Lime
Juice of 1 Small Orange
1 tsp. Powdered Sugar
$^1/_2$ oz. Apricot-Flavored Brandy
$2^1/_2$ oz. Light Rum
1 oz. Jamaica Rum
1 oz. Passion Fruit Syrup (if desired)
$^1/_2$ oz. 151-Proof Rum
Put all ingredients with a half cup of crushed ice into an electric blender. Blend at low speed for one minute and strain into frosted highball glass. Decorate with a stick of pineapple and one green and one red cherry. Carefully float rum and then top with sprig of fresh mint dipped in powdered sugar. Serve with straw.

SPECIAL SECTIONS

Eggnog

AMBASSADOR'S MORNING LIFT
☞ 32 oz. Prepared Dairy
    Eggnog
  6 oz. Cognac
  3 oz. Jamaica Rum
  3 oz. Crème de Cacao
    (Brown)
Combine in large punch
bowl and serve. Sprinkle
nutmeg on top of each
serving. Brandy or bourbon
may be substituted for
cognac.

BALTIMORE EGGNOG
☞ 32 oz. Prepared Dairy
    Eggnog
  5 oz. Brandy
  5 oz. Jamaica Rum
  5 oz. Madeira Wine
Combine in large punch
bowl and serve. Sprinkle
nutmeg on top of each
serving.

BRANDY EGGNOG
☞ 32 oz. Prepared Dairy
    Eggnog
  12 oz. Brandy
Combine in large punch
bowl and serve. Sprinkle
nutmeg on top of each
serving.

BREAKFAST EGGNOG
☞ 32 oz. Prepared Dairy
    Eggnog
  10 oz. Apricot-
    Flavored Brandy
  2¹/₂ oz. Triple Sec
Combine in large punch
bowl and serve. Sprinkle
nutmeg on top of each
serving.

CHRISTMAS YULE EGGNOG
☞ 32 oz. Prepared Dairy
    Eggnog
  12 oz. Blended
    Whiskey
  1¹/₂ oz. Light Rum
Combine in large punch
bowl and serve. Sprinkle
nutmeg on top of each
serving.

Eggnog

EGGNOG SUPREME
- 1 dozen Medium Eggs
- 1 cup Sugar
- 1½ quarts Whole Milk
- 1 pint Heavy Cream, whipped
- 1 750-ml bottle Cognac
- Powdered Nutmeg

Separate eggs; beat yolks in large serving bowl, adding sugar while beating. Stir in milk and cream. Slowly add cognac and refrigerate for 1 hour. Before serving, whip egg whites stiff. Mix into eggnog, dust with nutmeg.

IMPERIAL EGGNOG
- 32 oz. Prepared Dairy Eggnog
- 10 oz. Brandy
- 2 oz. Apricot-Flavored Brandy

Combine in large punch bowl and serve. Sprinkle nutmeg on top of each serving.

NASHVILLE EGGNOG
- 32 oz. Prepared Dairy Eggnog
- 6 oz. Bourbon
- 3 oz. Brandy
- 3 oz. Jamaica Rum

Combine in large punch bowl and serve. Sprinkle nutmeg on top of each serving.

PORT WINE EGGNOG **L**
- 32 oz. Prepared Dairy Eggnog
- 18 oz. Port Wine

Combine in large punch bowl and serve. Sprinkle nutmeg on top of each serving.

RUM EGGNOG
- 32 oz. Prepared Dairy Eggnog
- 12 oz. Light Rum

Combine in large punch bowl and serve. Sprinkle nutmeg on top of each serving.

SHERRY EGGNOG **L**
- 32 oz. Prepared Dairy Eggnog
- 18 oz. Cream Sherry

Combine in large punch bowl and serve. Sprinkle nutmeg on top of each serving.

WHISKEY EGGNOG
- 32 oz. Prepared Dairy Eggnog
- 12 oz. Blended Whiskey

Combine in large punch bowl and serve. Sprinkle nutmeg on top of each serving.

L indicates lower alcohol content

No-Alcohol Drinks

BEACH BLANKET BINGO

3 oz.   Cranberry Juice
3 oz.   Varietal Grape
        Juice (Chenin Blanc,
        etc.)

Pour ingredients over ice in a highball glass. Top with club soda and garnish with lime wedge.

CRANBERRY COOLER

2 oz.   Cranberry Juice
$^1/_2$ tbsp. Lime Juice
        Club Soda

Add juices to collins glass filled with ice. Top with club soda and stir. Garnish with twist of lime.

CREAMY CREAMSICLE

8 oz.   Orange Juice
2 Scoops Vanilla Ice
        Cream

Combine ingredients in electric blender. Blend at low speed. Pour in highball glass and garnish with orange slice.

FUZZY LEMON FIZZ

6 oz.   Peach Nectar
4 oz.   Lemon Soda

Pour ingredients over ice in a highball glass. Garnish with a lemon twist.

FRUIT SMOOTHIE

8 oz.   Chilled Orange
        Juice
1 Banana, Peeled and
        Sliced
$^1/_2$ cup Ripe
        Strawberries,
        Blueberries or
        Raspberries

Combine ingredients in electric blender. Blend at low speed. Pour in a highball glass and garnish with assorted fruits.

GRAPEBERRY

3 oz.   Cranberry Juice
3 oz.   Grapefruit Juice

Combine juices in large red-wine glass filled with ice. Add wedge of lime and short straw.

INNOCENT PASSION

4 oz.   Passion Fruit
        Juice
1 dash Cranberry Juice
1 dash Lemon Juice
        Club Soda

Combine juices in a highball glass filled with ice. Top with club soda, stir. Add a cherry and a long straw.

LEMON SQUASH

1 Lemon, peeled and
   quartered
2 tsp. Powdered Sugar

Muddle well in collins glass
until juice is well extracted.
Then fill glass with ice. Add
carbonated water and stir.
Decorate with fruits.

LEMONDADE
(CARBONATED)

2 tsp. Powdered Sugar
Juice of 1 Lemon

Dissolve in collins glass,
then add ice and enough
carbonated water to fill
glass and stir. Decorate
with slices of orange and
lemon, and a cherry. Serve
with straws.

LEMONADE (EGG)

Juice of 1 Lemon
2 tsp. Powdered Sugar
1 Whole Egg

Shake and strain into
collins glass over ice cubes.
Add enough water to fill
glass. Serve with straws.

LEMONADE (FRUIT)

Juice of 1 Lemon
2 tsp. Powdered Sugar
1 oz. Raspberry Syrup

Combine in collins glass.
Add ice cubes and enough
water to fill glass, and stir.
Decorate with slices of
orange and lemon, and a
cherry. Serve with straws.

LEMONADE (GOLDEN)

Juice of 1 Lemon
2 tsp. Powdered Sugar
1 Egg Yolk
6 oz. Water

Shake with ice and strain
into collins glass. Decorate
with slices of orange and
lemon, and a cherry.

LEMONADE (PLAIN)

2 tsp. Powdered Sugar
Juice of 1 Lemon

Stir. Then fill collins glass
with ice. Add enough water
to fill glass and stir well.
Decorate with slices of
orange and lemon, and a
cherry.

LIME COLA

Juice of 1/2 Fresh Lime
Cola

Add juice to tall glass of
ice. Fill with cola. Stir, add
long twist of lime.

LIME COOLER

1 tbsp.   Lime Juice
Tonic Water

Add lime juice to tall glass
filled with ice. Top with
tonic. Garnish with lime
wedge.

LIMEADE

Juice of 3 Limes
3 tsp. Powdered Sugar

Combine in collins glass,
then add ice and enough
water to fill glass. Stir and
add a wedge of lime and a
cherry in glass. Serve with
straws.

ORANGE AND TONIC
6 oz.   Orange Juice
4 oz.   Tonic Water
Pour ingredients over ice
in a highball glass. Garnish
with lime wedge.

ORANGE SMILE
1 Whole Egg
Juice of 1 Large Orange
1 tbsp.   Grenadine
Shake with ice and strain
into wine glass.

ORANGEADE
Juice of 2 Oranges
1 tsp. Powdered Sugar
Mix in collins glass. Add ice
cubes and enough water to
fill glass, and stir. Decorate
with slices of orange and
lemon, and two cherries.
Serve with straws.

PAC MAN
2 tsp.   Lemon Juice
1 tsp.   Grenadine
1 dash Bitters
Ginger Ale
Add grenadine, lemon
juice, and bitters to collins
glass filled with ice. Top
with ginger ale. Notch an
orange slice and slide
down side of glass.

PASSION FRUIT
SPRITZER
4 oz.   Passion Fruit
Juice
Club Soda
Pour juice in champagne
flute and fill with club
soda. Garnish with a lime
wedge.

PEACH MELBA
8 oz.   Peach Nectar
2 Scoops Vanilla Ice
Cream
1/2 Whole Sliced Peach
3 oz.   Ripe Raspberries
Combine ingredients in
electric blender. Blend at
low speed. Pour in a
highball glass and garnish
with raspberries.

PIKE'S PEAK COOLER
Cider
Juice of 1/2 Lemon
1 tsp.   Powdered Sugar
1 Whole Egg
Shake with ice and strain
into collins glass with
cracked ice. Fill with cider
and stir. Insert a spiral of
orange or lemon peel (or
both) and dangle over rim
of glass.

PUNCHLESS PIÑA
COLADA
1 oz.   Cream of
Coconut
1 oz.   Pineapple Juice
1 cup Ice
1 tsp.   Lime Juice
Combine ingredients in
blender. Pour into Collins
glass. Garnish with slice of
pineapple and cherry.

RUMLESS RICKEY

1 oz. Lime Juice
1 dash Grenadine
1 dash Bitters
Club Soda

Add juice, grenadine, and
bitters to old-fashioned
glass with three to four
large ice cubes. Top with
club soda. Stir. Garnish
with long twist of lime.

RUNNER'S MARK

4 oz. V-8 Vegetable
Juice
2 drops Tabasco Sauce
2 drops Lemon Juice
1 dash Worcestershire
Sauce

Combine ingredients in
old-fashioned glass over
ice. Stir, garnish with celery
or scallion.

SHIRLEY TEMPLE

Ginger Ale
1 dash Grenadine

Add grenadine to tall glass
filled with ice; top with
ginger ale, decorate with
orange slice and cherry.

TOMATO COOLER

8 oz.   Tomato Juice
2 tbsp. Lemon or Lime
Juice

Combine ingredients over
ice in a highball glass and
top with tonic water.
Garnish with a wedge of
lime, sprig of dill and
cucumber slice.

UNFUZZY NAVEL

3 oz.   Peach Nectar
1 tbsp.   Lemon Juice
3 oz.   Orange Juice
1 dash Grenadine

Combine the ingredients in
a shaker with ice. Strain
into wine glass. Garnish
with an orange slice.

VIRGIN MARY

4 oz.   Tomato Juice
1 dash Lemon Juice
$1/2$ tsp. Worcestershire
Sauce
2 drops Tabasco Sauce
Pepper, salt

Fill a large wine glass with
ice. Add tomato juice, then
rest of ingredients. Stir and
garnish with wedge of lime.

THE LIQUOR DICTIONARY

Much of the enjoyment of social drinking comes from a knowledge of the different types of alcoholic beverages available. This section will help you understand some of the subtle differences between one type of liquor and another, so that you can choose the flavor and style of spirit that suits the occasion and your taste.

First, here are a few common terms frequently misunderstood:

Alcohol (C_2H_5OH)—the common ingredient of all liquor. There are many types of alcohol, but for liquor only ethyl alcohol is used. Of the several types of ethyl alcohol, those spirits distilled from grain, grape, fruit, and cane are the most common.

Proof—a measurement of alcoholic strength or content. One degree of proof equals one-half of one percent of alcohol. An 80-proof product contains forty percent alcohol by volume; a 90-proof product, forty-five percent alcohol, etc.

For centuries the Scotch, British Gin, and Canadian Whisky sold in England, Scotland, and most of the rest of the world was 80 proof. America has only begun to appreciate the tasteful quality of the more moderate lower proofs. Practically all of the rum sold in America is now 80 proof, and vodka at 80 proof outsells higher-proof vodkas. For years the most expensive, famous-name cognacs have been imported at 80 proof, and now nearly all American-made brandy is also 80 proof.

Grain Neutral Spirits is a practically tasteless, colorless alcohol distilled from grain (like whiskey) but at 190 proof or above, whereas whiskey must be distilled at less than 190 proof. It is used in blended whiskeys, in making gin and vodkas, and in many other liquors.

Brandy

Brandy is distilled from fermented fruit, sometimes aged in oak casks, and usually bottled at 80 proof. Long enjoyed as an after-dinner drink, brandy is also widely used in mixed drinks and cooking. It is produced in a number of countries. The term *brandy,* used alone, means that the spirit has been distilled from grape wine.

Cognac is fine brandy known for its smoothness and heady scent. It is produced only in the Cognac region of France. (Hence, all cognac is brandy, but not all brandy is cognac.)

Armagnac is much like cognac but has a richer taste. This brandy is produced only in the Armagnac region of France.

American Brandy, virtually all of which is distilled in California, has its own taste characteristics. Unlike European brandies (whose farmer-distillers sell their brandies to the blender-shippers who control the brand names), California brandies are usually produced by individual firms that grow the grapes, distill, age, blend, bottle, and market the brandies under their own brand names. They are typically light and smooth.

Apple Brandy, Applejack, or Calvados are apple brandies distilled from cider made from apples. Calvados is produced only in Normandy, France. Applejack may be bottled-in-bond under the same regulations that apply to whiskey.

Fruit Brandies—eaux de vie—are water-white 80- to 90-proof spirits distilled directly from fruits. Fruit brandies made from cherries are called Kirsch or Kirschwasser, from pears, Poire, and from raspberries, Framboise. They are best served chilled or over ice. Fruit-Flavored Brandies are brandy-based liqueurs flavored with blackberries, peaches, apricots, cherries, etc. They are usually bottled at 70 or 80 proof.

Brandies fine enough to be drunk undiluted out of a snifter do not need to be heated over a candle. The warmth of a hand is sufficient to enhance the bouquet.

Liqueurs

The words *liqueur* and *cordial* are synonymous, describing liquors made by mixing or redistilling neutral spirits, brandy, whiskey, or other spirits with fruits, flowers, herbs, seeds, roots, plants, or juices to which sweetening has been added. Practically all liqueurs are sweet and colorful, with highly concentrated, dessertlike flavor.

Liqueurs are made in all countries. Several, made from closely guarded secret recipes and processes, are known throughout the world by their trade or proprietary brand names.

Here are brief descriptions of the liqueurs and flavorings mentioned most frequently in the recipes in this book.

Absinthe—anise seed (licorice) flavor; contains wormwood. Banned in the United States and virtually everywhere else. Replaced by Anis liqueurs, which have a similar flavor (see below).

Amaretto—Almond-flavored liqueur

Amer Picon—bitter, orange-flavored French aperitif cordial made from quinine and spices

Anis—Abisante, Abson, Anisette, Herbsaint, Mistra, Ojen, Oxygene, Pernod, Ricard

Bénédictine—secret herb formula first produced by Benedictine monks

Cassis—see *Crème de Cassis*

Chartreuse—yellow and green herb liqueurs developed by Carthusian monks

Cointreau—a triple sec (see below)

Cream Liqueurs—a relatively recent addition to the category. Usually flavored with chocolate, coffee, or orange.

Crème(s)—so called because high sugar content results in creamlike consistency
Crème de Cacao—from cacao and vanilla beans
Crème de Cassis—from black currants
Crème de Menthe—from mint
Crème de Noyaux—from almonds

Curaçao—orange-flavored, made from dried orange peel, from Dutch West Indies. May be blue or orange in color.

Forbidden Fruit—a domestic liqueur produced by blending shaddock fruit (a type of grapefruit) and imported cognac

Grand Marnier—a cognac-based liqueur flavored with bitter orange peel

Kümmel—caraway and anise seeds and other herb flavors

Maraschino—liqueur made from cherries grown in Dalmatia, Yugoslavia

Rock and Rye—sweetened rye whiskey sometimes bottled with rock candy or fruit slices

Schnapps—light-bodied liqueur, now available in a wide variety of flavors

Sloe Gin—a liqueur made from sloe berries (blackthorn bush)

Strega—Italian liqueur made from herbs, spices, and plants

Swedish Punch—Scandinavian liqueur made from Batavia Arak rum, tea, lemon, and other spices. Also known as Arrack Punsch and Caloric Punch (the latter because it gives off heat).

Gin

Gin was invented by a Dutch doctor some 300 years ago and was first drunk as a medicine. Its supposed curative powers became irrelevant—people *felt* better, so in the 17th century the English took the Dutch medicine back to their country and drank it liberally with or without toasting anyone's health.

Gins are little more than neutral spirits distilled from grain. But they are reprocessed and redistilled with a flavorist's grab-bag of assorted herbs and spices with the main ingredient being juniper berries. Gin, like other clear spirits, is basically clean and bracing in flavor, but has fruity and herby overtones as well.

The most common style of gin is the London Dry type made in Great Britain and the United States. English gins are 94 proof; American gins are 80 to 94 proof. Either way the two drinks are equally dry, which means unsweetened. Most gins are not aged.

Hollands gin, or genever, is still made and is more flavorful than the London Dry type.

Rum

Rum is made from sugar cane boiled down to a rich residue called molasses which is then fermented and distilled.

Light rums are clear to pale gold in color; dark rums amber to brown in color. Both light and dark are normally 80 proof.

Light rums are traditionally produced in Spanish-speaking islands like Puerto Rico. Because of their dryness and less intense flavor, they can be substituted in most cocktails calling for gin and vodka. (The lighter the rum, the better.)

Dark rum results from the addition of caramel coloring or aging. It is very aromatic and has a heavier, richer flavor than light rum. It comes from the tropics: Jamaica, Haiti, or Martinique. While supplying the punch in Planter's Punch and the rich flavor in a variety of tropical and hot drinks, the best can also be savored like a fine brandy.

Rums are aged from three to ten years (though some of the very light rums leave the cask in two years).

There are also 151-proof rums, which are excellent in desserts that call for flaming.

Whiskey

Whiskeys are distilled from a fermented mash of grain (usually corn, rye, barley, or wheat), and then aged in oak barrels. In this country, whiskey must be distilled at less than 190 proof (although whiskey with a special designation such as bourbon, rye, etc., cannot be distilled above 160 proof) and must be bottled at no less than 80 proof.

Whiskey, when placed in barrels to age, is a clear liquid. It is during the aging period that whiskey obtains its characteristic amber color, flavor, and aroma.

The major whiskey-producing countries are the United States, Canada, Scotland, and Ireland. Special grain characteristics, recipes, and distillation processes make the whiskey of each country distinct from that of the others.

American Whiskey—Although American whiskeys fall into two major categories, straight whiskey and blended whiskey, the United States government acknowledges thirty-three distinct types of whiskey. Only the major types (98 percent of the nation's consumption) are covered here.

Straight Whiskey is distilled from corn, rye, barley, or wheat (not blended with neutral grain spirits or any other whiskey) and aged in charred oak barrels for a minimum of two years. There are three major types of straight whiskey:

1. Bourbon Whiskey is distilled from a mash of grain containing not less than 51 percent corn and is normally aged four years in new charred oak barrels. Bourbon is amber in color and full-bodied in flavor, round and slightly sweet. When distilled in Kentucky, it is usually referred to as Kentucky Straight Bourbon Whiskey. Bourbon is named for Bourbon County in Kentucky where this type of whiskey originated. Bourbon and Bourbon-type whiskeys are also produced in Illinois, Indiana, Ohio, Pennsylvania, Tennessee, Missouri, and Virginia. Bourbon is more full-flavored than Scotch or Irish Whiskey.

2. Rye Whiskey is distilled from a mash of grain containing not less that 51 percent rye and is much like bourbon in color, but is different in taste and heavier in flavor.
3. Corn Whiskey is distilled from a mash of grain containing not less than 80 percent corn. Corn whiskey is commonly aged in re-used charred oak barrels.

Bottled-in-Bond Whiskey is straight whiskey, usually bourbon or rye, which is produced under United States government supervision. Though the government does not guarantee the quality of bonded whiskey, it does require that the whiskey be at least four years old, that it be bottled at 100 proof, that it be produced in one distillery by the same distiller, and that it be stored and bottled at a bonded warehouse under government supervision.

Blended Whiskey is a blend of one or more straight whiskeys and neutral grain spirits containing at least 20 percent straight whiskey bottled at not less than 80 proof.

A blend of straight whiskeys occurs when two or more straight whiskeys are blended together, to the exclusion of neutral grain spirits.

Canadian and Scotch Whisky—By tradition Scottish and Canadian distillers spell the spirit they make *whisky* (plural: *whiskies*).

Canadian Whisky—Canadian whiskies are blended whiskies, usually distilled from rye, corn, and barley. Produced only in Canada, under government supervision, most of the Canadian whisky sold in this country is at least four years old. Canadian whisky, usually lighter-bodied than American whiskey, is usually sold at 80 proof.

Scotch Whisky—Produced only in Scotland, Scotch whiskies are blended whiskies deriving their individual personalities from native barley grain and traditional pot stills. All Scotch blends contain malt whisky and grain whisky (similar to American grain neutral spirits). Scotch's distinctive smoky flavor comes from drying malted barley over peat fires. The malt whiskies of Scotland (also called single malts) are the product of nearly 100 distilleries, each of which produces its own distinctive spirit. Most malt whiskies are used in blends, but some are bottled unblended. These are best when cut with a dash of cool water and savored in a brandy snifter. All the Scotch imported in this country is at least four years old and is usually 80 or 86 proof. Scotch sold in the rest of the world is almost always 80 proof.

Irish Whiskey—Produced only in Ireland, Irish whiskey, like Scotch, is a blended product containing both barley malt whiskies and grain whiskies. Unlike Scotch, however, the malt is dried in coal-fired kilns and the aroma of the fires does not reach the malt. Irish whiskey is lighter flavored and less smoky than Scotch and is usually 86 proof.

Age is often believed to be the only indication of quality, but a whiskey, rum, or brandy can be aged too long as well as not long enough. Other factors affecting quality include variables in the distilling process itself, the types of grain used, the warehousing techniques employed, the rate of aging, and the degree of skill used in determining product maturity. Aging may make good whiskey better, but no amount of aging can make good whiskey out of bad.

Vodka

Vodka has humility. By law, vodkas produced in the United States must be colorless, tasteless, and odorless. Because of its purity, vodka will graciously assume the characteristics of whatever it is mixed with.

The higher the proof the less flavor, and vodka is also filtered through charcoal to remove any remaining hint of flavor. Imported vodkas are not subject to the same regulations as U.S. vodkas and sometimes have faint flavor nuances. There are also vodkas that are specially flavored with lemon, lime, mint, and even one flavored with buffalo grass.

Vodka is made from pure grain neutral spirits distilled from fermented corn, rye, or wheat. Russian vodka used to be made from potato mash in the days of the Czars. Today it's made from grain.

Taken straight, chilled vodka makes a fine aperitif with smoked salmon or hot sausage.

Beer

BEER

"Beer" refers to all brewed and fermented beverages that are made from malted grains and hops. Beer-making dates back to ancient Egyptian times.

There are five major types of beer: lager, ale, stout, porter, and bock. For all of these the stages of brewing are similar. The difference between light and dark beers comes from the amount of roasting, or "kilning," of the barley malt. The more roasting, the darker the color and the greater the caramelization of malt sugars.

Usually made from barley, beer begins with germination of the grain. Once germinated, the barley is called "malt."

The malt is next dried in a hot kiln. The temperature and duration of roasting determines both the color and sweetness of the final product. The longer the roast, the darker and sweeter the beer.

Next, the roasted malt is mixed with other cereals and water and cooked.

The type of water used for beer is important. Some waters make good beers. Other waters possess minerals or tastes more suitable for ale. That's why certain areas are noted for beer or ale but seldom produce both.

After cooking, liquid from this pre-alcoholic porridge is drained off. The liquid is call "wort." It's put into a brew kettle and infused with hops, a small, soft flower which adds a depth of flavor and a pleasantly bitter tang to beer.

After a few hours of boiling in the wort, the hops are strained out, the wort is cooled, and yeast is added which "attacks" the malt sugar, causing fermentation.

Yeast converts wort to beer. The pedigree of the yeast, the secret formula so carefully perpetuated so that the beer will have the same flavor year after year, is the brewmaster's "magic wand."

Two different types of yeasts make all the differences among beers. When "bottom" yeast finishes eating the sugar, it settles to the bottom of the tank. Lager is a "bottom fermented" beer. Practically all beers brewed in the United States are lagers.

Ale, on the other hand, is a "top fermented" beverage. "Top" yeast floats on the top of the tank when it finishes with the sugar.

You can taste the difference the two yeasts make. Ale is sharper and stronger than lager, with a more pronounced flavor of hops.

The ideal serving temperature is 45°F for beer and 50°F for ale. Beer goes flat if it's served too cold. Imported beers should be served at 50°F and English or Irish stout at 55°F.

Store bottled or canned beer in a cool, dark place. Extremely sensitive to sunlight, bottled beer must never be put in windows or it will acquire a "skunky" odor. At home, store cans or bottles in the lowest, coolest part of the refrigerator.

To serve beer, pour it so that the stream flows directly to the center of the glass, which should be stationary on the table. This produces a nice foam or "head." Beer naturally accompanies hamburger, stew, sausage, cold cuts, lobster, and sharp cheeses.

Here are some definitions:

Beer—a generic term for all brewed and fermented beverages made from cereal grains

Lager—bright, clear-bodied beer, effervescent. A "bottom fermented" brew. Most of the world's beers are lagers.

Ale—aromatic malt brew usually fuller-bodied, darker, and more bitter than lager. A "top fermented" brew.

Stout—a very dark beer, sometimes sweetish and quite strong with a pronounced hops taste

Porter—a type of ale with a rich, heavy foam. Sweeter than ale. Not quite as strong as stout.

Pilsner—a term put on labels of many light beers around the world. These are bright, lagered beers in the style made famous by Pilsner Urquell from Pilsner, Bohemia.

Bock Beer—a strong style of lager beer, originally seasonal (autumn and spring)

Malt Liquor—a beer with considerable variation from light to dark color, and from a strong, hoppy flavor to little. Higher alcoholic content than most other beers.

Sweet Beer—a combination of fruit juice and beer. Yields a sweeter drink and higher alcoholic content than lagers.

Sake—actually a type of beer in that it is a re-fermented rice brew of high alcoholic content

Light Beer—lagers, lower in alcohol and calories, mild in taste

Low-Alcohol Beer—similar to Light Beer, but contains even less alcohol and fewer calories

Although almost every country produces beer, only a handful are famous for their brews, notably Germany, Belgium, and Britain. The U.S. leads in volume, despite having far fewer breweries than, for example, Germany. Currently there is a revival of the small local breweries that were once so common in this country. Some of these are producing brews of great distinction, fully the equal of the best imports.

WINE

Wine, one of the oldest beverages known, is a natural product made entirely from grapes. Its probable Mediterranean origin predates written history, with the earliest known documents indicating that wine has been made since 4000 B.C. Wine, wine-making, and the cultivation of wine grapes gradually spread throughout the Western world via tradesmen, religious sects, and conquering armies. Today, almost every continent can enjoy wine from its own resources.

For many people, especially Europeans, wine is an integral part of life. It enhances the enjoyment of nearly every occasion. A bottle of wine on the table turns mere eating into dining.

But where to start? The world of wine can be overwhelming. The variety of labels seems endless, the terminology may appear confusing, and the customs related to serving it are varied and sometimes mystifying. Although becoming knowledgeable about wine has become a popular hobby in the United States in recent years, it is not essential to the enjoyment of the beverage. Wine is first and foremost a pleasant drink meant to accompany food. Wine appreciation is similar to the appreciation of food. It takes no special expertise, merely the enjoyment of harmonious and attractive flavors.

What makes the subject of wine fascinating, however, is that each wine has its own personality. Nature guarantees it will never have quite the same character every year, even if it comes from the same vineyard, winemaker, and process. This factor, combined with the ever-changing character of wine as it ages, results in a complex world of beverages that can satisfy nearly every taste and suit nearly every occasion and meal.

How Wine Is Made

Grapes are picked when ripe, usually from September to October (in the Northern Hemisphere), and put into a crusher-stemmer which removes the stems and produces grape "must." Must is pumped to a press to separate juice from the skins. The juice of virtually all wine grape varieties is white. The color of red wines comes from leaving the dark skins of red grapes in contact with their juice, which colors it during fermentation. The juice is pumped to a settling tank, then into a fermentation vat where the natural wine yeasts are augmented. When fermentation is complete, the wine is drawn off and placed in casks for aging, if desired. After aging, wine is filtered and bottled.

Wine Appreciation

There are only two things you need in order to become a discriminating wine connoisseur and a smart wine buyer: experience and a good memory. The more wines you experience, the better you'll be able to discriminate between what you do and don't like. Learning to assess quality wine is fun and can save you money. A twelve-dollar bottle may or may not be twice as good as a six-dollar bottle, but only your palate can make that decision.

Preferences in wine are subjective and everyone's taste differs. The guidelines that are commonly given for tasting, judging, and selecting wine are useful rules of thumb and often a help, but are only intended to enhance enjoyment. Such guidelines can be ignored whenever your taste dictates otherwise.

Wine Tasting

There are three criteria for judging wine: color, aroma, and taste. You must first examine the wine in a clear glass for color. The deeper the color, the fuller the flavor. The wine should be clear and appealing. Murkiness indicates something has happened to change the taste and quality of the wine.

Next, swirl the glass to aerate the wine. This helps release the bouquet or aroma. Most of anyone's judgment of wine is based on the aroma because the the sense of taste is dependent on smell. In a light white wine, a fruity, flowery, grapey perfume may arise. The big red wines may have a spicy berrylike character.

Now, taste it. Take some in your mouth and savor it before swallowing. Notice the components. Is it dry or sweet? Is it fruity or acidic? Is it too heavy, too light, or well-balanced? And most important—do you like it? If you do, write down the type, producer, and vintage of the wine. It will be helpful to have a list of a few names you can rely on for your next trip to a wine and spirits store.

Wine Storage

After purchase, wines should be stored in a cool, dry place such as a basement or storeroom, away from heat and wide variations in temperature. Screw-top wines can be stored standing up, but wines that have corks should be stored on their sides so that the cork remains moist. If the cork dries out, air will enter the bottle and oxidize the wine. Once opened, keep the leftover wine corked tightly and place in the refrigerator. Most wines will keep like this for only a few days. After that, the wine absorbs oxygen and begins to turn to vinegar.

If wine, particularly red wine, has been stored for a number of years, a sediment may form on the side of the bottle. This is a natural side effect of aging and does not mean the wine has been spoiled. However, before serving, pour the wine slowly and carefully into a clean decanter or pitcher holding the shoulder of the bottle over a flashlight, so you can stop pouring when the sediment reaches the neck. The wine in the decanter will be clear.

Wine Service

When serving wine, as with serving food, it's usually better to serve lighter beverages before more substantial ones. Hence, white wine is normally served before red, light wine before heavy, and dry before sweet. Red wines should be served at room temperature (65°) or slightly cool to the touch. White wines, rosés, and light reds such as Beaujolais are best served with a slight chill. For maximum effervescense, Champagne and sparkling wine are best served very cold (45°) but not so chilled that the delicate flavors are lost.

For each wine type there is a proper kind of glass that provides optimum enjoyment, but in practice only a couple of styles are necessary. The best all-purpose glass for both red and white wine is an eight-to-ten-ounce clear glass that has a large bowl at the base and is slightly tapered inward on the top. The bowl allows plenty of room for swirling and the tapered top concentrates the scent. For Champagne, a tall, clear flute-shaped glass ensures that the wine will retain the long stream of bubbles the wine-maker went to such great effort to offer you. Shallow, bowl-shaped glasses give the wine a broad surface area from which the bubbles dissipate rapidly and cause the wine to go flat, if not spill.

It is common to have more than one glass at a table setting if you're serving more than one kind of wine.

Wine and Food

In deciding which wine to serve with a particular meal or dish, remember that ideally the wine and food should make each other taste better. Consider the occasion: A picnic calls for something simple, a holiday dinner something special. Consider regional affinities. Italian wines, not surprisingly, go very well with Italian dishes. Consider too the intensity of the dish: Subtle, mild food goes well with delicate wines. Rich, spicy foods are best paired with big, full-flavored wines. Wines can be chosen to harmonize with the dish—a red wine and steak, for example—or provide a pleasant contrast, such as a lemon-sharp, crisp white with a rich, oily salmon steak.

Here are some suggested types of wine for various occasions, meals, dishes, and courses.

Apertif hour—Champagne and sparkling wine, crisp whites such as Macon, California, Fumé Blanc, dry Fino Sherry. These wines have crisp acidity and are pleasantly sharp and savory in taste, which stimulates the appetite and refreshes the palate. Their cutting flavor makes an attractive contrast to rich canapes, caviar, oysters, nuts.

Fish—Normally, crisp whites are best, because their high acidity accents fish flavors in much the same way a squeeze of lemon does. Shellfish, for example, is excellent with sharper whites such as Muscadet. Lobster, however, has an affinity with rich, round whites such as Chardonnay or White burgundy. But exceptionally rich fish dishes, such as salmon, will pair nicely with a light red or dry rosé.

Chicken, veal, pork, and mild cheeses—These lighter, versatile foods can be paired with lighter, less tannic reds, such as Beaujolais, Chianti, Pinot Noir, or flavorful whites such as Rieslings, Chenin Blanc, Chardonnay, and Gewürztraminer.

Lamb, game, and strong cheeses—These flavorful foods are best with Bordeaux, Cabernet Sauvignon, rich red Burgundies, Barolos, Riojas, Rhône wines, and other intense reds whose flavors naturally complement red meat and whose astringent tannins balance the fattiness of meats and cheeses.

Baked Ham and turkey, sausages—Best with fine dry rosés.

Beef and steak—Excellent with Pinot Noirs, Cabernet Sauvignon, Merlots, Zinfandels, and other medium-bodied reds. Prime ribs call for an elegant, subtle red such as Pinot Noir; a charcoal-broiled steak with pepper sauce needs an equally assertive red, such as a spicy Zinfandel.

Desserts—Over-sugary desserts overpower fine sweet wines. Mild fruit tarts, cakes, berries, etc., are delicious with sweet Rieslings, Sauternes, and Muscats. Mild chocolate desserts are best paired with ruby Port.

A Glossary of Basic Wine Terms

Acidity—A term used to indicate pleasant tartness or sharpness to the taste due to the presence of fruit acids.

Aroma—That portion of the wine's odor derived from the grape variety and fermentation.

Balance—A tasting term denoting complete harmony among the main components of a wine.

Body—The weight or fullness of wine on the palate.

Bouquet—That portion of a wine's odor that develops after it is bottled.

Dry—A tasting term to denote the absence of sweetness in wine.

Enology—the study of wine-making.

Fermentation—The process of converting natural grape sugar into alcohol and carbon dioxide by the addition of yeast.

Generic Wine—Wine blended with several grape varieties in which the character of any one variety does not dominate. These wines are labeled with a generalized term such as chablis, burgundy, or rhine.

Nose—The total odor of wine composed of aroma, bouquet, and other factors.

Residual Sugar—The natural grape sugar that is left in a wine which determines the sweetness level.

Tannin—The components in a wine that have an astringent, puckery, and sometimes bitter quality, and a mouth-drying aftertaste.

Varietal Wine—Wine made from one grape variety.

Vintage Wine—Wine made from grapes that are harvested in one given year.

Wines of the United States

Although California, New York, Oregon, and Washington are the chief wine-producing states in America, many other states, such as Virginia and Texas, produce small quantities of wine, some quite excellent. This is partly due to the discovery that a great many areas in the U.S. are suitable for growing some types of wine grapes, given skillful wine-making.

The East
The most important eastern wine-producing state is New York. The traditional wines of New York are dissimilar to the wines of California and Europe because of the different grape species used for wine production. Instead of the classic European grape varieties, the grapes used are either native American varieties such as Concord, Isabella, Catawba, and Delaware, or are the hybrids such as Baco and Seyval Blanc. These grape varieties produce wines that range from sweet and simple to dry and distinguished. In recent years some very fine white wines made from European grape varieties have been produced.

The West
Oregon and Washington are new and important wine-producing states; however, California out-produces them by far. The production of wine has a long history in California, dating back to the early Spanish missions. In the 1960s California had only a handful of wineries. Now over 575 wineries exist, and more are opening each year.

The principal grape varieties used on the West Coast are the same classic varieties used in Europe. These wines are identified by the grape variety. The reason for this is that any one grape variety can flourish in several geographic districts and any one district can produce good grapes of several different varieties.

West Coast grape-growing regions include the Yakima valley in Washington, the Willamette valley in Oregon, and dozens more in California, from north of San Francisco down to San Diego. The major fine wine-producing areas in California are Napa, Sonoma, Mendocino, Monterey, and the Central Coast. Each region has characteristics different from the others due to dissimilar climate, soil, and topography. Within these regions are smaller areas with unique microclimates that produce wines that have singular qualities unlike those of the surrounding area. Thus one grape variety can do well in many regions and produce completely different results.

While there are differences among wines from year to year, there are few poor California vintages. Cabernet Sauvignons are usually the only California wines that are better if aged, but not too long—five to ten years after the vintage date.

While producer and geographical information is always given on California and Northwest wine labels, the major clue to the wine's style is the grape used. Except for generic blends and a few specialty bottlings, many fine wines are labeled by varietal—the name of the grape variety used. Here are some of the major varieties and their characteristics as wines:

Whites
Johannisberg (or White) Riesling:—Pale color, flowery scent, delicate, fruity flavor, lively acidity; dry to slightly sweet; golden-colored, late-harvest dessert types are very sweet.

Sauvignon (or Fumé) Blanc:—Pale straw color, herb and spice aroma, very dry, crisp, appetizing savory taste. Medium-bodied.

Chardonnay:—Pale gold color; full, rich aroma, applelike, often with nuances of vanilla from aging in oak barrels. Dry, crisp, but full and rich.

Chenin Blanc:—Fruity aroma, somewhat peachlike; dry to slightly sweet.

White Zinfandel:—A fruity-sweet, simple wine made from red Zinfandel grapes, hence often slightly pink in color.

Reds

Cabernet Sauvignon:—Deep, rich red; aroma of berries and herbs, sometimes cedarlike hints. Thick-textured, mouth-filling, powerful; tannic edge to flavor softens with age.

Merlot:—Soft-textured red similar in flavor to Cabernet Sauvignon, with which it is often blended.

Pinot Noir:—Deep red; medium-bodied, less tannic than Cabernet; fruity and subtle.

Zinfandel:—Dark red; spicy-berry aroma; powerful assertive taste, direct flavor.

All regions in California produce a wide selection of wine types, and wine-making technology in the state is among the most advanced in the world. Ideal climate, modern wine-making, and restless experimentation have enabled California to produce wines that now rival the world's best.

Wines of France

Without France the wine world would never be where it is today. Fortunately for us, since 500 B.C. France has continued to perfect grape-growing and wine-making techniques. It not only produces most of the important wine types in the world but also many of the greatest examples of each.

French wine production is governed by a system of appellation laws which go beyond guaranteeing that the wine in a French bottle comes from the region indicated on the label to specify which types of grapes may be grown in a region and how the wine may be made. The result is that certain wine styles are associated with certain regions. The red wines of Bordeaux, for example, share similar characteristics because they are made only in a certain manner from certain grapes.

There are several famed wine districts in France that produce very different wines. The most notable are presented in the following section.

Bordeaux

Bordeaux is actually a city in southwest France sur-
rounded by regions of vineyards. It is mainly known for its
red wines, but their dry and sweet white wines are among
the finest made. Within Bordeaux are several sub-districts
that use similar grape varieties yet produce wines of different character. The primary grape varieties are Cabernet
Sauvignon, Cabernet Franc, and Merlot. Red wines that are
medium to full bodied, fragrant, and complex in flavor come
from these regions: St. Estèphe, Pauillac, St. Julien, Médoc,
Margaux, and Graves. Some thicker-textured, softer red wines
come from St. Émilion and Pomerol.

There are over three thousand individual châteaux or
estates in Bordeaux, the best of which bottle wine from
their own vineyards. Bordeaux lasts and improves in the
bottle for a decade or more.

Red Bordeaux are vintage-dated and much is made of
the wines from the very best years (harvests). But wines
from these years may take years to be at their best. There
is often more enjoyment to be had from a mature wine
from a good but not great year than from an immature
"great" wine. Wines from good years are lighter but not
necessarily inferior to wines from great years.

Red Bordeaux Vintage Chart

Great Years: For drinking now, 1961, '70. For drinking or
keeping, 1975. For keeping until 1990, 1982.

Good Years: For drinking now, 1966, '71, '76. For drinking
or keeping, 1978, '79, '81. For keeping until 1990, 1983,
'85.

The Graves district also produces austere dry whites
from the grape varieties Sauvignon Blanc and Sémillion.
Other white wine areas are Sauternes and Barsac. Both use
the same grape varieties as the white Graves but the grapes
are harvested overripe. These sweet wines are golden in

color with the rich flavor of ripe pears and apricots. Sauternes can last for decades.

White Bordeaux (Sauternes) Vintage Chart:

Great Years: For drinking now, 1967, '71. For drinking or keeping, 1975, '83.

Good Years: For drinking now, 1970, '76, '79, '80, '81.

Burgundy

Located in eastern France, Burgundy is much smaller than Bordeaux and is divided into five main districts. The wines are made either by the vineyard owner or by *negociants* who buy wines from the various growers, blend them together, and sell the final product from their particular firm. In purchasing a bottle of Burgundy, it is just as important to know the reputation of the producer or *negociant* as it is to know the reputation of the vineyard. The five main districts of Burgundy are:

Chablis—Producing excellent austere white wines from the Chardonnay grape. These crisp, dry wines have an almost mineral tang and are best matched with delicate seafoods and shellfish.

Maconnais—Producing popular, light dry wines primarily from Chardonnay grapes. The most well-known wines are Macon-Villages, Pouilly-Fuissé, and St.-Védran.

Chalonnais—Producing light dry reds and dry whites.

Beaujolais—Producing light fruity red wines from the Gamay grape variety, intended to be enjoyed young.

Côte d'Or—Within this region are two sub-regions—the Côte de Nuits (north) and the Côte de Beaune (south). The Côte de Nuits is responsible for the greatest red Burgundies, such as Chambertin, Vosne-Romanée, Vougeot, Musigny, and Nuits St.-Georges. These wines are made from Pinot Noir grapes and in character are generally medium-full bodied, fragrant, and wonderfully complex.

The Côte de Beaune is responsible for the greatest white Burgundies, such as Meursault, Chassagne-Montrachet, Puligny Montrachet, and Le Montrachet. The wines are made from the Chardonnay grape varietal and in character are generally medium-full bodied, rich, and buttery.

Burgundy Vintage Chart:

Great Years: For drinking now, 1969, '71, '76. For drinking or keeping, 1978. For keeping until 1988, 1983.

Good Years: For drinking now, 1972, '79, '80.

Champagne

Thanks to the discoveries of the seventheenth-century monk Dom Perignon, sparkling wines are enjoyed the world over. Champagne is made by a costly time-consuming process called *méthode champenoise.* Essentially, this is the process by which still wine is made sparkling by allowing it to ferment a second time in the bottle, thus producing the characteristic bubbles in champagne. There are other ways to make a wine sparkling, but this produces the finest results and is the only process allowed in the Champagne region.

The still base wine or *cuvée* must be near flawless. For the base, Chardonnay or Pinot Noir grape varieties are used singularly or in a blend. If the label says "Blanc de Noir," the wine is made entirely from the clear juice of the Pinot Noir. If the term "Blanc de Blanc" is used, the wine is 100 percent Chardonnay. Most wines are a blend of both varieties.

Each Champagne House, or firm, produces a standard nonvintage bottling that is a blend of several vintages, and in the best years, a vintage-dated wine made solely from that harvest. Champagne, at best, is a versatile elegant beverage with toasty, lemony flavors. Each wine is labeled according to its sweetness level. Brut is the dryest; Extra Dry is slightly sweeter; Demi-Sec is fairly sweet.

Rhône

The vineyards of the Rhône valley are located in southern France on steep, sun-drenched granite cliffs. This area produces red and white wines that are deep in color, very hearty, and big. Most of the finer Rhône wines are pressed from one kind of grape, sometimes two or three—with the exception of Chateauneuf-du-Pape, in which up to thirteen grapes are allowed. The principal red grape varieties are Syrah and Grenache. The principal white variety is Voignier. Côtes du Rhône is the basic label of the Rhône valley. Smaller areas producing finer wines include Côte Rotie (red), Hermitage (red and white), and Chateauneuf-du-Pape (red and white).

Rhône Vintage Chart:

Great Years: For drinking now, 1978. For drinking or keeping, 1983. For keeping until 1990, 1985.

Loire Valley

Although there is almost no wine sold under the label Loire, there are a number of well-known vineyard areas along the river, including Vouvray, Sancerre, Pouilly, and Muscadet.

Vouvray—Perhaps the best-known district. Made from Chenin Blanc grapes, the wines are light and delicately fruity with a hint of sweetness. A substantial amount of sparkling and some semi-sparkling wines are also made.

Sancerre and *Pouilly-sur-Loire*—Both primarily produce dry white wines from the grape varietal Sauvignon Blanc. The wines have a strong varietal character and at best are excellent.

Muscadet—Produces delightful light dry white wines with a crisp finish. The wines are made from mélon variety.

In addition, there are fine sweet wines made from the Chenin Blanc grape, and light reds made from Cabernet Franc.

Alsace

Located in northeast France, Alsace borders Germany and, in fact, produces dry white wines made from varieties associated with German wines: (Johannisberg) Riesling and Gewürztraminer. Gewürztraminer has a very flowery aroma and an exotic spicy flavor.

Alsace Vintage Chart:

Great Years: For drinking or keeping, 1983, '85.

Wines of Germany

Germany's vineyards lie as far north as grapes can ripen. The vineyards are located on steep hillsides with the best vines facing south for maximum exposure to the sun. Most of the wines of Germany are white and range from sweet to sweeter to sweetest. Once you can decipher a German wine label, you can buy a German wine with confidence.

At the very top of the label is the name of the growing region. Just under that is the year of harvest.

In bold type across the wine label are the town and vineyard that produced the wine. An *er* suffix is placed on a village name, so a wine from the town Bernkastel, for example, becomes Bernkastel*er* on the bottle.

Just under the town name you'll see the grape variety. The most important varieties are (Johannisberg) Riesling, Sylvaner, and Müller-Thurgau. The label then tells if the wine is dry (trocken) or semi-dry (halbtrocken).

The last two lines, which look like fine print on a contract, tell the ripeness of the grapes at harvest, the official passed-quality-control number, and whether or not the wine was estate-bottled or -produced by a cooperative of growers.

There are eleven wine districts in Germany. They are Nahe, Franconia (Franken), Baden and Württemburg, Ahr, Rheinhessen, Palatinate (Pfalz), Rheingau, Middle Rhine, Mosel (with Saar and Ruwer), and Bergstrasse. The two most important districts are the Mosel-Saar-Ruwer producing stylish elegant wines, and the Rheingau, producing fuller, more lush wines than the Mosel with ripe, apricotlike fruitiness.

Further, the label tells you what level of sweetness you are buying. Apart from *Tafelwein* (table wine), which is rarely exported, there are two main types:

Qualitätswein (Quality Wine), or QbA for short, indicates a basic level of quality.

Qualitätswein mit Prädikat (Quality Wine with Special Attributes) is the highest-quality category. The Pradikats or special attributes refer to five levels of ripeness and sweetness.

1. *Kabinett*—Slightly sweet.

2. *Spätlese*—Late picked. Riper flavors, fairly sweet.

3. *Auslese*—Selected late picked. Very sweet, intense flavors.

4. *Beerenauslese*—Berry-selected, late picked. Concentrated and very sweet.

5. *Trockenbeerenauslese*—Dried berry-selected, late picked. Extremely sweet.

Eiswein is wine from grapes picked and crushed frozen, and is very sweet.

German Vintage Chart:

Great Years: For drinking now, 1975, '76, '83, '85.

Wines of Italy

Decades ago Italian wines suffered not only from the haphazard methods of wine-making but also from an easygoing attitude concerning nomenclature. But in July 1963 regulations for controlling place names, or Denomination of Origin, were made law. Italy's best wines are now labeled *Denominazione di Origine Controllata* (D.O.C.) and some now carry an additional *Garantita* of quality as well (D.O.C.G.).

There are some 18 district wine-growing regions in Italy located throughout the country. The most well known are *Piedmont,* producing Barolo, Barbaresco, Gattinara, Barbera, Asti Spumante, and others; *Tuscany,* producing Chianti and Brunello di Montalcino; *Veneto,* producing Soave, Bardolino, and Valpolicella.

Popular Italian Wines

Amarone—Red wines made from grapes that are dried, like raisins, to concentrate sugar and increase alcoholic content (up to 15 percent). Heavy flavor.

Asti Spumante—Muscat grapes go into this sparkling white wine that's grapey and fruity–sweet and enjoyable. Very popular in Italy and growing in popularity in the United States.

Barbaresco—A rough tannic red wine from Nebbiolo grapes. One of Italy's best reds; better and smoother when aged.

Barbera d'Alba—Fruity red wine with high tannic overtones.

Barbera d'Asti—"More refined" relative of the wine above; should be aged four to eight years.

Bardolino—Light red table wine.

Barolo—The "king" of Piedmont reds. A strong wine with an earthy, pungent bouquet. Tannic when young but smooth when aged.

Great Years: For drinking now, 1978. For keeping until 1990, 1982.

Chianti—Medium-light bodied, bright-flavored red wines. Very aromatic. Made from Sangiovese grapes (about 70 percent) and the rest a blend of up to five other varieties.

Great Years: For drinking now or keeping, 1985.

Frascati—Fruity, dry young white wines.

Gattinara—Like a Barolo but more refined. Hearty and full-flavored.

Grignolino—Rose or light red wine with ample bouquet.

Lambrusco—Light, simple, lively red. Serve chilled.

Orvieto—Fruity dry light wines.

Pinot Grigio—A little fruitier than most Italian whites. Dry.

Soave—Popular light dry white wine made in the town of Soave near Verona. Drink young.

Spanna—Another name for the Nebbiolo grape and a red wine produced from it in Piedmont. Rich, full flavor.

Valpolicella—Light red wine, good slightly chilled. Soft. Ruby-colored. The Italian equivalent of Beaujolais.

Verdicchio—Light, crisp, dry white wine. Pale green.

Wines of Spain

Spain has more vineyards than any other country in Europe. Currently, there is an expansion of grape growing and the gradual utilization of modern wine-making methods. The main quality regions are Jerez, Rioja, and Catalonia.

Rioja, located in northern Spain, is known for its red table wines. These are made in the style of French Bordeaux and aged in oak at least two years, and often longer. The result is a smooth, dry red with flavor, aromatic bouquet and a warm aftertaste of oak. In northeast Spain, *Catalonia* produces a wide variety of wines but is best known in the United States for its sparkling wine.

Spain is best known for its sherry, and *Jerez de la Frontera* is the center of sherry country. The chalky soil there adds special characteristics and fineness to the wine. Sherry is a fortified wine to which grape brandy has been added to increase the alcoholic content. The Palomino grape is the primary grape variety.

Sherry is not known by vineyard or vintage. The vintage is lost in the "Solera." This progressive system employs a series of casks graduated by age, ranging from fine old sherry to fresh youthful sherry. When ready to bottle, a portion of the oldest sherry leaves the cask or "butt." An equal quantity is drawn from the next-oldest sherry butt and replaces the wine in the oldest butt. Then, to replace the wine lost in the second-oldest sherry butt, an equal quantity is drawn from the next-older butt—and so on. The sherry is essentially "ageless."

Types of Sherry
Fino—A pale light gold wine in which "flor," a wine-yeast, develops on top during production, adding character. The wine is very dry, has a fresh appley nose and delicate flavors. To be drunk young.

Manzanilla—This is both a fino wine and a wine in its own right. Produced near the sea, the salt air affects the flavor, giving a special tang. A fresh light tart wine.

Amontillado—A softer, darker-colored sherry than fino. The best Amontillados are old finos with nutty powerful flavor and usually slightly sweet.

Oloroso—This sherry is fuller in body than the Amontillado. The wine is strong, nutty, and pungent. It is the basis for the best sweeter sherries, often known as milk or cream.

Wines of Portugal

There are regions in Portugal that make table wines, such as Dao, which produces wines similar to the Riojas of Spain. But Portugal's main claim to fame is Port and Maderia.

Madeira

Madeira is an island located off the coast of Morocco. Wine has been a major product there for over 400 years. Fame came once Madeira was made suitable for export by being fortified by brandy, and the long sea voyages through tropical heat speeded up the long maturing process, resulting in the caramel tang by which all Madeira can now be recognized.

Today, the wines are "baked" to achieve this tang, and the shippers of Madeira use the Spanish solera system to blend their wine into consistent brands.

There are four distinct types of Madeira named after the grapes from which they are produced, ranging in levels of sweetness. From dry to sweet they are: Sercial, Verdelho, Bual (Boal), and Malmsey (Malvasia). Rainwater is a blend and may be dry or medium sweet.

Port

Port's name was derived from the city from where it was shipped at the mouth of the Douro, Oporto. A blend of many grape varieties, the wine is made by running off partially fermented red wine into a barrel a quarter full of brandy while the wine still has half of its grape sugar. The brandy stops the fermentation so that the wine is strong and sweet.

When completed, the wine is a deep opaque purple, rich in fruit, tannins and very long lived. There are several types of port.

White Port—Port made from white grapes. Similar to a dry sherry.

Tawny Port—Port aged many years in oak, producing a tawny color. Very fine quality and smooth.

Ruby Port—Young port aged in wood a relatively short period of time. Deep in color, fruity but rough.

Vintage Port—This is among the world's best wines. Not produced every year, the wine is made entirely from one exceptional year and bottled early for laying away and aging. It must be aged at least ten years and has to be decanted before serving.

Best Years: For drinking now, 1960, '63, '66, '67. For keeping or drinking, 1970, '75. For keeping until 1995, 1977, '80, '82, '83.

Late-Bottled Vintage Port—Wine of a good year kept much longer in wood than Vintage Port. A lighter wine.

The Wines of Other Countries

The spread of modern grape-growing methods and scientific winemaking has enabled good, and often outstanding fine wines to be made in countries with climates once thought unsuitable for wine production. Excellent wines are now produced in Australia, New Zealand, South Africa, Chile, Argentina, even Lebanon. In some cases the wines resemble the bottlings produced in Europe and the U.S., but many have their own distinct personalities. Among the most distinctive wines of Australia are the Shiraz, a deep, powerful red, and Semillon, a fine rich white. The Sauvignon Blancs of New Zealand are particularly noteworthy. Chile produces some fine Cabernet Sauvignons. Wines from these and other countries are often not only good, but also attractively priced, because they do not yet have the reputation of well-known European or California wines.

Shopping Suggestions

When shopping to stock your home bar, we recommend the following quality products:

Kentucky Tavern Bourbon Whiskey
Yellowstone Bourbon Whiskey
Mellow Mash Bourbon Whiskey
Old Thompson Blended Whiskey
Glenmore Gin
Glenmore Vodka
Expresso Coffee Liqueur
Boston Cordials
Boston Schnapps
Chi-Chi's Margarita
Tequila Cooler
Hot Shot Tropical Fruit Liqueur
Mr. Boston Flavored Brandies
Elduris Icelandic Vodka
Desmond & Duff 12-Year-Old Scotch
Felipe II Spanish Brandy
Gavilan Tequila

INDEX

If you know the name of the mixed drinks you desire, you need not use this index: All drinks are listed alphabetically throughout the book.

This index is arranged so that you may choose specific types of drinks, such as cocktails, fizzes, highballs, etc., or cocktails made with gin, vodka, whiskey, or other ingredients.

ABSINTHE SUBSTITUTE DRINKS

Absinthe is illegal in the U.S. but there are various substitutes available with the same taste and viscosity for use in mixed drinks.

Absinthe Drip Cocktail.	37
Absinthe Special Cocktail	37
Blarney Stone Cocktail.	54
Bombay.	56
Brazil Cocktail.	62
Button Hook Cocktail	64
Café de Paris Cocktail	65
Cognac Coupling	75
Deep Sea Cocktail	81
Dempsey Cocktail.	82
Dixie Cocktail	83
Du Barry Cocktail	84
Duchess.	84
Eye-Opener.	87
Green Opal.	104
Hasty Cocktail.	105
Irish Whisky	111
Jean Lafitte Cocktail	115
Jeyplak Cocktail.	115
Knock-Out Cocktail	118
Lawhill Cocktail.	122
Linstead Cocktail	123
Mandeville	129
Merry Widow Cocktail No. 1	131
Modern Cocktail	134
Montreal Club Bouncer	136
Morning Cocktail	136
Morning Glory Fizz	137
Peggy Cocktail	146
Phoebe Snow	146
Picadilly Cocktail	146
Presto Cocktail	152
Rattlesnake Cocktail	155
Robert E. Lee Cooler	158
Saucy Sue Cocktail	164
Special Rough Cocktail	174
Swiss Family Cocktail	177
Temptation Cocktail	178
Third Degree Cocktail	181
Third Rail Cocktail	181
T.N.T. No. 1	182
Turf Cocktail.	184
Tuxedo Cocktail.	184
Ulanda Cocktail	186
Whip Cocktail	195
Whiskey Orange	197

ADES

California Lemonade	66
Lemonade (Carbonated)	209
Lemonade (Claret)	122
Lemonade (Egg).	209
Lemonade (Fruit)	209
Lemonade (Golden).	209
Lemonade (Modern)	122
Lemonade (Plain)	209
Lemon Squash	209
Limeade.	209
Orangeade	210
Orange Smile	210

AMARETTO DRINKS

Alabama Slammer 32, 38
Amaretto and Cream	39
Amaretto Mist	39
Amaretto Rose	39
Amaretto Sour	40
Amaretto Stinger	40
Amaretto Tea	40
Boccie Ball.	56
Café de Amaretto	65
Ferrari.	89
French Connection	91
Godchild	100
Godfather.	100
Godmother.	100
Golden Friendship	101
Hot Gold	108
Italian Coffee	112
Italian Sombrero.	112
Ritz Fizz	158
Road Runner	158
Scooter	165
Stiletto	175
Sweet Maria	177
Toasted Almond. 35, 182

AMER PICON DRINKS

Amer Picon Cocktail	41
Quebec	153

ANISETTE DRINKS

Apricot Anise Collins	44
Baltimore Bracer	48
Blanche	54
Crème de Café	79
Dream Cocktail	83
Fontainbleau Special	91

Green Opal 104
Johnnie Cocktail 116
Ladies Cocktail 121
Malmaison 129
Narragansett 138
Shanghai Cocktail 168
Snowball 172
Suissesse Cocktail 176
Typhoon 185
White Lily Cocktail 199
Yellow Parrot Cocktail 202
Yolanda 202

APPLE BRANDY DRINKS

Angel Face 41
Ante 42
Apple Blow Fizz 42
Apple Brandy Cocktail 42
Apple Brandy Highball 42
Apple Brandy Rickey 42
Apple Brandy Sour 42
Apple Pie No. 1 44
Bentley 50
Bolero 56
Deauville Cocktail 81
Dempsey Cocktail 82
Depth Bomb 82
Golden Dawn 101
Harvard Cooler 105
Honeymoon Cocktail 107
Jack-in-the-Box 113
Jack Rose Cocktail 113
Jersey Lightning 115
Joulouville 116
Liberty Cocktail 123
Lugger 125
Moonlight 136
Prince's Smile 152
Royal Smile Cocktail 160
Saucy Sue Cocktail 164
Soother Cocktail 173
Special Rough Cocktail 174
Star Cocktail 174
Star Daisy 174
Third Rail Cocktail 181
Tulip Cocktail 184
Wembly Cocktail 194

APPLEJACK DRINKS

A.J. 38
Ambrosia 40
Applecar 42
Applejack Punch 44
Apple Rum Rickey 44
Barton Special 49
Frozen Apple 93
Puerto Apple 152

APPLE SCHNAPPS DRINKS

Apple Colada 42
Apple Pie No. 2 44
Indian Summer 35, 111

APRICOT BRANDY DRINKS

After Dinner Cocktail 38
After Supper Cocktail 38
Angel Face 41
Apricot Anise Collins 44
Apricot Brandy Rickey 44
Apricot Cocktail 45

Apricot Cooler 45
Apricot Fizz 45
Apricot Lady 45
Aprihot 45
Aqueduct 45
Babbie's Special Cocktail 48
Banana Punch 49
Bermuda Bouquet 51
Bermuda Rose 51
Boston Cocktail 57
Breakfast Eggnog 62, 205
Button Hook Cocktail 64
Charlie Chaplin 70
Claridge Cocktail 74
Cuban Cocktail No. 2 80
Darb Cocktail 81
Devil's Tail 82
English Rose Cocktail 86
Ethel Duffy Cocktail 86
Fairy Belle Cocktail 88
Favorite Cocktail 89
Fifth Avenue 89
Flamingo Cocktail 90
Frankenjack Cocktail 91
Golden Dawn 101
Golden Slipper 101
Hop Toad 107
Imperial Eggnog 110, 207
K.G.B. Cocktail 117
Leave-it-to-Me Cocktail No. 1 122
Lil Naue 123
Lugger 125
Midnight Cocktail 132
Nevins 139
Paradise Cocktail 145
Prince's Smile 152
Princess Pousse Café 152
Red Cloud 155
Resolute Cocktail 156
Rose Cocktail (English) 159
Saucy Sue Cocktail 164
Spencer Cocktail 174
Tempter Cocktail 180
Thanksgiving Special 181
Tulip Cocktail 184
Valencia Cocktail 187
Webster Cocktail 194
Wembly Cocktail 194
Western Rose 195
What the Hell 195
Why Not? 200
Yellow Parrot Cocktail 202
Zombie 203

BEER

Beer Buster 50
Depth Charge 82
Shandy Gaff 168
Tomboy 183

BENEDICTINE DRINKS

Aunt Jemima 46
B & B 48
Bobby Burns Cocktail 56
Brighton Punch 62
Cabaret 65
Frisco Sour 93
Froupe Cocktail 93
Honeymoon Cocktail 107

Honolulu Cocktail No. 2 107	Brandy Toddy (Hot) 61
Hoot Mon Cocktail 107	Brandy Vermouth Cocktail 61
Kentucky Colonel Cocktail 117	Brantini 61
Merry Widow Cocktail No. 1 131	Brighton Punch 62
Pousse L'Amour 151	Bull's Eye 63
Preakness Cocktail 151	Bull's Milk 64
Queen Elizabeth 153	Button Hook Cocktail 64
Rolls-Royce 159	Café Royale 65
Twin Hills 185	Caledonia 66
Widow's Dream 200	Cardinal Punch 68
Widow's Kiss 200	Carrol Cocktail 69
	Champagne Cup 69
BLACKBERRY BRANDY DRINKS	Champagne Punch 69
Allegheny................. 39	Champs Élysées Cocktail 70
Bee Stinger............... 50	Charles Cocktail 70
Cadiz 65	Cherry Blossom 71
Polonaise 149	Chicago Cocktail 72
Poop Deck Cocktail 149	Chocolate Daisy 72
Warsaw Cocktail 192	Chocolate Flip 72
Windy Corner Cocktail 200	Cider Cup 73
	Claret Cup 73
BRANDY	Claret Punch 74
Adam and Eve.............. 37	Classic Cocktail 74
Alexander Cocktail No. 2 38	Coffee Cocktail 75
Ambassador's Morning Lift..... 40, 205	Coffee Flip 75
Ambrosia 40	Cold Deck Cocktail 76
American Beauty Cocktail........ 40	Combo 76
Andalusia 41	Creamy Orange 78
Angel's Kiss 41	Cuban Cocktail No. 2 80
Angel's Wing 41	Deauville Cocktail 81
Aunt Jemima............... 46	Delmonico No. 1 81
B & B................... 48	Depth Bomb 82
Baltimore Bracer 48	Diana Cocktail 82
Baltimore Eggnog............ 48, 205	Dream Cocktail 83
Bermuda Highball............ 51	East India Cocktail No. 1 85
Betsy Ross 51	Egg Sour 85
Between-the-Sheets 51	English Highball 86
Blackjack 52	Fancy Brandy 88
Black Russian 29, 52	Fantasio Cocktail 88
Bombay Cocktail 56	Fish House Punch 90
Bombay Punch 56	Fog Cutter 91
Bosom Caresser 57	Fontainbleau Special 91
Boston Sidecar 57	Froupe Cocktail 93
Brandied Madeira 58	Frozen Berkeley............. 93
Brandied Port 58	Frozen Brandy and Rum........ 93
Brandy Alexander............. 29, 58	Georgia Mint Julep 95
Brandy and Soda 58	Glögg 100
Brandy Blazer 58	Gloom Lifter.............. 100
Brandy Cassis 58	Grapefruit Nog 103
Brandy Cobbler 58	Harvard Cocktail 105
Brandy Cocktail 58	Hot Brandy Flip............ 107
Brandy Collins.............. 59	Imperial Eggnog............ 110, 207
Brandy Crusta Cocktail 59	Jamaica Granito 113
Brandy Daisy 59	Japanese 115
Brandy Eggnog............. 59, 205	Kiss the Boys Goodbye 118
Brandy Fix 59	Lady Be Good.............. 121
Brandy Fizz 59	La Jolla 121
Brandy Flip 59	Lil Naue 123
Brandy Gump Cocktail.......... 60	Loving Cup 125
Brandy Highball............. 60	Lugger 125
Brandy Julep 60	Luxury Cocktail 125
Brandy Milk Punch 60	Mariposa 130
Brandy Punch 60	Metropolitan Cocktail......... 132
Brandy Sangaree 60	Mikado Cocktail............ 132
Brandy Sling 61	Mississippi Planter's Punch 134
Brandy Smash 61	Mocha Mint 134
Brandy Sour 61	Montana 134
Brandy Squirt 61	Morning Cocktail 136
Brandy Swizzle 61	Nashville Eggnog........... 138, 207
Brandy Toddy 61	Netherland 138

Olympic Cocktail 141
Panama Cocktail 143
Phoebe Snow 146
Polonaise 149
Poop Deck Cocktail 149
Port Wine Cocktail 150
Port Wine Sangaree 150
Pousse Café 151
Pousse L'Amour 151
Prairie Oyster 151
Presto Cocktail 152
Quaker's Cocktail 153
Red Swizzle 156
Rhine Wine Cup 156
St. Charles Punch 163
Santini's Pousse Café 164
Saratoga Cocktail 164
Sauterne Cup 164
Scooter 165
Sherry Twist Cocktail 169
Shriner Cocktail 169
Sidecar Cocktail 170
Sir Walter Cocktail 171
Sloppy Joe's Cocktail No. 2 172
Soother Cocktail 173
Spanish Coffee 173
Special Rough Cocktail 174
Stinger 175
Stirrup Cup 175
Strawberry Fields Forever 176
Third Rail Cocktail 181
Three Miller Cocktail 182
Thunder-and-Lightning 182
Thunderclap 182
Tom-and-Jerry 183
Vanderbilt Cocktail 187
Victor 189
Washington Cocktail 193
Wassail Bowl 193
Waterbury Cocktail 194
Weep-No-More Cocktail 194
Whip Cocktail 195
Widow's Kiss 200
Yolanda 202

CAMPARI DRINKS

Americano 40
Negroni 138
Rosita 159

CHAMPAGNE

Ambrosia 40
Arise My Love 46
Black Velvet 54
Bombay Punch 56
Boom Boom Punch 56
Bucks Fizz (Mimosa) 63
Cardinal Punch 68
Caribbean Champagne 68
Champagne Cocktail 69
Champagne Cup 69
Champagne Punch 69
Champagne Sherbet Punch 70
Count Currey 78
Duke Cocktail 84
French "75" 93
Kir Royale 118
London Special 124
Luxury Cocktail 125
Mimosa 133

Passion Mimosa 35, 145
Ritz Fizz 158
Tequila Punch 180
Typhoon 185

CHARTREUSE (GREEN) DRINKS

Bijou Cocktail 51
Everybody's Irish Cocktail 86
Jewel Cocktail 115
Pousse Café 151
St. Patrick's Day 163
Sand-Martin Cocktail 163
Spring Feeling Cocktail 174
Tailspin Cocktail 178
Tipperary Cocktail 182

CHARTREUSE (YELLOW) DRINKS

Alaska Cocktail 38
Champs Élysées Cocktail 70
Chocolate Cocktail 72
Golden Slipper 101
Pousse Café 151
Widow's Kiss 200
Xanthia Cocktail 201
Yellow Parrot Cocktail 202

CHERRY BRANDY DRINKS

Aquarius 45
Blood-and-Sand Cocktail 54
Canadian Cherry 66
Cherie 71
Cherry Blossom 71
Cherry Fizz 71
Cherry Flip 71
Cherry Rum 71
Cherry Sling 71
Dubonnet Fizz 84
Gilroy Cocktail 97
Hudson Bay 109
Kiss-in-the-Dark 118
Lady Finger 121
Merry Widow Cocktail No. 2 131
Nightmare 139
Orange Oasis 142
Polynesian Cocktail 149
Rose Cocktail (French) 159
Scotch Holiday Sour 165
Singapore Sling 170
Stirrup Cup 175
Vanderbilt Cocktail 187
Wedding Belle Cocktail 194
Xanthia Cocktail 201

CHERRY VODKA DRINKS

Cherry Cooler 71
Rococo 158

CHERRY WINE DRINKS

Cherry Wine Cocktail 71

COBBLERS

These tall drinks are generally made with
plenty of shaved ice, fruit, and liquor, and
served in a large goblet.
Brandy Cobbler 58
Claret Cobbler 73
Gin Cobbler 97
Port Wine Cobbler 150
Rum Cobbler 160
Sherry Cobbler 168
Whiskey Cobbler 195

COFFEE

Black Maria	52
Café Di Amaretto	65
Café Royale	65
Irish Coffee	111
Italian Coffee	112
Jamaica Coffee	112
Mexican Coffee	132
Spanish Coffee	173

COFFEE BRANDY DRINKS

Almeria	39
Black Maria	52
Black Russian	52
Cappucino Cocktail	68
Cara Sposa	68
Coffee Grasshopper	75
Coffee Sour	75
Crème de Café	79
Jamaica Coffee	113
Jamaica Hop	115
Moon Quake Shake	136
Queen Bee	153
Sombrero	172
South of the Border	173
Torridora Cocktail	183

COFFEE LIQUEUR DRINKS

Black Magic	52
Brave Bull	62
Hummer	109
Mexican Coffee	132
Toasted Almond	182
White Russian	199

COGNAC

Ambassador's Morning Lift	40, 205
Cognac Coupling	75
Cognac Highball	75
Eggnog Supreme	85, 207
French Connection	91

COLLINS

These tall, cool drinks belong to the punch family, with Tom and John the best known members.

Apricot Anise Collins	44
Brandy Collins	59
Gables Collins	95
John Collins	116
Mint Collins	133
Rum Collins	160
Sloe Gin Collins	171
Tequila Collins	180
Tom Collins	31, 183
Victory Collins	189
Vodka Collins	190
Whiskey Collins	195

COOLERS

A cooler is a tall warm weather drink not unlike an individual punch.

Apricot Cooler	45
Boston Cooler	57
Cherry Cooler	71
Floradora Cooler	90
Gin Cooler	97
Harvard Cooler	105
Highland Cooler	106
Klondike Cooler	118
Lone Tree Cooler	124
Pineapple Cooler	147
Remsen Cooler	156
Robert E. Lee Cooler	158
Rock and Rye Cooler	158
Rum Cooler	160
Scotch Cooler	165
Vodka Cooler	190
Wine Cooler	200

CRÈME DE BANANA DRINKS

Banana Cow	49
Banshee	49
Boston Gold	57
Capri	68
Caribbean Champagne	68
Hyatt's Jamaican Banana	109
La Jolla	121
Top Banana	183
West Indian Punch	195

CRÈME DE CACAO (BROWN) DRINKS

Ambassador's Morning Lift	40, 205
Brandy Alexander	29, 58
Caledonia	66
Chocolate Rum	72
Fifth Avenue	89
Fox River Cocktail	91
Toreador	183
Velvet Hammer No. 1	187

CRÈME DE CACAO (WHITE) DRINKS

Alexander Cocktail No. 1	38
Alexander Cocktail No. 2	38
Angel's Kiss	41
Angel's Tip	41
Angel's Wing	41
Aunt Jemima	46
Banshee	49
Barbary Coast	49
Barnaby's Buffalo Blizzard	49
Button Hook Cocktail	64
Capri	68
Cole's Raspberry Cream	76
Eye-Opener	87
Flying Grasshopper	90
Golden Cadillac	101
Grasshopper	103
Hyatt's Jamaican Banana	109
Jamaica Hop	115
Jockey Club Cocktail	115
Kretchma Cocktail	120
Maxim	131
Mocha Mint	134
Ninotchka Cocktail	140
Panama Cocktail	143
Peach Bunny	143
Peppermint Pattie	146
Peppermint Stick	146
Pink Squirrel	148
Poppy Cocktail	149
Purple Mask	152
Robin's Nest	158
Russian Bear Cocktail	162
Russian Cocktail	162
Savannah	164
Silk Stockings	170
Tropical Cocktail	184

Velvet Hammer No. 2 189
Vodka Grasshopper 190

CRÈME DE CASSIS DRINKS

Brandy Cassis 58
Kir 117
Kir Royale 118
Parisian 145
Pousse Café 151
Vermouth Cassis 189

CRÈME DE MENTHE (GREEN) DRINKS

Alexander's Sister Cocktail 39
Arise My Love 46
Caruso 69
Continental 76
Crème de Menthe Frappé 79
Emerald Isle Cocktail 86
Everybody's Irish Cocktail 86
Flying Grasshopper 90
Grasshopper 103
Greenback 103
Green Devil 103
Green Dragon 104
Green Fizz 104
Green Swizzle 104
Jade 113
Jocose Julep 116
Mint Highball 133
Port and Starboard 150
St. Patrick's Day 163
Shamrock 168
Tequila Mockingbird 180
Vodka Grasshopper 190
Zero Mist 203

CRÈME DE MENTHE (WHITE) DRINKS

Amaretto Stinger 40
American Beauty Cocktail 40
Bee Stinger 50
Chocolate Rum 72
Coffee Grasshopper 75
Cold Deck Cocktail 76
Crème de Gin Cocktail 79
Diana Cocktail 82
Dixie Whiskey Cocktail 83
Ethel Duffy Cocktail 86
Fallen Angel 88
Fantasio Cocktail 88
Knock-Out Cocktail 118
Lady Be Good 121
Miami 132
Mint on Rocks 134
Mocha Mint 134
Monte Carlo Imperial Highball 136
Pall Mall 143
Peppermint Pattie 146
Pousse Café 151
Scotch Cooler 165
Stinger 175
Virgin 189
Vodka Stinger 191
White Way Cocktail 200

CRÈME DE NOYAUX DRINKS

Gables Collins 95
Mikado Cocktail 132
Pink Squirrel 148

CUPS

These delectable wine cocktails are made with brandy and triple sec mixed with wine, champagne or cider.

Champagne Cup 69
Cider Cup 73
Claret Cup 73
Loving Cup 125
Rhine Wine Cup 156
Sauterne Cup 164
Stirrup Cup 175

CURAÇAO DRINKS

Aqueduct 45
Blanche 54
Blue Devil Cocktail 55
Blue Hawaiian 55
Blue Lagoon 55
Blue Margarita 55
Blue Moon Cocktail 55
Classic Cocktail 74
Crystal Slipper Cocktail 79
Marmalade 130
Napoleon 138
Ritz Fizz 158
Sauterne Cup 164
Stars and Stripes 174
Yale Cocktail 202

DAISIES

These overgrown cocktails are made of liquor, grenadine or liqueurs, and lemon or lime juice, and usually shaken with cracked ice.

Brandy Daisy 59
Canal Street Daisy 68
Chocolate Daisy 72
Gin Daisy 72
Rum Daisy 160
Star Daisy 174
Vodka Daisy 190
Whiskey Daisy 197

DUBONNET DRINKS

Ante 42
Antoine Special 42
Bentley 50
Bushranger 64
Chocolate Soldier 73
Coronation Cocktail 78
Dubonnet Cocktail 84
Dubonnet Fizz 84
Dubonnet Highball 84
Mary Garden Cocktail 131
Napoleon 138
Opera Cocktail 141
Peggy Cocktail 146
Phoebe Snow 146
Rum Dubonnet 160
Soul Kiss Cocktail 173
Temptation Cocktail 178
Trois Rivières 184
Wedding Belle Cocktail 194
Weep-No-More Cocktail 194
Zaza Cocktail 203

EGGNOGS

Dating back to 1775, these punches can be made using almost any liquor. Prepared eggnogs may be substituted for eggs and sugar in any of these recipes. Top with a sprinkle of nutmeg.

Ambassador's Morning Lift 40, 205
Baltimore Eggnog 48, 205
Brandy Eggnog 59, 205
Breakfast Eggnog 62, 205
Christmas Yule Eggnog, ... 73, 205
Cider Eggnog 73
General Harrison's Eggnog 95
Imperial Eggnog. 110, 207
Nashville Eggnog 138, 207
Port Wine Eggnog 150, 207
Rum Eggnog 161, 207
Sherry Eggnog 169, 207
Whiskey Eggnog 197, 207

FIXES

These sweet miniature cobblers are served in highball glasses.

Brandy Fix 59
Gin Fix 98
Rum Fix 161
Whiskey Fix 197

FIZZES

Fizzes are made with liquor, citrus juices, and sugar, then filled with the "fizz" (carbonated beverage).

Alabama Fizz 38
Albemarle Fizz 38
Apple Blow Fizz 42
Apricot Fizz 45
Bird-of-Paradise Fizz 51
Brandy Fizz 59
Bucks Fizz (Mimosa) 63
Cherry Fizz. 71
Chicago Fizz. 72
Cream Fizz 78
Derby Fizz 82
Diamond Fizz 82
Dubonnet Fizz 84
Gin Fizz 98
Golden Fizz 101
Grand Royal Fizz 103
Green Fizz 104
Imperial Fizz. 110
Japanese Fizz 115
Lady Love Fizz 121
Manila Fizz 130
May Blossom Fizz 131
Merry Widow Fizz 132
Morning Glory Fizz 137
New Orleans Gin Fizz 139
Peach Blow Fizz 145
Pineapple Fizz 147
Pink Rose Fizz 148
Ramos Fizz. 155
Royal Gin Fizz 159
Ruby Fizz 160
Silver Fizz 170
Silver Stallion Fizz 170
Sloe Gin Fizz 171
South-Side Fizz 173
Tequila Fizz 180

FLIPS

This combination eggnog and fizz is made with liquor, eggs, sugar and shaken well with cracked ice.

Brandy Flip 59
Cherry Flip 71
Chocolate Flip 72
Coffee Flip 75
Hot Brandy Flip 107
Ice Cream Flip. 110
Port Wine Flip 150
Sherry Flip 169
Sloe Gin Flip 171
Whiskey Flip 197

GALLIANO DRINKS

Barnaby's Buffalo Blizzard 49
Golden Cadillac 101
Golden Dream 101
Harvey Wallbanger 105

GIN

Abbey Cocktail 37
Adam and Eve 37
Alabama Fizz 38
Alaska Cocktail 38
Albemarle Fizz 38
Alexander Cocktail No. 1 38
Alexander's Sister Cocktail 39
Allen Cocktail 39
Allies Cocktail. 39
Angel Face 41
Angler's Cocktail 41
Apricot Anise Collins 44
Apricot Cocktail 45
Artillery. 46
Babbie's Special Cocktail 48
Bachelor's Bait Cocktail 48
Barbary Coast 49
Baron Cocktail. 49
Barton Special 49
Beauty Spot Cocktail 50
Belmont Cocktail 50
Bennett Cocktail. 50
Bermuda Bouquet 51
Bermuda Highball 51
Bermuda Rose 51
Biffy Cocktail 51
Bijou Cocktail 51
Billy Taylor 51
Bird-of-Paradise Fizz 51
Bloodhound Cocktail 54
Blue Bird 55
Blue Devil Cocktail. 55
Blue Moon Cocktail 55
Boomerang 56
Boston Cocktail 57
Brantini 61
Bronx Cocktail 62
Bronx Cocktail (Dry) 62
Bronx Golden Cocktail 62
Bronx Silver Cocktail 63
Bronx Terrace Cocktail 63
Brown Cocktail 63
Bulldog Cocktail 63
Bulldog Highball 63
Cabaret 65
Café de Paris Cocktail 65
Caruso 69
Casino Cocktail 69
Chelsea Sidecar 70
Chocolate Soldier 73
Claridge Cocktail 74
Clover Club Cocktail 74
Clover Leaf Cocktail 74
Club Cocktail 74
Colonial Cocktail 76

261

INDEX

Cooperstown Cocktail 76
Cornell Cocktail 78
Coronation Cocktail 78
Count Currey 78
Cream Fizz 78
Crème de Gin Cocktail. 79
Crimson Cocktail 79
Crystal Slipper Cocktail 79
Damn-the-Weather Cocktail. 81
Darb Cocktail 81
Deep Sea Cocktail 81
Delmonico No. 1 81
Delmonico No. 2 81
Dempsey Cocktail. 82
Diamond Fizz 82
Dixie Cocktail 83
Dr. Cook 83
Double Standard Sour 83
Du Barry Cocktail 84
Dubonnet Cocktail 84
Eclipse Cocktail 85
Emerald Isle Cocktail 86
Emerson 86
English Highball 86
English Rose Cocktail 86
Fairy Belle Cocktail 88
Fallen Angel 88
Fancy Gin 88
Fare Thee Well 88
Farmer's Cocktail 89
Favorite Cocktail 89
Fifty-Fifty Cocktail 89
Fine-and-Dandy Cocktail 89
Fino Martini 89
Flamingo Cocktail 90
Floradora Cooler 90
Florida 90
Flying Dutchman 90
Fog Cutter 91
Fog Horn 91
Frankenjack Cocktail 91
Free Silver 91
French "75" 93
Froth Blower Cocktail 93
Gentle Ben 95
Gilroy Cocktail 96
Gimlet. 30, 97
Gin Aloha 97
Gin and Bitters 97
Gin Buck 97
Gin Cobbler 97
Gin Cocktail 97
Gin Cooler 97
Gin Daisy. 97
Gin Fix 98
Gin Fizz 98
Gin Highball 98
Gin and It 98
Gin Milk Punch 98
Gin Rickey. 98
Gin Sangaree. 98
Gin and Sin 98
Gin Sling 98
Gin Smash 99
Gin Sour 99
Gin Squirt 99
Gin Swizzle 99
Gin Thing 99
Gin Toddy 99
Gin Toddy (Hot) 99
Gin and Tonic 30, 100
Golden Dawn 101

Golden Daze 101
Golden Fizz 101
Golf Cocktail 101
Grand Royal Fizz 103
Grapefruit Cocktail 103
Greenback 103
Green Devil 103
Green Dragon 104
Green Fizz 104
Green Opal 104
Green Swizzle 104
Gypsy Cocktail 104
Harlem Cocktail 105
Hasty Cocktail 105
Hawaiian Cocktail 106
Hoffman House Cocktail 106
Hokkaido Cocktail 106
Homestead Cocktail 106
Honolulu Cocktail No. 1 107
Honolulu Cocktail No. 2 107
Hotel Plaza Cocktail 108
H.P.W. Cocktail 108
Hudson Bay 109
Hula-Hula Cocktail 109
Ideal Cocktail 110
Imperial Cocktail 110
Income Tax Cocktail 111
Jamaica Glow 113
Jean Lafitte Cocktail 115
Jewel Cocktail 115
Jeyplak Cocktail 115
Jockey Club Cocktail 115
Joulouville 116
Journalist Cocktail 116
Judge Jr. Cocktail. 116
Judgette Cocktail 116
K.G.B. Cocktail. 117
Kiss-in-the-Dark. 118
Knickerbocker Cocktail 118
Knock-Out Cocktail 118
Kup's Indispensible Cocktail 120
Lady Finger 121
Lady Love Fizz 121
Lasky Cocktail 121
Leap Frog Highball. 122
Leap Year Cocktail 122
Leave-it-to-Me Cocktail No. 1 122
Leave-it-to-Me Cocktail No. 2 122
Little Devil Cocktail 123
London Buck 124
London Cocktail. 124
Lone Tree Cocktail 124
Lone Tree Cooler 124
Long Island Tea 35, 124
Maiden's Blush Cocktail. 128
Maiden's Prayer. 128
Major Bailey 129
Mamie's Sister. 129
Manila Fizz 130
Martinez Cocktail 130
Maurice Cocktail 131
Maxim 131
Melon Cocktail 131
Merry Widow Cocktail No. 1 131
Million Dollar Cocktail 133
Mr. Manhattan Cocktail 134
Monte Carlo Imperial Highball 136
Montmartre Cocktail 136
Montreal Club Bouncer 136
Montreal Gin Sour 136
Morro 137
Napoleon 138

Negroni 138	Snowball 172
New Orleans Gin Fizz 139	Snyder. 172
Nightmare 139	Society Cocktail 172
North Pole Cocktail. 140	Southern Bride. 173
Opal Cocktail 141	Southern Gin Cocktail 173
Opera Cocktail. 141	South-Side Cocktail. 173
Orange Blossom 141	South-Side Fizz 173
Orange Buck. 142	Spencer Cocktail 174
Orange Oasis 142	Sphinx Cocktail 174
Paisley Martini 143	Spring Feeling Cocktail 174
Pall Mall 143	Stanley Cocktail. 174
Palm Beach Cocktail 143	Star Daisy 174
Papaya Sling 143	Straight Law Cocktail 175
Paradise Cocktail 145	Strawberry Dawn 176
Parisian 145	Sunshine Cocktail. 176
Park Avenue 145	Sweet Patootie Cocktail 177
Peach Blossom 145	Tailspin Cocktail 178
Peach Blow Fizz 145	Tango Cocktail 178
Peggy Cocktail 146	Thanksgiving Special. 181
Perfect Cocktail 146	Third Degree Cocktail 181
Peter Pan Cocktail 146	Three Stripes Cocktail 182
Piccadilly Cocktail 146	Thunderclap 182
Pink Lady 147	Tidbit 182
Pink Pussy Cat 147	Tom Collins 31, 183
Pink Rose Fizz 148	Trinity Cocktail 184
Plaza Cocktail 148	Turf Cocktail. 184
Pollyanna 149	Tuxedo Cocktail 184
Polo Cocktail 149	Twin Six Cocktail. 185
Pompano 149	Typhoon 185
Poppy Cocktail 149	Ulanda Cocktail 186
Prairie Chicken 151	Union Jack Cocktail 186
Prince's Smile 152	Verboten 189
Princeton Cocktail 152	Victor 189
Queen Elizabeth 153	Virgin 189
Racquet Club Cocktail 155	Waikiki Beachcomber 192
Ramos Fizz. 155	Wallick Cocktail 192
Red Cloud 155	Wallis Blue Cocktail 192
Remsen Cooler 156	Webster Cocktail 194
Renaissance Cocktail 156	Wedding Belle Cocktail 194
Resolute Cocktail 156	Wembly Cocktail 194
Robert E. Lee Cooler 158	Western Rose 195
Rolls-Royce 159	What the Hell 195
Rose Cocktail (English) 159	White Cargo Cocktail 199
Rose Cocktail (French). 159	White Elephant 199
Roselyn Cocktail 159	White Lady. 199
Royal Clover Club Cocktail. 159	White Lily Cocktail. 199
Royal Cocktail. 159	White Rose Cocktail 199
Royal Gin Fizz 159	White Way Cocktail 200
Royal Smile Cocktail 160	Why Not? 200
Rum Runner 161	Will Rogers 200
Russian Cocktail 162	Woodstock 200
Sake Martini (Sakini). 163	Xanthia Cocktail 201
Salty Dog 163	Yale Cocktail 202
Sand-Martin Cocktail 163	Yellow Rattler 202
San Sebastian 164	Yolanda 202
Savannah 164	Zaza Cocktail 203
Seaboard 167	
Sensation Cocktail 167	**HIGHBALLS**
Seventh Heaven Cocktail 167	
Shady Grove 168	These are all-time favorites and simple to
Silver Bullet 170	make. Any liquor may be used in
Silver Cocktail 170	combination with ice, soda, or water.
Silver Fizz 170	Apple Brandy Highball 44
Silver King Cocktail 170	Bermuda Highball. 51
Silver Stallion Fizz 170	Billy Taylor 51
Silver Streak 170	Bitters Highball 52
Singapore Sling 170	Bourbon Highball. 58
Smile Cocktail 172	Brandy Highball 60
Smiler Cocktail 172	Bulldog Highball 63
	Bull's Eye 63

Cablegram Highball 65
Cognac Highball 75
Cuba Libre 79
Dubonnet Highball 84
English Highball 86
Gin Highball 98
Gin and Tonic 30, 100
Horse's Neck 107
Irish Whisky Highball 111
Jamaica Granito 113
Leap Frog Highball 122
London Buck 124
Mamie Gilroy 129
Mint Highball 133
Monte Carlo Imperial Highball 136
Rum Highball 161
Rye Highball 162
Scotch Highball 165
Spritzer 174
Stone Fence 175
Susie Taylor 177
Vodka and Tonic 190
Whiskey Highball 197

HOT DRINKS

American Grog 40
Aprihot 45
Blue Blazer 55
Brandy Blazer 58
Brandy Toddy (Hot) 61
Café Di Amaretto 65
Café Royale 65
Gin Toddy (Hot) 99
Glögg 100
Hot Brandy Flip 107
Hot Brick Toddy 107
Hot Buttered Rum 108
Hot Buttered Wine 108
Hot Gold 108
Indian Summer 35, 111
Irish Coffee 111
Jamaica Coffee 113
Mexican Coffee 132
Mulled Claret 137
Night Cap 139
Port Wine Negus 150
Rum Toddy (Hot) 162
Spanish Coffee 173
Tom-and-Jerry 183
Wassail Bowl 193
Whiskey Skin 198
Whiskey Toddy (Hot) 198

IRISH WHISKY DRINKS

Blarney Stone Cocktail 54
Cameron's Kick Cocktail 66
Everybody's Irish Cocktail 86
Irish Coffee 111
Irish Rickey 111
Irish Shillelagh 111
Irish Whisky 111
Irish Whisky Highball 111
Paddy Cocktail 143
Rory O'More 159
St. Patrick's Day 163
Shamrock 168
Tipperary Cocktail 182

JULEPS

Native to Kentucky, juleps are cool and refreshing anywhere. Traditionally made with Kentucky bourbon and fresh mint leaves and served in a frosted glass with straws.

Brandy Julep 60
Dixie Julep 83
Georgia Mint Julep 95
Jocose Julep 116
Mint Julep 133
Mint Julep (Southern Style) 134

KIRSCHWASSER DRINKS

Blackjack 52
Florida 90
Lady Finger 121

KÜMMEL DRINKS

Allies Cocktail 39
Green Dragon 104
K.G.B. Cocktail 117
Silver Bullet 170
Silver Streak 170
Tovarich Cocktail 184

LEMON VODKA DRINKS

Alfie Cocktail 39

LIME LIQUEUR DRINKS

Limey 123

LIME VODKA DRINKS

Green Hornet (Dry) 104
Lime Giant 123
Outrigger 142
Queen Bee 153

LOW-ALCOHOL DRINKS

These are drinks that contain $1/3$ to $1/2$ less alcohol than a standard drink (5 oz. of wine, 12 oz. of beer, or a drink containing $1 1/2$ oz. of spirits). They are marked throughout book with the symbol **Ⓛ**

Adonis Cocktail 37
Amer Picon Cocktail 41
Angel Face 41
Bamboo Cocktail 48
Bellini 32, 50
Bitters Highball 52
Bittersweet 52
Bucks Fizz (Mimosa) 63
Café Royale 65
Country Club Cooler 78
Dubonne® Highball 84
Duke Cocktail 84
East India Cocktail No. 2 85
Eclipse Cocktail 85
Hot Springs Cocktail 108
Kir 117
Mimosa 133
Mint Gin Cocktail 133
Passion Mimosa 35, 145
Picon Cocktail 146
Pineapple Cooler 147
Plain Vermouth Cocktail 148
Port Milk Punch 150
Port Wine Flip 150, 207
Port Wine Negus 150

Queen Charlotte 153
Reform Cocktail 156
Royal Purple Punch 160
Sangria 164
Shandy Gaff 168
Sherry-And-Egg Cocktail 168
Sherry Cobbler 168
Sherry Cocktail 169
Sherry Eggnog 169, 207
Sherry Flip 169
Sherry Milk Punch 169
Spritzer 174
Tomboy 183
Vermouth Cocktail 189
Wine Cooler 200
Xeres Cocktail 201

MARTINIS

The original martini recipe called for half dry gin and half dry vermouth. Today, popular proportions for an extra dry martini range from 5-to-1 to an 8-to-1 ratio. The greater proportion of gin to vermouth, the "drier" the martini. Always pour the gin first then the vermouth.

Boston Bullet 57
Dillatini 82
Dry Martini 84
Fino Martini 89
Gibson 95
Martini 130
Martini (Extra Dry) 30, 130
Martini (Medium) 130
Martini (Sweet) 130
Paisley Martini 143
Rum Martini 161
Sake Martini (Sakini) 163
Tequini 181

MELON LIQUEUR DRINKS

Green Demon 103
Melon Ball 35, 131
Shady Lady 168

MINT GIN DRINKS

Mint Collins 133
Mint Gin Cocktail 133

NO-ALCOHOL DRINKS

Beach Blanket Bingo 208
Bitters Highball 52
Cranberry Cooler 208
Creamy Creamsicle 208
Fuzzy Lemon Fizz 208
Fruit Smoothie 208
Grapeberry 208
Innocent Passion 208
Lemon Squash 209
Lemonade (Carbonated) 209
Lemonade (Egg) 209
Lemonade (Fruit) 209
Lemonade (Golden) 209
Lemonade (Plain) 209
Lime Cola 209
Lime Cooler 209
Limeade 209
Orange and Tonic 210
Orange Smile 210
Orangeade 210
Pac Man 210
Passion Fruit Spritzer 210

Peach Melba 210
Pike's Peak Cooler 210
Punchless Piña Colada 210
Rumless Rickey 211
Runners Mark 211
Shirley Temple 211
Tomato Cooler 211
Unfuzzy Navel 211
Virgin Mary 211

ORANGE LIQUEUR DRINKS

Waterloo 194

ORANGE GIN DRINKS

Leap Year Cocktail 122

PEACH BRANDY DRINKS

Corkscrew 76
Fish House Punch 90
Georgia Mint Julep 95
Golden Daze 101
Judgette Cocktail 116
Outrigger 142
Peach Bunny 145
Peach Sangaree 146

PEACH SCHNAPPS DRINKS

Fuzzy Navel 23, 94
Woo Woo 35, 200

PEPPERMINT SCHNAPPS DRINKS

Depth Charge 82
Hot Pants 108
Peppermint Iceberg 146
Peppermint Stick 146
Shavetail 168

POUSSE CAFÉS

These sweet, striped wonders are made from a series of liqueurs poured in succession so that one floats on top of another. Follow the recipes exactly to get the layers of ingredients in the right order.

Angel's Delight 41
Angel's Kiss 41
Angel's Tip 41
Angel's Wing 41
Fifth Avenue 89
Port and Starboard 150
Pousse Café 151
Pousse L'Amour 151
Princess Pousse Café 152
Santini's Pousse Café 164
Stars and Stripes 174

PUNCHES

Perfect for gatherings, punches can be mixed in endless variety.

Ambassador's Morning Lift 40
Applejack Punch 44
Banana Punch 49
Bombay Punch 56
Boom Boom Punch 56
Brandy Milk Punch 60
Brandy Punch 60
Brighton Punch 62
Cardinal Punch 68
Champagne Punch 69
Champagne Sherbet Punch 70
Claret Punch 74
Fish House Punch 90

Gin Milk Punch 98
Glögg 100
Irish Shillelagh 111
Milk Punch 133
Planter's Punch No. 1 148
Planter's Punch No. 2 148
Port Milk Punch 150
Royal Purple Punch. 160
Rum Milk Punch 161
St. Charles Punch 163
Scotch Milk Punch 165
Sherry Milk Punch 169
Tequila Punch 180
West Indian Punch 195
Whiskey Milk Punch 197

RICKEYS

A cross between a collins and a sour,
rickeys are always made with lime,
cracked ice, and a carbonated beverage.
Apple Brandy Rickey 44
Apple Rum Rickey 44
Apricot Brandy Rickey. 44
Fog Horn 91
Gin Rickey 98
Irish Rickey 111
Rum Rickey 161
Scotch Rickey 167
Sloe Gin Rickey. 171
Twister 185
Whiskey Rickey 197

ROCK AND RYE DRINKS

Hair Raiser 105
Rock and Rye Cocktail 158
Rock and Rye Cooler 158

RUM DRINKS

Acapulco 37
Almeria 39
Ambassador's Morning Lift 40, 205
American Grog 40
Andalusia 41
Apple Pie No. 1. 44
Apple Rum Rickey 44
Apricot Lady 45
Bacardi Cocktail. 48
Bahama Mama 32, 48
Baltimore Eggnog 48, 205
Banana Cow 49
Banana Daiquiri 49
Barbary Coast 49
Beachcomber 49
Between-the-Sheets 51
Bikini 51
Black Devil 52
Black Maria 52
Blue Hawaiian 55
Bolero 56
Boom Boom Punch 56
Borinquen 57
Boston Cooler 57
Boston Sidecar. 57
Brown Cocktail 63
Buck Jones 63
Bull's Milk 64
Burgundy Bishop 64
Bushranger 64
Calm Voyage 66
Canado Saludo. 68

Cape Codder 68
Cardinal Punch 68
Caribbean Champagne 68
Casa Blanca 69
Chateau Briand's Rum Cow 70
Cherie 71
Cherry Rum 71
Chicago Fizz. 72
Chinese Cocktail 72
Chocolate Rum 72
Christmas Yule Eggnog 73, 205
Cocomacoque 75
Continental 76
Corkscrew 76
Cream Puff. 78
Crème de Café. 79
Creole 79
Cuba Libre 79
Cuban Cocktail No. 1 80
Cuban Cocktail No. 2 80
Cuban Special 80
Daiquiri 29, 81
Derby Daiquiri 82
Devil's Tail 82
East India Cocktail No. 1 85
El Presidente Cocktail No. 1 86
El Presidente Cocktail No. 2 86
Eye-Opener 87
Fair-and-Warmer Cocktail 88
Fireman's Sour 89
Fish House Punch. 90
Fog Cutter 91
Fort Lauderdale 91
Free Silver 91
Frozen Berkeley 93
Frozen Brandy and Rum. 93
Frozen Daiquiri 94
Frozen Mint Daiquiri 94
Frozen Pineapple Daiquiri 94
Gaugin 95
Golden Friendship 101
Green Demon 103
Havana Cocktail 106
Hop Toad. 107
Hot Buttered Rum 108
Hudson Bay 109
Hummer 109
Huntsman Cocktail 109
Hurricane 109
Hyatt's Jamaican Banana 109
Imperial Fizz 110
Irish Shillelagh 111
Jade 113
Jamaica Coffee 113
Jamaica Glow 113
Judge Jr. Cocktail 116
Knickerbocker Special Cocktail 118
Liberty Cocktail 123
Limey 123
Little Devil Cocktail 123
Little Princess Cocktail 123
Long Island Tea 35, 124
Look Out Below 125
Mai-Tai 128
Malmaison 129
Mandeville 129
Mariposa 130
Mary Pickford Cocktail 131
Miami 132
Mississippi Planters Punch .

Modern Cocktail 134
Moon Quake Shake. 136
Morro 137
Nashville Eggnog 138, 207
Nevada Cocktail. 138
New Orleans Buck 139
Night Cap 139
Palmetto Cocktail 143
Parisian Blonde 145
Passion Daiquiri 145
Piña Colada 30, 147
Pineapple Cocktail 147
Pineapple Fizz 147
Pink Creole 147
Planter's Cocktail 148
Planter's Punch No. 1 148
Planter's Punch No. 2 148
Poker Cocktail 149
Puerto Apple 152
Quaker's Cocktail 153
Quarter Deck Cocktail 153
Red Swizzle 156
Robson Cocktail 158
Rum Cobbler 160
Rum Collins 160
Rum Cooler 160
Rum Daisy 160
Rum Dubonnet 160
Rum Eggnog 161, 207
Rum Fix 161
Rum Highball 161
Rum Martini 161
Rum Milk Punch 161
Rum Old Fashioned 161
Rum Rickey 161
Rum Screwdriver 161
Rum Sour 161
Rum Toddy 161
Rum Toddy (Hot) 161
San Sebastian 164
Santiago Cocktail 164
Santini's Pousse Café 164
Saxon Cocktail 165
September Morn Cocktail 167
Sevilla Cocktail 168
Shanghai Cocktail 168
Sir Walter Cocktail 171
Sloppy Joe's Cocktail No. 1 172
Spanish Town Cocktail 174
Stanley Cocktail 174
Stone Cocktail 175
Strawberry Daiquiri 175
Susie Taylor 177
Tahiti Club 178
Tchoupitolas Street Guzzle 178
Third Rail Cocktail 183
Three Miller Cocktail 182
Tom-and-Jerry 183
Torridora Cocktail 183
Van Vleet 187
Vesuvio 189
Waterloo 194
West Indian Punch 195
White Lady Cocktail 199
White Lion Cocktail 199
X.Y.Z. Cocktail 201
Zombie 203
S̄ ̶ ̶DRINKS
. . . . 106
. . . . 163

SANGAREES
These are taller, sweet old-fashioneds
without bitters.
Brandy Sangaree 60
Gin Sangaree. 98
Peach Sangaree 146
Port Wine Sangaree 150
Sherry Sangaree 169
Whiskey Sangaree 198

SCOTCH
Affinity Cocktail 38
Barbary Coast 49
Barton Special 49
Beadlestone Cocktail 50
Beals Cocktail 50
Blood-and-Sand Cocktail 54
Bobby Burns Cocktail 56
Cameron's Kick Cocktail 66
Derby Fizz 82
Flying Scotchman 90
Godfather 100
Highland Cooler. 106
Highland Fling Cocktail 106
Hole-in-One 106
Hoot Mon Cocktail 107
Mamie Gilroy 129
Miami Beach Cocktail 132
Modern Cocktail 134
Morning Glory Fizz 137
Paisley Martini 143
Rob Roy 158
Rusty Nail 162
Scotch Bird Flyer 165
Scotch Bishop Cocktail 165
Scotch Cooler 165
Scotch Highball 165
Scotch Holiday Sour 165
Scotch Milk Punch 165
Scotch Mist 165
Scotch Old Fashioned 167
Scotch Rickey 167
Scotch Sour 167
Scotch Stinger 167
The Shoot 169
Stone Fence 175
Thistle Cocktail 181
Walters 192
Woodward Cocktail. 200

SLINGS
These are like sangarees, but made with
the addition of lemon juice and a twist of
lemon peel.
Brandy Sling 61
Gin Sling 98
Papaya Sling 143
Singapore Sling 170
Vodka Sling 190
Whiskey Sling 198

SLOE GIN DRINKS
Alabama Slammer 32, 38
Angel's Delight 41
Angel's Kiss 41
Black Hawk 52
Blackthorn 52
Charlie Chaplin 70
Chocolate Flip 72
Clove Cocktail 74
Eclipse Cocktail 85

Irish Shillelagh 111
Johnnie Cocktail. 116
Kiss the Boys Goodbye 118
Lemonade (Modern) 122
Love Cocktail 125
McClelland Cocktail 131
Merry Widow Fizz 132
Moulin Rouge 137
Ping-Pong Cocktail 147
Ruby Fizz 160
San Francisco Cocktail 163
Shriner Cocktail 169
Sloeberry Cocktail 171
Sloe Driver 171
Sloe Gin Cocktail 171
Sloe Gin Collins 171
Sloe Gin Fizz 171
Sloe Gin Flip 171
Sloe Gin Rickey 171
Sloe Tequila 172
Sloe Vermouth. 172
Union Jack Cocktail 186

SMASHES

These are junior-sized juleps.
Brandy Smash 61
Gin Smash 99
Whiskey Smash 198

SOURS

Sours are tart lemony cocktails similar to
highly concentrated punches.
Amaretto Sour 40
Apple Brandy Sour 42
Boston Sour 57
Brandy Sour 61
Coffee Sour 75
Double Standard Sour 83
Egg Sour 85
Fireman's Sour 89
Frisco Sour 93
Gin Sour 99
Montreal Gin Sour 136
New York Sour 139
Rum Sour. 162
Scotch Holiday Sour 165
Scotch Sour 167
Tequila Sour 181
Vodka Sour 191
Whiskey Sour 198

STRAWBERRY LIQUEUR DRINKS

Watermelon 194

STRAWBERRY SCHNAPPS DRINKS

Affair 37
Strawberries and Cream 175
Strawberry Daiquiri 175
Strawberry Fields Forever 176
Strawberry Margarita. 176
Strawberry Sunrise 176

STREGA DRINKS

Calm Voyage 66
Velvet Hammer No. 2 187

SWEDISH PUNCH DRINKS

Biffy Cocktail 51
Lasky Cocktail 121
May Blossom Fizz 131

SWIZZLES

These drinks originally came from the
West Indies where a swizzle stick was a
twig having three to five forked branches
on the end.
Brandy Swizzle 61
Gin Swizzle 99
Green Swizzle 104
Red Swizzle 156
Rum Swizzle. 162
Whiskey Swizzle 198

TEQUILA DRINKS

Bloody Bull 54
Bloody Maria 54
Blue Margarita. 32, 55
Brave Bull 62
Chapala 70
Frozen Margarita 94
Frozen Matador 94
Gentle Ben 95
Hot Pants 108
Hot Shot Margarita 108
Margarita 30, 130
Mexicana 132
Mexican Coffee 132
Mexicola 132
Montezuma 136
Prado 151
Rosita 159
Shady Lady 168
Silk Stockings 170
Sloe Tequila 172
South of the Border. 173
Strawberry Margarita 176
Tequila Cocktail 180
Tequila Collins 180
Tequila Fizz 180
Tequila Manhattan 180
Tequila Matador 180
Tequila Mockingbird 180
Tequila Old Fashioned 180
Tequila Pink 180
Tequila Punch 180
Tequila Sour 181
Tequila Straight 181
Tequila Sunrise 30, 181
Tequini 181
Tequonic 181
T.N.T. No. 2 182
Toreador 183
Viva Villa 190

TODDIES

These may be served either hot or cold.
Brandy Toddy 61
Brandy Toddy (Hot) 61
Gin Toddy (Hot) 99
Hot Brick Toddy 107
Hot Buttered Rum 108
Pendennis Toddy 146
Rum Toddy 162
Rum Toddy (Hot) 162
Whiskey Toddy (Cold). 198
Whiskey Toddy (Hot) 198

TRIPLE SEC DRINKS

Acapulco 37
After Dinner Cocktail 38
After Supper Cocktail . . . . .
Alfie Cocktail . . . . .

Ambrosia	40
Angel's Delight	41
Ante	42
Applecar	42
Apricot Lady	45
Banana Daiquiri	49
Baron Cocktail	49
Beachcomber	49
Bermuda Bouquet	51
Betsy Ross	51
Between-the-Sheets	51
Blanche	54
Blarney Stone Cocktail	54
Blue Bird	55
Blue Monday Cocktail	55
Bombay Cocktail	56
Bombay Punch	56
Bosom Caresser	57
Boston Sidecar	57
Brandy Crusta Cocktail	59
Brandy Punch	60
Breakfast Eggnog	62, 205
Broken Spur Cocktail	62
Cadiz	65
Canadian Cocktail	66
Cara Sposa	68
Casa Blanca	69
Champagne Cup	69
Champagne Punch	69
Chapala	70
Chapel Hill	70
Chelsea Sidecar	70
Cherie	71
Cherry Blossom	71
Chicago Cocktail	72
Chinese Cocktail	72
Cider Cup	73
Claret Cup	73
Claret Punch	74
Claridge Cocktail	74
Combo	76
Cuban Special	80
Damn-the-Weather Cocktail	81
Deauville Cocktail	81
Derby Fizz	82
Dixie Whiskey Cocktail	83
Dream Cocktail	83
Duke Cocktail	84
East Indian Cocktail No. 1	85
Egg Sour	85
Ethel Duffy Cocktail	86
Eye-Opener	87
Fair-and-Warmer Cocktail	88
Fancy Brandy	88
Fancy Gin	88
Fancy Whiskey	88
Fare Thee Well	88
Fine-and-Dandy Cocktail	89
Florida	90
Flying Dutchman	90
Frankenjack Cocktail	91
Frozen Daiquiri	94
Frozen Margarita	94
Gin Aloha	97
Golden Dream	101
Hawaiian Cocktail	106
Hokkaido Cocktail	106
Jade ~~ ~~ Cocktail	107
~~ ~~	110
~~ ~~	111
~~ ~~	113

Jamaica Granito	113
Jean Lafitte Cocktail	115
Johnnie Cocktail	116
Journalist Cocktail	116
Kamikaze	35, 117
Knickerbocker Special Cocktail	118
Limey	123
Little Devil Cocktail	123
Long Island Tea	124
Loving Cup	125
Maiden's Blush Cocktail	128
Maiden's Prayer	128
Mai-Tai	128
Margarita	30, 130
Martinez Cocktail	130
McClelland Cocktail	131
Midnight Cocktail	132
Mikado Cocktail	132
Millionaire Cocktail	133
Montmartre Cocktail	136
Morning Cocktail	136
Netherland	138
New Orleans Gin Fizz	139
Olympic Cocktail	141
Opal Cocktail	141
Oriental Cocktail	142
Parisian Blonde	145
Planter's Punch No. 2	148
Ramos Fizz	155
Rebel Charge	155
Red Raider	156
Rhine Wine Cup	156
Rococo	158
St. Charles Punch	163
San Sebastian	164
Santini's Pousse Café	164
Sauterne Cup	164
Scotch Bird Flyer	165
Scotch Bishop Cocktail	165
Sherry Twist Cocktail	169
Sidecar Cocktail	170
Sir Walter Cocktail	171
Sloppy Joe's Cocktail No. 1	172
Sloppy Joe's Cocktail No. 2	172
Snyder	172
Soother Cocktail	173
Southern Gin Cocktail	173
Spanish Town Cocktail	174
Strawberry Margarita	176
Sweet Patootie Cocktail	177
Tango Cocktail	178
Temptation Cocktail	178
Trois Rivières	184
Ulanda Cocktail	186
Waikiki Beachcomber	192
Wallick Cocktail	192
Wallis Blue Cocktail	192
Whip Cocktail	195
White Lady Cocktail	199
Will Rogers	200
X.Y.Z. Cocktail	201

TROPICAL FRUIT LIQUEUR DRINKS

Hot Shot Margarita	108
Sunburn	176
Suntan	176
Tahitian Tea	178
Tropical Heart	184
Woo Woo	35, 200

VANILLA LIQUEUR DRINKS

Creamsicle 78

VERMOUTH DRINKS

Adonis Cocktail 37
Affinity Cocktail 38
Algonquin 39
Allegheny 39
Allies Cocktail 39
American Beauty Cocktail 40
Americano 40
Antoine Special 42
Apple Pie No. 1 44
Artillery 46
Bamboo Cocktail 48
Baron Cocktail 49
Beadlestone Cocktail 50
Beals Cocktail 50
Beauty Spot Cocktail 50
Bermuda Highball 51
Bijou Cocktail 51
Bittersweet 52
Black Devil 52
Blackthorn 52
Blood-and-Sand Cocktail 54
Bloodhound Cocktail 54
Bobby Burns Cocktail 56
Bolero 56
Bombay Cocktail 56
Boom Boom Punch 56
Boomerang 56
Brandied Madeira 58
Brandy Vermouth Cocktail 61
Brantini 61
Brazil Cocktail 62
Broken Spur Cocktail 62
Bronx Cocktail 62
Bronx Cocktail (Dry) 62
Bronx Golden Cocktail 62
Bronx Silver Cocktail 63
Bronx Terrace Cocktail 63
Brown Cocktail 63
Cabaret 65
Cardinal Punch 68
Carrol Cocktail 69
Caruso 69
Charles Cocktail 70
Claridge Cocktail 74
Clove Cocktail 74
Club Cocktail 74
Cold Deck Cocktail 76
Combo 76
Cooperstown Cocktail 76
Corkscrew 76
Coronation Cocktail 78
Country Club Cooler 78
Damn-the-Weather Cocktail 81
Darb Cocktail 81
Deep Sea Cocktail 81
Delmonico No. 1 81
Delmonico No. 2 81
Devil's Cocktail 82
Diplomat 83
Dixie Cocktail 83
Dry Martini 84
Du Barry Cocktail 84
Duchess 84
East India Cocktail No. 2 85
El Presidente Cocktail No. 2 86
Emerson 86
English Highball 86

English Rose Cocktail 86
Extra Dry Martini 30, 130
Fair-and-Warmer Cocktail 88
Fantasio Cocktail 88
Fare Thee Well 88
Farmer's Cocktail 89
Favorite Cocktail 89
Ferrari 89
Fifty-Fifty Cocktail 89
Flying Scotchman 90
Fontainbleau Special 91
Fort Lauderdale 91
Frankenjack Cocktail 91
Froupe Cocktail 93
Gilroy Cocktail 97
Gin and It 98
Golden Friendship 101
Golf Cocktail 101
Gypsy Cocktail 104
Harvard Cocktail 105
Hasty Cocktail 105
Highland Fling Cocktail 106
Hoffman House Cocktail 106
Hole-in-One 106
Homestead Cocktail 106
Hoot Mon Cocktail 107
Hotel Plaza Cocktail 108
H.P.W. Cocktail 108
Ideal Cocktail 110
Imperial Cocktail 110
Income Tax Cocktail 111
Jersey Lightning 115
Jewel Cocktail 115
Jeyplak Cocktail 115
Joulouville 116
Journalist Cocktail 116
Judgette Cocktail 116
Kangaroo Cocktail 117
Kiss-in-the-Dark 118
Knickerbocker Cocktail 118
Knock-Out Cocktail 118
Kup's Indispensable Cocktail 120
Lady Be Good 121
Lawhill Cocktail 122
Leap Year Cocktail 122
Leave-it-to-Me Cocktail No. 1 122
Little Princess 123
Lone Tree Cocktail 124
Lone Tree Cooler 124
Los Angeles Cocktail 125
Manhasset 129
Manhattan 30, 129
Manhattan (Dry) 129
Martinez Cocktail 130
Martini 130
Martini (Extra Dry) 30, 130
Martini (Medium) 130
Martini (Sweet) 130
Mary Garden Cocktail 131
Maurice Cocktail 131
Maxim 131
Merry Widow Cocktail No. 1 131
Metropolitan Cocktail 132
Miami Beach Cocktail 132
Million Dollar Cocktail 133
Mint Gin Cocktail 133
Montana 134
Montmartre Cocktail 136
Morning Cocktail 136
Moulin Rouge 137
Mountain Cocktail 137

Narragansett	138
Negroni	138
Old Pal Cocktail	141
Opening Cocktail	141
Oriental Cocktail	142
Paddy Cocktail	143
Paisley Martini	143
Pall Mall	143
Palm Beach Cocktail	143
Palmetto Cocktail	143
Parisian	145
Park Avenue	145
Peggy Cocktail	146
Perfect Cocktail	146
Peter Pan Cocktail	146
Piccadilly Cocktail	146
Plaza Cocktail	148
Poker Cocktail	149
Pollyanna	149
Pompano	149
Preakness Cocktail	151
Presto Cocktail	152
Princeton Cocktail	152
Quebec	153
Queen Elizabeth	153
Racquet Club Cocktail	155
Reform Cocktail	156
Rob Roy	158
Rock and Rye Cocktail	158
Rolls-Royce	159
Rory O'More	159
Rose Cocktail (English)	159
Rose Cocktail (French)	159
Roselyn Cocktail	159
Rosita	159
Rum Martini	161
Sand-Martin Cocktail	163
San Francisco Cocktail	163
Scotch Bishop Cocktail	165
Scotch Holiday Sour	165
Shamrock	168
Sherry Twist Cocktail	169
Silver Cocktail	170
Sloe Gin Cocktail	171
Sloe Vermouth	172
Sloppy Joe's Cocktail No. 1	172
Smiler Cocktail	172
Snyder	172
Society Cocktail	172
Soul Kiss Cocktail	173
Soviet	173
Sphinx Cocktail	174
Star Cocktail	174
Sunshine Cocktail	176
Surf Rider	177
Swiss Family Cocktail	177
Tailspin Cocktail	178
Tango Cocktail	178
Tequila Manhattan	180
Tequila Pink	180
Tequini	181
Thanksgiving Special	181
Third Degree Cocktail	181
Thistle Cocktail	181
Three Stripes Cocktail	182
Tipperary Cocktail	182
Trilby Cocktail	184
Trinity Cocktail	184
Tropical Cocktail	184
Tulip Cocktail	184
Turf Cocktail	184
Tuxedo Cocktail	184
Twin Six Cocktail	185
Vermouth Cassis	189
Vermouth Cocktail	189
Vesuvio	189
Victor	189
Wallick Cocktail	192
Warsaw Cocktail	192
Washington Cocktail	193
Watermelon	194
Webster Cocktail	194
Wembly Cocktail	194
Western Rose	195
What the Hell	195
Whip Cocktail	195
White Elephant	199
Why Not?	200
Will Rogers	200
Woodward Cocktail	200
Yale Cocktail	202
Yellow Rattler	202
Yolanda	202

VODKA DRINKS

Aqueduct	45
Banana Punch	49
Barnaby's Buffalo Blizzard	49
Beer Buster	50
Bikini	51
Black Magic	52
Black Russian	29, 52
Bloody Mary	29, 54
Blue Lagoon	55
Blue Monday Cocktail	55
Boston Gold	57
Bull Frog	63
Bull Shot	64
Cape Codder	32, 68
Cappucino Cocktail	68
Cherry Wine Cocktail	71
Chi-Chi	72
Clamato Cocktail	73
Cole's Raspberry Cream	76
Creamy Screwdriver	79
Devil's Tail	82
Flying Grasshopper	90
Gables Collins	95
Gentle Ben	95
Gibson	95
Godchild	100
Godmother	100
Grape Vodka Froth	103
Green Demon	103
Hair Raiser	105
Harvey Wallbanger	105
Headless Horseman	106
Huntsman Cocktail	109
Kamikaze	35, 117
Kangaroo Cocktail	117
Kretchma Cocktail	120
Long Island Tea	35, 124
Madras	128
Melon Ball	35, 131
Moscow Mule	137
Ninotchka Cocktail	140
Pink Pussy Cat	147
Polynesian Cocktail	149
Purple Mask	152
Purple Passion	152
Red Apple	155
Road Runner	158

Robin's Nest	158
Rock and Rye Cooler	158
Rococo	158
Russian Bear Cocktail	162
Russian Cocktail	162
Salty Dog	163
Screwdriver	30, 167
Seabreeze	167
Shalom	168
Soviet	173
Surf Rider	177
Sweet Maria	177
Top Banana	183
Tovarich Cocktail	184
Twister	185
Velvet Hammer No. 1	187
Victory Collins	189
Vodka and Apple Juice	190
Vodka and Tonic	190
Vodka Collins	190
Vodka Cooler	190
Vodka Daisy	190
Vodka Gimlet	190
Vodka Grasshopper	190
Vodka on the Rocks	190
Vodka Salty Dog	190
Vodka "7"	190
Vodka Sling	190
Vodka Sour	191
Vodka Stinger	191
Warsaw Cocktail	192
White Russian	199
Woo Woo	35, 200

WHISKEY DRINKS

(Bourbons, Blends, Rye, or Canadian)

Algonquin	39
Allegheny	39
Ambassador's Morning Lift	40, 205
Aquarius	45
Black Hawk	52
Blue Blazer	55
Boston Sour	57
Bourbon Highball	58
Brighton Punch	62
Buddy's Favorite	63
Cablegram	65
California Lemonade	66
Canadian Cherry	66
Canadian Cocktail	66
Canadian Pineapple	66
Canal Street Daisy	68
Chapel Hill	70
Christmas Yule Eggnog	73, 205
Commodore Cocktail	76
Cowboy Cocktail	78
Creole Lady	79
Dinah Cocktail	83
Dixie Julep	83
Dixie Whiskey Cocktail	83
Double Standard Sour	83
Elk's Own Cocktail	86
Fancy Whiskey	88
Fox River Cocktail	91
Frisco Sour	93
Gloom Lifter	100
Godfather	100
Horse's Neck	107
Hot Brick Toddy	107
Imperial Fizz	110
Incider Cocktail	110

Japanese Fizz	115
Jocose Julep	116
John Collins	116
Kentucky Cocktail	117
Kentucky Colonel Cocktail	117
King Cole Cocktail	117
Klondike Cooler	118
Ladies Cocktail	121
Lawhill Cocktail	122
Limestone	123
Linstead Cocktail	123
Los Angeles Cocktail	125
Manhasset	129
Manhattan	30, 129
Manhattan (Dry)	129
Milk Punch	133
Millionaire Cocktail	133
Mint Julep	133
Mountain Cocktail	137
Narragansett	138
Nashville Eggnog	138
Nevins	139
New York Cocktail	139
New York Sour	139
Old Fashioned	141
Old Pal Cocktail	141
Opening Cocktail	141
Oriental Cocktail	142
Palmer Cocktail	143
Pendennis Toddy	146
Preakness Cocktail	151
Quebec	153
Rattlesnake Cocktail	155
Rebel Charge	155
Red Raider	156
Rye Highball	162
Rye Whiskey Cocktail	162
Seaboard	167
Soul Kiss Cocktail	173
Stiletto	175
Stone Cocktail	175
Swiss Family Cocktail	177
Temptation Cocktail	178
Thunderclap	182
T.N.T. No. 1	182
Trilby Cocktail	184
Trois Rivières	184
Twin Hills	185
Ward Eight	192
Whiskey Cobbler	195
Whiskey Cocktail	195
Whiskey Collins	195
Whiskey Daisy	197
Whiskey Eggnog	197, 207
Whiskey Fix	197
Whiskey Flip	197
Whiskey Highball	197
Whiskey Milk Punch	197
Whiskey Orange	197
Whiskey Rickey	197
Whiskey Sangaree	197
Whiskey Skin	198
Whiskey Sling	198
Whiskey Smash	198
Whiskey Sour	31, 198
Whiskey Squirt	198
Whiskey Swizzle	198
Whiskey Toddy (Cold)	198
Whiskey Toddy (Hot)	199
Whispers-of-the-Frost Cocktail	199
White Plush	199

WINE DRINKS

Adonis Cocktail	37
Andalusia	41
Baltimore Eggnog	48, 205
Bamboo Cocktail	48
Bellini	32, 50
Betsy Ross	51
Bishop	52
Bombay Punch	56
Bosom Caresser	57
Brandied Madeira	58
Brandied Port	58
Brazil Cocktail	62
Broken Spur Cocktail	62
Buck Jones	63
Burgundy Bishop	64
Cadiz	65
Cardinal Punch	68
Champagne Sherbet Punch	70
Chicago Fizz	72
Chocolate Cocktail	72
Chocolate Daisy	72
Claret Cobbler	73
Claret Punch	74
Clove Cocktail	74
Cocomacoque	75
Coffee Cocktail	75
Coffee Flip	75
Cognac Coupling	75
Creamy Orange	78
Creole Lady	79
Crimson Cocktail	79
Devil's Cocktail	82
East India Cocktail No. 2	85
Elk's Own Cocktail	86
Fino Martini	89
General Harrison's Eggnog	95
Gin Sangaree	98
Glögg	100
Golden Frappe	101
Hot Buttered Wine	108
Hot Springs Cocktail	108
Jamaica Glow	113
Japanese Fizz	115
Kir	117
Lemonade (Claret)	122
Lemonade (Modern)	122
Lil Naue	123
Loving Cup	125

Malmaison	129
Mint Gin Cocktail	133
Montezuma	136
Mulled Claret	137
Nightmare	139
Pineapple Cooler	147
Polonaise	149
Poop Deck Cocktail	149
Port Milk Punch	150
Port Wine Cobbler	150
Port Wine Cocktail	150
Port Wine Eggnog	150, 207
Port Wine Flip	150
Port Wine Negus	150
Port Wine Sangaree	150
Quarter Deck Cocktail	153
Queen Bee	153
Queen Charlotte	153
Reform Cocktail	156
Renaissance Cocktail	156
Rhine Wine Cup	156
Rock and Rye Cocktail	158
Royal Purple Punch	160
St. Charles Punch	163
Sangria	164
Sauterne Cup	164
Sevilla Cocktail	168
Shalom	168
Sherry-and-Egg Cocktail	168
Sherry Cobbler	168
Sherry Cocktail	169
Sherry Milk Punch	169
Sherry Eggnog	169, 207
Sherry Flip	169
Sherry Sangaree	169
Sherry Twist Cocktail	169
Sloppy Joe's Cocktail No. 2	172
Soviet	173
Spritzer	174
Stone Cocktail	175
Straight Law Cocktail	175
Tempter Cocktail	180
Tequila Punch	180
The Shoot	169
Wassail Bowl	193
Whispers-of-the-Frost Cocktail	199
Wine Cooler	200
Xeres Cocktail	201